FOR MORE THAN ONE VOICE

FOR MORE THAN ONE VOICE

Toward a Philosophy of Vocal Expression

Adriana Cavarero

Translated and with an
Introduction by Paul A. Kottman

STANFORD UNIVERSITY PRESS

STANFORD, CALIFORNIA

2005

Stanford University Press
Stanford, California

For More than One Voice was originally published in Italian ander the title
A più voci: Per una filosofia dell'espressione vocale ©2003 (Mil Feltrinelli).

Printed in the United States of America on acid-free, arc al-quality paper

Library of Congress Cataloging-in-Publication Data

Cavarero, Adriana.
  [A più voci. English]
  For more than one voice : toward a philosophy of vocal expression /
Adriana Cavarero ; translated by Paul Kottman.
    p. cm.
  Includes bibliographical references and index.
  ISBN 0-8047-4954-X (hardcover : alk. paper) —
  ISBN 0-8047-4955-8 (pbk. : alk. paper)
  1. Speech—Philosophy. 2. Language and languages—Philosophy.
3. Philosophy—History. I. Title.
P95.C38613 2005
401—DC22

                                                    2004013437

Original Printing 2005

Last figure below indicates year of this printing:
14 13 12 11 10 09 08 07 06 05

Contents

Translator's Introduction

My ears have not yet drunk a hundred words
Of thy tongue's uttering, yet I know the sound.
—William Shakespeare, *Romeo and Juliet*

After some hesitation, Romeo takes a risk—he speaks up out of the darkness and presents himself to Juliet. Rather than introduce himself by name, however, he alerts Juliet to his presence in the very act of speaking, or, more precisely, through the sound of his voice, by which she in turn recognizes him.

The singularity of the voice, which Shakespeare foregrounds in this well-known scene, is the essential point of departure for Cavarero's text. She tries to rethink the relation between speech and politics—announced in Aristotle's formula whereby man's nature as a political animal [*zoon politikon*] is bound up with man's characterization as that animal that has speech [*zoon logon echon*]—by focusing her attention on the embodied uniqueness of the speaker as it is manifested in that speaker's voice, addressed to another.[1] In this way, she radically departs from more traditional conceptions of what constitutes "political speech," such as the signifying capacity of the speaker, the communicative capacity of discourse, or the semantic content of a given statement. As in her earlier work, Cavarero continues to develop and deepen a number of themes foregrounded by Hannah Arendt, who asserts in *The Human Condition* that what matters in speech is not signification or "communication" but rather the fact that "in acting and speaking, men show who they are, reveal actively their unique personal identities and thus make their appearance in the human world."[2] From Arendt's perspective, speech is not a mere faculty that distinguishes man from animal, or a general capacity for signification that allows human beings to communicate with one another; rather, speech is first and foremost a privileged way in which the speaker actively, and therefore politically, distinguishes him- or herself to others. By focusing her attention on the uniqueness of the speaker—as it is manifested in the unique sound of the voice—Cavarero is able to offer in *For More than One Voice* a novel account of political speech that takes Arendt's reflections one step further. Refining the radically phenomenological perspective that Arendt puts forth in her work, Cavarero locates the political sense of speech in the singularity of the speaker's voice, the acoustic emission that emits from mouth to ear. For Cavarero this politics emerges from "the reciprocal communication of voices," wherein what comes to the fore is above all the embodied singularity of the speakers in relation to others, no matter what they say. Her text is ambitious in its theoretical scope; I will try to say something about that particular ambition in what follows.

This is the fourth book by Cavarero to be translated into English; the trajectory of her thought has been introduced to an English-speaking audience in different ways in each of the previous three.³ So when Cavarero invited me to provide a preface to this volume, I decided that instead of providing an introductory overview, I wanted to contribute an essay of affinity and propinquity. Perhaps because she and I share a fondness for Shakespeare, or perhaps because Verona has been for me the scene of many memorable conversations with her, I want to preface—and at the same time take the risk of engaging with—her work by way of the balcony scene from *Romeo and Juliet*. For Cavarero's text strives—not unlike Shakespeare's nocturnal scene—to amplify the resonance of voices in order to open the possibility of a different mode of political existence.

The tragedy of *Romeo and Juliet* is above all a tragedy of the name, of designation, *semantike*.⁴ The story or plot of Romeo and Juliet—the "death mark'd love" of the two young lovers—would not be what it is without this more general tragedy of the name or of naming, which unfolds wherever anyone suffers or dies on account of what they are called. "Civil brawls," as the Prince says in the first scene of Shakespeare's play, "bred of an airy *word/* By thee, old Capulet and Montague" (1.1.87–88).⁵ Particularly in Shakespeare's theatrical staging of the myth, Romeo and Juliet themselves seem to understand that their story—what is happening to them alone—is also this "other" tragedy of the name into which they too have been "born"—"from forth the fatal loins of these two foes." Juliet, especially, analyzes their predicament in precisely this way during the balcony scene—moving from their names to names in general, from "Montague" to "Rose," from "Romeo" to "love." Indeed, it is this collision of their lives—their desire, their relationship, their interactions—with their names that lies at the source of the tragedy, the heart of its mythos.

However, in the balcony scene—and, in fact, through this very analysis—the tragic myth itself is suspended. For on this scene the essence of the tragedy is exposed, elaborated, and—for the scene's duration at least—superseded by the relation that emerges from the exchange between the two in the context of this exposure. First, and most apparently, what this laying bare of the tragedy's essence in fact reveals is the extent to which the "ancient grudge," which in principle prohibits the sort of relationship desired by Romeo and Juliet, is rooted in the enmity of the name ("'tis but thy name that is my enemy," says Juliet [2.2.38]). It is this enmity that separates them, so to speak, or—within the ambit of the tragedy—that makes their union impossible. Yet insofar as the balcony scene exposes this violence of the name to interrogation by the lovers, it also serves to suspend the tragic myth. Put differently, although this scene is clearly essential to the tragedy—for what would the story mean without this encounter, without Romeo and Juliet's reciprocal profession of desire?—in Shakespeare's theatrical rendering, the scene's essentiality and its centrality lie at the same time in its power to interrupt or forestall the play's trajectory.

Indeed, if one takes seriously Aristotle's suggestion that mythos ("plot" or "story") is the most essential part of tragedy, then Shakespeare's *Romeo and Juliet* at once demonstrates the authority of the tragic myth while at the same time suspending its power through its theatrical staging. The play has often been called Shakespeare's most "classical" tragedy, precisely because (among other features, like "fortune") it is the one play by Shakespeare in which the plot or story seems to transcend the dramatic script[6]—yet it turns out that precisely where tragedy as myth in the classical sense seems strongest in Shakespeare's drama, the power of a theatrical scene to interrupt and undo that tragic myth is most essential; namely, in the balcony scene, which has in fact come to stand (after Shakespeare) as *the* scene of the story.

How might the balcony scene—as a theatrical resonance of two voices—work to disrupt tragedy and its mythic trajectory? And how might that disruption be recuperated from Shakespeare's drama in a way that gestures toward a different definition of the political sphere, such as the one proposed by Arendt when she suggests that theatrical mimesis is "the political art *par excellence*"?[7] As Cavarero says toward the end of the present text, perhaps this drama authorizes us to imagine the story of Romeo and Juliet without its tragic end, to "imagine another story for the community of lovers" within a public sphere whose boundaries are not determined by "what" the lovers are called, and that does not demand their death or separation.

Let me recall Shakespeare's staging of their encounter, which departs sharply from the earlier, lyrical (that is, nontheatrical) renderings of the story, on which Shakespeare seems to have relied for the plot. First—in contrast to Arthur Brook's 1562 lyrical translation of the tale, and the immediate Italian sources from which it is taken—in Shakespeare's rendering, the lovers do not see one another. And this lack of reciprocal visibility means, of course, that the lovers do not encounter each another simultaneously, as in the earlier poetic versions, where they spy one other at the same moment. Instead, Juliet is seen by Romeo well before Romeo, in turn, reveals himself to Juliet by speaking up. In fact, the scene (as it is transposed into the theater by Shakespeare) comes to be structured dramatically on this marked disjunction between seeing and speaking, between the visual and the acoustic. Surprisingly, Shakespeare's staging of the tale does not merely expose the lovers to each other's gaze (or to the gaze of the spectators), as one might expect when a myth moves from lyrical epic to a theatrical tragedy. Rather, in transferring the tale to the theater, Shakespeare's scene (and indeed much of the play) works under the cover of night, in a penumbra that frustrates the primacy of spectacle—a primacy that classically divides theatrical tragedy from lyrical poetry. Consequently, and remarkably, what comes to the fore in this scene is not a privileging of visibility but above all the spoken exchange between the lovers. At stake, I will suggest, is not simply a general distinction between verbality and visuality; rather, it is the way in which speech constitutes action, or *inter*action, in a way that the gaze alone cannot.[8] After all, it is only when Romeo takes the initiative to move from merely *looking* at Juliet to engaging her in conversation that their relationship emerges. Only when they audibly address one another does the scene become relational.

The emphasis on verbality in the balcony scene has been read by some critics as a "dramatic equivalent" of Philip Sidney's sonnet sequence *Astrophil and Stella;* or, by other readers like Joel Fineman, as a further instance of Shakespeare's "corruptingly linguistic verbal duplicity," which opposes the ideal specularization of a sonnet tradition extending back to Petrarch, and to which Sidney belongs.[9] To avoid confusion, therefore, let me assert from the start that in drawing attention to the *spoken* exchange of the lovers at night, I do not wish to highlight the poetic language of the scene. Rather, I want to underscore very simply that they are *speaking* aloud to one another; the scene is therefore first of all the resonance of two unique voices—what Cavarero calls "the reciprocal communication of voices."

To be sure, this is an exceptional dialogue. The spoken exchange in fact begins with Romeo's epideictic response to the appearance of Juliet, a response that invokes a disjunction between the act of speaking and the fact of "communicating" or "saying something." From Romeo, we in fact learn that Juliet is speaking before we come to know what she is saying. "She speaks," he tells us, "yet she says nothing. What of that?" (2.2.12). And even when her voice becomes audible to Romeo (and to the audience), Juliet's speech remains enigmatically irreducible to signification. "Ay me," she sighs, letting this vocalization resonate by itself before continuing (2.2.24).

Indeed, when her speech finally—thirty-three lines into the scene—begins to signify in a way that is recognizable to Romeo (and to the audience), it does so only in order to denounce the name and signification more generally. Without knowing he is there, Juliet invokes Romeo's name through the famous apostrophe ("O Romeo, Romeo, wherefore art thou Romeo"), calling him beyond his name, or without his title ("refuse thy name" [2.2.33]). In other words, her discourse comes to signification only in order to then call past it; her speech "signifies," it turns out, in order to defy the power of designation itself. The problem, therefore, is not, as Fineman calls it, the duplicity of Shakespeare's language as it revises the idealizing poetic speech of earlier sonneteers. What comes to the fore in the theatrical scene is in fact the spoken suspension of the semantic register.

As everyone familiar with the play knows, the suspension of the tragedy staged by this scene unfolds first of all through Juliet's cold, detached analysis of the disjunction between the name "Romeo" and "that dear perfection which he owes/without that title." Her soliloquy proceeds as a critique not only of the proper name—"Romeo" or "Montague"—but of designation in general—"that which we call a rose/By any other name would smell as sweet." Juliet knows that the name "Romeo" is not who she desires—it names nothing of his body, as she says, nothing "belonging to a man." On the contrary, the problem for Juliet is that the name "Romeo Montague" evokes the uniqueness of the one who carries that name without, however, revealing who he uniquely is. This is, of course, the point of her elaboration: namely, to underscore the separation between Romeo himself—the one she desires—and the name he bears; between who he is and what he is called. Indeed, her desire is made possible by—or perhaps is itself the occasion of—the separation of "who" Romeo is from his name.

On the one hand, therefore, the semantic content of Juliet's speech, as scripted by Shakespeare, serves to foreground the irreducibility of

Romeo himself—the one she desires—to the name "Romeo." In this sense, Romeo's and Juliet's relationship is conditioned on, and is itself the occasion of, the separation of who they are from what they are called.[10]

On the other hand, it is precisely this irreducibility of who Romeo is to what he is called that is, so to speak, mise-en-scène by the dialogue itself, over and beyond the radical analysis of the name scripted by Shakespeare for Juliet. That is to say, the disjunction between the name and its bearer, between who he is and what he is called, is not only posited philosophically by Juliet as she speaks into the darkness in a kind of virtual monologue (because she speaks to no one in particular, certainly not yet to Romeo who has already told us "'tis not to me she speaks" [2.2.14]). Rather, this separation is enacted or affirmed on the scene itself at the moment when this monologue is broken and becomes dialogue—that is, when it ceases to be a general, philosophical reflection on the name as such and becomes theatrical speech-in-relation, here and now in the dark of night.

For as the audience knows, Juliet's discourse has in fact found a listener: Romeo himself, who has clandestinely marked her speech at every step (repeating, at each interval, "she speaks, O speak again bright angel," or "Shall I hear more, or shall I speak at this?" [2.2.25–26, 36]). Of course, in contrast to the audience, or unlike a generalizable "auditor" that might accidentally overhear Juliet's discourse, Romeo hears himself called by this analysis. To be sure, this appeal could hardly be more ambiguous, for on the one hand, Juliet does not address Romeo directly ("'Tis not to me she speaks"), and, on the other hand, her apostrophe calls out to Romeo beyond, or in spite of, his name—calling him by name (in principle) in order to separate him from it. "Romeo, doff thy name, / And for thy name, which is no part of thee, / Take all myself" (2.2.47–49).

At least, this is how Romeo hears himself called at this moment. And, it is worth noting, he must hear this call like no one else hears it, because this appeal concerns him alone. In other words, Juliet's call to Romeo beyond his name—insofar as it is heard by Romeo himself—affirms the tension of a desire, of a relation, that is theirs alone. In fact, the absolute singularity of their relation is precisely what the theatricality of the scene presupposes, even as it is staged for a larger audience. In other words, it is as if we (the audience) and not Romeo are the real eavesdroppers, listening in on a private discourse without ever possibly hearing it as they themselves do.

But how, then, can Romeo respond to such an address, one that calls to him by name by at the same time calling him beyond his name? How can he answer, so to speak, as himself and not just as "Romeo"?

"I take thee at thy word," he answers, "call me but love and I'll be new baptized" (2.2.49–50). His response is keen: in taking Juliet at her word, he refuses to identify himself by a proper name, because "love" is not a name with which one could be christened; rather, it is the name of the phenomenon in question, so to speak, whereby one becomes separable from one's name, one's family, one's genealogy. Indeed, it is almost as if Romeo only comes to see himself as separable from his name, from his father, when he hears himself called that way by Juliet. In other words, only through the spoken interaction of the scene does Romeo see that it is possible to answer as "himself" and not as "Romeo."

Juliet, for her part, is understandably startled by the unexpected voice that emits from the darkness—a darkness that she (or Shakespeare) once more underlines: "What man art thou," she asks, "that thus bescreen'd in night/So stumblest upon my counsel?" (2.2.52–53).

Romeo's reply is, once again, insistently enigmatic: "By a name/I know not how to tell thee who I am: My name, dear saint, is hateful to myself/Because it is an enemy to thee/Had I it written I would tear the word" (2.2.48–51). Now, on the surface it would seem that the cleverness of Romeo's response—both his refusal to identify himself by any name, and his more radical insistence that who he is cannot be revealed by what he is called—affirms his agreement with Juliet. In other words, the semantic content of his words, scripted by Shakespeare, succinctly expresses the separation of his name from who he is.

However, the expression of this separation does not simply occur at the semantic level of Juliet's or Romeo's speech—that is, at the level that can be read on the page of Shakespeare's text or cited by me here. Rather, it occurs more precisely, and more forcefully, in the vocalized utterance, in Romeo's resonant appeal to Juliet. Or, better, it occurs through the emergence of a singular relation that this convocation at once affirms and brings into being on the scene. For when Romeo says, "by a name I know not how to tell thee who I am," he is not simply communicating to Juliet, through this enigmatic claim, that he agrees with her analysis of the name in general. He is not, in other words, simply declaring—in the content of his discourse—"yes, you are right Juliet, no name can reveal who anyone is." On the contrary, what Romeo professes here regards himself alone—

in his relation to Juliet; that is, he refuses, in the very act of speaking to her here and now, to name to her who he himself is. What is heard by Juliet at this moment is therefore not simply a random or impersonal agreement with her thesis regarding the general heterogeneity of a name to its bearer. Instead, she hears *this* man "thus bescreen'd in night" say, "by a name I know not how to tell *thee* who *I* am."

What she hears, finally, is a singular voice—which, as it happens, is one that she recognizes. "My ears have not yet drunk a hundred words / Of thy tongue's uttering," she exclaims, "yet I know the sound. / Art thou not Romeo and a Montague?" (2.2.58–60). She thus identifies him by the unique timbre of his voice alone, without being able to see his face or hear him say his name. Indeed, she identifies him by his voice in spite of the fact that his voice pronounces words that explicitly renounce such identification.

What Romeo's enigmatic refusal to present himself by name produces, therefore, is a scene in which the singularity of his voice—in the act of speaking to Juliet here and now—confounds and defeats what is ostensibly the very problem at hand; that is, the name's powerlessness to reveal or to represent the one who bears it. The "uttering" of Romeo's tongue, as it is heard by Juliet, thus enacts the separation of the name "Romeo" from the one who speaks, allowing Juliet to recognize who is speaking there in the darkness, in spite of the fact that this speaker does not identify himself by name.

What finally opposes the tragedy of the name, therefore—what really subverts it, I think—is not, as is often claimed, Juliet's theoretical appeal to a "dear perfection," to some "Romeo-ness" that is not reducible to any title or appellation. Rather what radically suspends the tragedy of the name is the scene itself; that is, the audible manifestation of Romeo's uniqueness through his voice, his active communication of himself to her *hic et nunc*—as Cavarero would say, "it is the embodied uniqueness of the speaker and his convocation of another voice."

Or, better, the scene suspends the tragedy by affirming their singularity (and the singularity of their relationship) through their spoken interaction.[11] Although this is a singularity that at some level resists appellation, it can be manifested through their reciprocal convocation. Indeed, what this convocation makes clear is the extent to which the vocal sphere of the interactive scene is, so to speak, broader that the sphere of the name—the acoustic resonance of their voices, as they are heard here and now, exceeds the words they utter. "When the register of speech is totalized," writes Cavarero, "for instance, when it is identified with a system of language of which the voice would be a mere function—it is indeed inevitable that the vocal emission not headed for speech is nothing but a remainder." However, "rather than a mere leftover," she continues, "what is really at stake is an originary excess."

This excess is, in fact, what the scene opens up. Put another way, the spoken interaction of the two lovers—the simple fact that they call out to one another in the darkness—is coextensive with a scene that both affirms their relation and at the same time bestows on it a new sense. What their very interaction makes possible—at least for the scene's duration—is thus a kind of alternative political space whereupon the central question is not "what" the actors are called, or even what they say to one another, but rather "who is speaking?"[12]

After all, it is clear that Juliet desires Romeo not because of what he says; on the contrary, his words fail to convince her. (He speaks too much like "the numbers that Petrarch flowed in," says Mercutio at a certain point [2.4.40].) For when Romeo starts to profess his love by swearing on the moon, on himself, and so on, Juliet admonishes him, "do not swear," in a manner that expresses a typically Shakespearean blurring of vow and perjury ("Yet if thou swear'st," Juliet says, "Thou mayst prove false. At lovers' perjuries,/They say, Jove laughs" [2.2.91–93]). From a rhetorical perspective, we might conclude more generally from Juliet's remarks that persuasion here has little to do with what is said, with the conventional poetics of lovers' oaths or of refined sonnets, and everything to do with who is saying it—everything to do, that is, with the relationship between this speaker and this listener.

"Thou knowest the mask of night is on my face," says Juliet, "Else would a maiden blush bepaint my cheek/For that which thou hast heard me speak tonight" (2.2.85–87). But of course what this overt reference to the masking of the face makes clear is that in the end, what cannot be masked are their voices. Everything else can be masked—their faces, their gestures, even the words they use; words can, after all, designate everything and its opposite, through the trope of oxymoron that Romeo himself practices in his first lines in the play ("O brawling love, O loving hate/O any thing, of nothing first create" [1.1.174–75]). Hence Juliet's inherent mistrust of Romeo's vows. Unlike his words, however, Romeo's voice—whatever it says—inevitably communicates one thing: the embodied uniqueness of one who emits it.[13]

It turns out, in other words, that over and beyond the words put down by William Shakespeare, the act of speaking first and foremost reveals the speaker, communicating above all the one who speaks to the one who listens. Obviously, as Cavarero's work shows, this happens on every scene of spoken interaction, not just this highly idiosyncratic one involving a balcony from Shakespeare's play. Indeed, as Arendt articulates it, this kind of active revelation of oneself in word and deed is what defines the space of interaction, or what Cavarero calls the "local." Such spaces are not defined by the "space" on which they are played out; rather, this "space of interaction" is what is created wherever at least two actors actively communicate themselves to one another, bringing into being a relation between them. In this sense, I think, Shakespeare's play opens itself to a mode of interaction that the work, as a scripted or choreographed production, cannot fully contain or govern.

Thus the balcony scene not only posits—analytically, discursively, philosophically—the suspension of the tragic association of the name with its bearer through Juliet's famous speech, and Romeo's enigmatic response. Brilliant as these lines are, the power of the scene to suspend the tragedy and subvert the force of the name is nevertheless irreducible to what is said—no matter how radical Romeo and Juliet's discourse is. Rather, over and beyond the scripted language, the scene performs, through the resonance of the lovers' very voices, the suspension of the tragedy of the name. Or, put differently, the scene not only describes but moreover actively affirms the separation of the name "Romeo" from who Romeo is—above all, through his relation to Juliet.

Surprisingly, therefore, the fact that the balcony scene suspends or interrupts the tragedy of the name is not attributable simply to the supreme refinement of Shakespeare's language, to the exquisite sophistication of Juliet's monologue, or to the shrewd response that it elicits from Romeo. Put another way, as a result of Romeo's revelation of himself to Juliet by speaking up, under the cover of night, it not only becomes possible to actively separate "Romeo" from his name, but it now becomes possible to separate their interaction from Shakespeare's language, from what Juliet and Romeo say to each other. For what finally emerges from the profundity of the verbal exchange scripted by William Shakespeare is a scene whereupon a singular relationship is enacted and affirmed—one in which what matters is not only what is said, but rather who is saying it.[14] In fact, in spite of the memorable lines that Shakespeare has left us, what Juliet and Romeo do and say to each other is finally less crucial, as far as the tragedy is concerned, than the fact that they reveal who they are to one another in spite of what they say. It is the priority of this revelation that distinguishes Shakespeare's version of the story.

In other words, not only is the act of speaking not reducible here to communication-as-signification, but also, precisely because of this irreducibility, the act of speaking communicates above all the one who speaks to those who listen. In this way, the tragedy of the name is suspended by something that, so to speak, cannot be scripted: that is—in the first instance—the spoken interaction of the two lovers' voices, and—in the second instance—the relation that this convocation brings into being and affirms here and now. For this vocalization, like the relation it makes possible, cannot be fully inscribed or archived by any mark or sign.

Now, in a simple sense, Juliet's recognition of Romeo's voice is obviously scripted in advance by Shakespeare in the lines "my ears have not yet drunk a hundred words of thy tongues' uttering/And yet I know the sound." Yet it is quite apparent (especially here) that Shakespeare's text depends in an essential way on the prior fact, as it were, of the singularity of Romeo's voice. For it is first of all the singularity of this speaker's voice, and therefore the singularity of this speaker, that is manifested in the sonority of Romeo's utterance. The fact that who is speaking is singular (even before being identifiable by name), and the fact that this singularity can be manifested in that speaker's voice, is finally the only thing in this scene that Shakespeare must take for granted. And it is precisely this "vocal phenomenology of uniqueness" (to use Cavarero's phrase) that Shakespeare exploits to such great effect.

It is a given that Romeo communicates first of all himself in the act of speaking, just as it is taken for granted that Juliet can recognize Romeo through his voice; and these givens turn out to be the ontological conditions of possibility for the scene itself. The "relational character of speech" (as Cavarero puts it), rooted as it is in the singularity of each speaker, which makes itself manifest in the uniqueness of their voice, is the only thing that Shakespeare's scene must perforce take for granted as its ontological horizon. The name, the family, civil strife, the law of the enemy— all of these things can be, and are, subject to radical question and revision in Shakespeare's play. But what the play, like all theater and all political life, cannot suspend is the fact that speaking up implies that someone is re-

vealed, here and now, through the sound of their voice. This is true
whether one is being heard for the first time, or whether the voice is familiar—as Romeo's is to Juliet.

Put quite simply, Shakespeare's text depends on the fact of Romeo's
unique voice—that it can be and is recognizable to Juliet as a manifestation of Romeo's singularity beyond his name and beyond the words he utters.[15] Were this not the case, Shakespeare could have set the scene under
the harsh light of the sun, with the sort of reciprocal visibility represented
in Sidney's or Brooke's lyrical rendering. For even if it were played under
the bright light of day, the meaning of the dialogue—the call for Romeo
to doff his name—would not have changed. But the point is that in bringing the scene into being, Shakespeare needed the cover of night. Night
here is not a mere scenographic choice. Rather, visibility is eclipsed because
Romeo's voice—unseen, and therefore unidentifiable through the gaze—
is the immediate, acoustic revelation of that embodied uniqueness that
Juliet wanted to separate from his name.

The active revelation of who Romeo is to Juliet—embodied, as
Cavarero would say, with a voice that is like no other—in fact responds to
her desire for his body, which is, as she herself indicates, separable from his
name. The name "Romeo," after all, is "not hand, nor foot, nor arm"—
much less the singular flesh that she desires. Romeo's voice, on the other
hand, does emit from his body; and in its acoustic resonance, his "tongue"
reaches her "ears." Clearly, the singularity that Romeo's voice manifests is
first of all an embodied singularity. Obviously, what Juliet desires is not
merely the philosophical claim of her discourse—namely, that there is
uniqueness, or that human beings are all unique. What she desires is this
one, who lives, breathes, and speaks.

Again, as Cavarero notes repeatedly, this embodied uniqueness can
be perceived visibly as well. When Romeo and Juliet see each other for the
first time, their immediate appearance to one another explicitly carries with
it this recognition of embodied singularity dissociated from the name (as
Juliet says, on learning from the nurse that Romeo is a Montague: "to early
seen unknown, and known too late" [1.5.138]).[16] However, from Cavarero's
point of view, the acoustic exchange of voices has the value of being more
"bodily" than the gaze. In other words, from her perspective, the difference
between the gaze or face-to-face encounter and a verbal or vocal exchange
serves to highlight how the acoustic sphere might provide a more fruitful

phenomenological position from which to radically reconfigure a meta-physical-political tradition going back to Plato that is rooted in theory (and a whole lexicon constructed on sight, contemplation, intellectual detach-ment, and so forth) by opening an ontological horizon founded on the ma-terial, contextual relation of embodied unique existents. The theoretical ar-ticulation of this ontological horizon—rooted in the phenomenal relationality of the voice—is, as the reader will note, the central aim of her argument in this book. I will say more about this aim momentarily.

However, although her position, as she articulates it, certainly has the merit of providing a radical critique of the metaphysical tradition of politi-cal philosophy, as well as of many twentieth-century critics of this tradition (including Levinas), there is perhaps another way to recuperate the differ-ence between a visual face-to-face encounter and a vocal exchange. Return-ing to *Romeo and Juliet*, what could be emphasized is that the revelation of embodied uniqueness through the voice carries with it an interactive sense that a visible encounter does not. For one can look upon, or be looked upon by, another without acting or interacting, and therefore without the possi-bility of any active relationship. (Romeo could have simply continued to admire Juliet's physical appearance in the window, as he in fact does for the first part of the scene, without ever speaking up.) If, as Cavarero notes fol-lowing Hannah Arendt, the human condition of plurality guarantees an on-tological horizon of relationality between unique existents—and if this horizon can be either visual or vocal (although, again, Cavarero privileges the vocal)—then it is also true, following Arendt in a different vein, that without speech, this horizon of relationality remains inactive, unaffirmed, a "brute physical appearance."[17] In other words, the difference between vocal exchange and a visual face-to-face encounter might also be recuperated—over and beyond the analysis of this difference that Cavarero provides in the following pages—as a way of underscoring the disjunction between (on the one hand) a material, ontological horizon of plurality, a kind of sheer rela-tionality between embodied uniquenesses that simply comes with being alive in the world among others, and (on the other hand) what Arendt calls the "political" space of action, a kind of relation that results from interaction and that gives sense to political existence.

Nowhere is this made clearer in Shakespeare's play than in Romeo's final speech, uttered as he looks upon what he believes to be the dead body of Juliet. Praising her beauty in the same Sidney-esque language with which he praised it when they first met, he here dwells on the fact that she still appears beautiful in spite of the fact that she can no longer speak ("O my love,/Death that hath suck'd the honey of thy breath/Hath had no power yet upon thy beauty" [5.3.92–93]). Indeed, the commonplace fact that a dead corpse can no longer be heard but can be seen is here employed by Shakespeare as the very disjunction that ultimately kills not only the lovers' bodies but more importantly ends their relation. For what is peculiar about the deaths of the two lovers, within the context of Shakespeare's play, is that they die to each other before dying corporally. That is to say, their active relation, the living sense of their interaction, does not expire in the same instance as their bodies (which remain visible, tangible, kissable)—but rather expires along with the lack of breath or voice with which to speak, or along with the death of interaction. Each sees the other dead, making clear that what is at stake in death is not simply the body's demise, but rather the severing of an active relation, which is marked explicitly in *Romeo and Juliet* as the impossibility of ever hearing the other's voice again.

Put differently, the relationality of the balcony scene—and the tension of desire between Juliet and Romeo that runs throughout the play itself—is rooted in the embodied singularity of the two lovers without, however, being reducible to their embodiedness. Romeo's voice, through which Juliet recognizes "who" he is in the darkness of the balcony scene, clearly emits from this actor (who passes air through his vocal cords) toward Juliet who hears it. But this very emission that goes out from Romeo to Juliet means that although their spoken interaction is ontologically grounded in their embodied uniqueness, it has, so to speak, a relational sense that exceeds its sheer physicality. The relational character of the scene does not arise only from the fact that the two actors have a "throat of flesh" or can move their bodies or pass air through their larynx, but moreover from the fact that they speak to one another, from the new relationship (or the new sense for this relationship) that this speech brings into being.

Again, for Cavarero, the difference between the face-to-face and vocal exchange serves chiefly to underscore the embodied materiality of a vocal, relational ontology as a forceful challenge to the disembodied universal claims of metaphysical political theory. Although I agree with this emphasis, I would suggest additionally that this difference might also serve to highlight the rupture or break between a sheer, ontological horizon of embodied relationality (whether visual, vocal, tactile, or olfactory) and what Arendt calls a "political" sphere of relationality that depends on action [*praxis*]. For the vocalized utterance as it is "destined to speech" (to use Cavarero's phrase) is not solely a manifestation of one's embodied uniqueness, although it is also always such a manifestation. Every utterance is moreover an action, which at once manifests one's embodied uniqueness to others in the context of a material, ontological relation here and now and which also initiates, or alters, a relation whose sense exceeds this sheer manifestation of one's corporeal uniqueness. In other words, action—especially vocal utterance—is the way in which the actor affirms and manifests his or her embodied uniqueness, and also inaugurates a new sense for that uniqueness by fostering a relationship whose character is more than solely ontological, but also political. Put formulaically, while it is important to insist with Cavarero (for reasons I will now explain, and which she explains at length) on an ontological horizon of relationality, or plurality, among embodied uniqueses, it is also important, from my point of view, to bear in mind the extent to which the category of relationality is not solely ontological, but moreover a category that appertains to the political sphere of action as it distinguishes itself from an ontological horizon of embodied plurality.[18]

As I indicated at the outset, Cavarero's aim in *For More than One Voice* is deceptively ambitious. It is nothing short of laying the ground— through a radical rethinking of the role of voice in the relation between logos and politics—for an antimetaphysical ontology founded not on the activity of thinking, or on abstract entities like Man or Individual or Justice, but rather irremediably rooted in a radically embodied, contextual, relational ontology that takes seriously Arendt's notion of the human condition as a "plurality" of unique existents. Indeed, in a sense, Cavarero's insistence on the importance of providing the theoretical or discursive framework for such an ontological grounding is even more deep-seated than Arendt's own. For as Cavarero puts it, only by redefining the ontological horizon itself—which, for her, means the obligatory work not only of "deconstructing" the central figures of metaphysical ontology but moreover of recuperating an entirely different sense for those figures—can a new form of political existence emerge.[19] She thus proceeds to dis-figure the central theme that has defined the bond between ontology and politics since Plato—namely logos—by focusing on the theme of the voice as that literal phenomenon that undoes the metaphysical figuration of the term *logos* itself, because what is undeniable in the sound of each voice is the embodied, relational uniqueness of each existent. For Cavarero, politics should now inscribe itself in this disfigured, antimetaphysical, material, contextual, relational ontology.

It is precisely because her aim is so ambitious that Cavarero argues so forcefully for the irreducibility of this ontological horizon, this plurality of embodied, unique existents. Indeed, the reader will note that Cavarero insists on the corporeality of the voice in order to "return" speech to the body—that is, in order to reverse the philosophical tendency to subordinate speech (as in the semantic destiny of the term *logos* itself) to a mute, immaterial order of signification. Her reading of Plato, her analysis of the figure of the Sirens, of opera, and of biblical texts convincingly demonstrates that "the voice and body reinforce one another" in the western tradition. And Cavarero makes use of this inextricable bond between voice and body to, as it were, rescue both the voice and the body from the figuration to which they have been subjected by the politicophilosophical tradition of the west.[20] Wherever Plato makes use of the voice or the body as a figure that valorizes an order of "signifieds" that is neither bodily nor sonorous, Cavarero seeks out the unique bodies beneath the figuration, the singular sounds of a plurality of voices that disturb the mute working of the mind. If the Sirens, according the history of their figuration, have been robbed of both their "original" bodily shape and their voice, then Cavarero aims to rescue "future" Sirens from the fate to which this figuration would condemn them (and, implicitly, women in general).

It could thus be said that the recuperation of the bodily act of speech plays an essential role in Cavarero's analysis of the voice insofar as this bodily voice is, for her, not a figure. Indeed, not only is the voice absolutely not figural for Cavarero, it in fact turns out to be a central phenomenon through which the figural impulse of metaphysics can be subverted. She proceeds in *For More than One Voice* to read various figurations of the bodily voice in western philosophy, music, and literature in order to, finally, rescue the voice from figuration in general. The voice, for her, is stubbornly, insistently, unabashedly bodily—it is the voice of this one, this throat of flesh, heard by this other. Her insistence on the fleshy nature of the voice may strike some readers as too essentialist, which is why I want to stress that this avowal should be understood in the context of her broad, highly ambitious reworking of a politicophilosophical tradition that seeks to eliminate the bodily singularity of every existent in the name of a universal, figural abstraction.

Much of *For More than One Voice* is thus devoted to overturning "the old metaphysical strategy that subordinates speech to thought" through the articulation of an entirely different ontological horizon that takes the acoustic resonance of a plurality of unique voices as its phenomenological beginning. Cavarero writes:

An antimetaphysical strategy, like mine, aiming to valorize an ontology of uniqueness finds in the voice a decisive—indeed, obligatory—resource. The point is not simply to revocalize logos. Rather, the aim is to free logos from its visual substance, and to finally mean it as sonorous speech—in order to listen, in speech itself, for the plurality of singular voices that convoke one other in a relation which is not simply sound, but above all resonance.

Cavarero's affirmation of the ontological status of a material, relational, contextual plurality of unique existents, as she herself points out, has something in common with contemporary philosophers like Giorgio Agamben and Jean-Luc Nancy, for whom a radical response to the political-philosophical tradition of the west implies the articulation of a "relational" ontology of plurality and uniqueness.[21] She writes:

> The political, for Nancy, corresponds precisely to the *in* of this being in common. Favoring, particularly in less recent works, the term *community*, he in fact grounds politics in the *with*, the *among*, the *in*—which corresponds in Arendt's lexicon to the in-between—that is, in any particle that alludes to the original, ontological relation inscribed in the plurality of singular beings. Politics is the bond—a bond inscribed in the ontological status of singularity, insofar as this implies plurality and relation. These three categories of uniqueness, plurality, and relation—which generate each other—determine the coincidence of ontology and politics.

Significantly, however, even as she affirms her affinity with this line of thought, she also criticizes Nancy for being too quick to conflate ontology and politics. "For Nancy, this coincidence [between ontology and politics] is absolute. . . . Politics consists immediately in the given relation of the ontological condition." For Cavarero, unlike Nancy, the articulation of an antimetaphysical, relational, embodied ontology of plural uniqueness is a necessary condition for rethinking politics—but it is not sufficient for the emergence of such a politics. Instead, she claims (following Arendt) that "ontology and politics are in a necessary relation, but they are not the same thing; they do not coincide." Symptomatically, what accounts for the difference between ontology and politics is, in fact—for both Arendt and Cavarero—action. Action is something more than, or other than, simply "being"—it is its "consequence and response." "Without action in a shared space of reciprocal exhibition," writes Cavarero, "uniqueness remains a mere ontological given—the given of an ontology that is not able to make itself political." In short, the point I wish to draw attention to here is the fact that—even as Cavarero repeatedly and methodically articulates an antimetaphysical ontology from which a new politics might emerge—for her, this ontology does not fully result in, or coincide with, politics in the absence of action.

Given her remarks in the context of her discussion of Nancy's work, it is therefore curious that Cavarero's own analysis of the voice—which, naturally, is the chief focus of the book—does not push itself toward ulterior implications for the notion of action that she herself invokes as the category that separates the ontological from the political. In *For More than One Voice*, the act of speaking or vocalization is employed primarily as a "resource" with which to "valorize an (antimetaphysical) ontology of uniqueness" that radically subverts the classical definition of logos in relation to politics. Vocalization is not conceived by Cavarero as a "political" action, but rather as a phenomenon through which an antimetaphysical, relational ontology might find its most forceful articulation.[22] Given the methodological and philosophical aims of the book, not to mention inevitable limits of scope in a project so ambitious, this is perfectly comprehensible. However, I'd like briefly to imagine at least one way in which conceiving vocalization as action might produce an important critical purchase on the disjunction or noncoincidence of ontology and politics.

In her account of action, Arendt is careful to point out through explicit reference to the voice that what is essential to action is not solely the fact that it is rooted in the body of the singular actor, or that it reveals the embodied singularity of the actor; rather, she adds, what is essential to action is moreover the capacity of this embodied, singular actor to initiate or begin something new.[23] Arendt even goes so far as to claim that this capacity for beginning is made possible by the actor's embodied uniqueness, but yet not fully conditioned or determined by that actor's body, or his/her material, contextual, ontological relation to others. In other words, the capacity for action emerges from, but at some point exceeds, the "human condition" of materiality, plurality—what Arendt calls "worldliness."[24] She makes this point when she argues that action (unlike "labor" or "work") "is not forced upon us by necessity . . . [action] may be stimulated by the presence of others whose company we wish to join, but it is never conditioned by them; its impulse springs from the beginning that came into the world when we were born and to which we respond by beginning something new on our own initiative."[25] This "impulse" to appear, or to reveal oneself in word or deed, is the sine qua non of politics, over and beyond the ontological horizon from which it emerges. Although such a politics clearly corresponds to (and depends on) the relational ontology that Cavarero articulates in *For More than One Voice*, in Arendt's account the act (especially the act of speaking) is an "initiative" that emerges out of, and is distinct from, the ontological horizon of the human condition.

"Action," put differently, is not a given—like the sheer fact of the voice's singularity or the uniqueness of one's own embodiment. Being born with "a voice like no other" does not, in the end, guarantee or determine the actions performed by that singular voice. On the contrary, as Shakespeare's *Romeo and Juliet* makes clear, such action can by no means be taken for granted; rather, it always entails a certain risk, or initiative on the part of the agents themselves. It is worth remembering, after all, that Romeo and Juliet risk their lives by speaking to one another—not just because of "what" they say, or because they are subject to policing or censorship, but because "speaking up" in this context is tantamount to a relationship. "Bondage is hoarse," says Juliet, "and may not speak aloud" (2.2.160), expressing perfectly the essential bond between silence and oppression, between the voice and freedom, that hangs over their exchange. Obviously, their spoken interaction is already—as soon as Romeo makes a sound—an act of transgression; as Juliet reminds him, "the place is death considering who thou art/If any of my kinsman find thee here" (2.2.64–65). Romeo's voice—his act of speaking up ("shall I hear more, or shall I speak at this?")—is inseparable from this risk. It is not simply what he says to Juliet that puts them in danger, but the very usage of his voice— a usage that almost got him killed by Tybalt earlier in the play, when the Capulet recognized Romeo's voice ("This by his voice should be a Montague/Fetch me my rapier" [1.5.53–54]).

The risk of speaking up is, finally, inseparable from the freedom that such action might bring about. For using one's voice—to sing, to tell a story, to soothe a child—is not only an essential phenomenon that reveals the ontological horizon described by Cavarero in the following pages; it is, moreover, often (regardless of whether the speaker is aware) a risk that adheres to the radical contingency of action.

What if Romeo had not spoken up, but merely admired Juliet's form while listening to her discourse? Ontologically, the horizon would be the same; politically, however, his actions made all the difference. After all, nothing within the tragic myth (before Shakespeare) guaranteed, governed, or predicted what Romeo's utterance would bring about—namely, a scene of speaking in which the voice itself, in all of its fragility, confounds the limits and conditions of its own resonance.

FOR MORE THAN ONE VOICE

Introduction

A voice means this: there is a living person, throat, chest, feelings, who sends into the air this voice, different from all other voices.
—Italo Calvino, "A King Listens"

The Voice According to Calvino

In one of his last, ingenious texts, Italo Calvino leaves us the extraordinary figure of a king who listens. Part of a collection dedicated to the five senses, the king in question represents hearing. He is seated immobile on the throne, ears pricked in order to intercept and decipher the sounds that surround him. Besieged by the logic of his own power, the only activity of the monarch consists in an acoustic control of the realm. In the palace, which, like "a great ear," has "pavilions, ducts, shells, labyrinths," every sound is a sign of either fidelity or betrayal.[1] There are many hidden spies to interpret: whispers, rumors, vibrations, crashes, oceans of silence. Naturally, there are also human voices in the palace. But "every voice that knows it is heard by the King acquires a cold glaze"; it becomes a courtly voice, artificial, false—not so much for what it says, but in its very sonorous materiality. The king who listens knows this, or better, he hears it [*lo sente*].

In keeping with a tradition that goes back to the ancient tyrant, Calvino's king is prisoner of his own system. The logic is obsessive, violent, persecutory, and suspicious. Because he is always threatened by his imminent overthrow, the king's power imposes on him a vigilant insomnia. However, his vigilance is, in this case, exclusively auditory. As if in a sonorous nightmare, the regal ear is amplified to a level of perception that is as acute as it is impotent. The king can do nothing except listen, intercept sounds, and try to interpret their meaning. The words, which are reduced to their sonorous materiality as sounds among sounds, do not count for their semantic valence but only for their phonic substance. Paying little attention to what the courtiers say, the king spies on the vocal timbre of their voices, which is, again, artificial, false, "cold" like death. In fact, the throats of the court are no longer able to emit the true and unmistakable voice of life—namely, the voice that "involves the throat, saliva, infancy, the patina of experienced life, the mind's intentions, the pleasure of giving a personal form to sound waves."

One fine day, "when in the darkness a woman's voice is released in singing, invisible at the sill of an unlighted window," the insomniac king happens to hear her. And he is aroused; he finally remembers life and rediscovers in her voice an object for his long-lost desires. The king's new emotion certainly does not depend on the song she sings, which he had heard many times before; nor does it depend on the woman herself, whom he has never seen. Rather, Calvino explains, the king is "attracted by that voice as a voice, as it offers itself in song." What attracts him, in other words, is "the pleasure this voice puts into existing: into existing as voice; but this pleasure leads you to imagine how this person might be different from every other person, as the voice is different." In short, the king discovers the uniqueness of each human being, as it gets manifested in the uniqueness of the voice. In fact, he discovers something more: "the voice could be the equivalent of the hidden and most genuine part of the person," a sort of invisible, but immediately perceptible, nucleus of uniqueness. And this voice emerges from the world of the living that is outside the deadly logic of power. Thus, for the regal ear, it opens a horizon of perception whose existential status is totally opposed to that which confines him to the acoustic games of the palace. For it is no longer a matter of capturing and deciphering threatening sounds, but rather of enjoying the sound of the "vibration of a throat of flesh." Alive and bodily, unique and unrepeatable, overcoming with her simple sonorous truth the treacherous din of the realm, a woman sings. And the king listens, distracted from his obsessive vigilance.

Taking up the theme of the voice, Calvino's story offers a series of ideas that implicitly unsettles one of philosophy's cornerstones. Prior to the entrance of the woman who sings, we are dealing with a voice that emerges from a background of acoustic signals in which vocal emission does not occupy a special role with respect to the other sounds and noises of the palace. The identification of the king with the sense of hearing in fact reduces even the words pronounced by the human beings in the palace to pure sound. And here, precisely, Calvino's fundamentally antiphilosophical intuition springs into action. In contrast to what philosophy has done for centuries, the king-ear—motivated by the essential falsity of political discourse—concentrates on the vocal and ignores the semantic.

In the context of the palace, the vocal itself is a sign of the uncertain sounds of the palace. Not only are the words of the courtiers false, but their voices are false as well; in fact, they are concordant with the threatening noises of the entire system. As with the sound of a closing door, in these voices there is a cold and artificial sound. There is no life. Which means that the human voice—as it is perceived by the ear that lies at the center of power—becomes an acoustic sign among others, a depersonalized noise to be captured and decoded. The human source of these sonorous emissions reveals nothing that is particularly human, but rather dissolves into a general order of political acoustics that controls the realm.

In fact, the female voice that is capable of remaining such without confusing itself with noises, and that is therefore capable of revealing what is peculiarly human, comes from a place that is outside of the political. This revelation has absolutely no surprising characteristics. On the contrary, it concerns the most obvious aspect of what Hannah Arendt calls the human condition: namely, the uniqueness that makes of everyone a being that is different from all the others. "That voice certainly comes from a person, unique, inimitable like every person," observes Calvino. This uniqueness would be perceptible from the gaze as well; but, in centering the story on the sense of hearing and putting the woman who sings outside the window in the darkness, Calvino proceeds in his privileging of the acoustic sphere, pulling our attention to the voice. As long as the ear shows its natural talent for perceiving the uniqueness of a voice that is alone capable of attesting to the uniqueness of each human being, the one who emits that voice must remain invisible. Calvino's text is precise. No appearance of a face corresponds to the phonic emission. Sight does not even have the role of anticipating or confirming the uniqueness captured by the ear.

The king's ear, which is accustomed to the depersonalizing effect of the acoustic order of the realm, is obviously surprised by the message of this voice. As often happens with the ear of politics—and, for similar reasons, with the ear of philosophy—it rarely strains itself to perceive the voice of the human existent as unique. Symptomatically, what escapes it is precisely this "vibration of a throat of flesh" that repeats words with an unrepeatable voice. Put differently, what escapes it is the simple vocal self-revelation of the existence, which ignores every semantic interference. The typical freedom with which human beings combine words is never a sufficient index of the uniqueness of the one who speaks. The voice, however, is always different from all other voices, even if the words are the same, as often happens in the case of a song. This difference, as Calvino underlines, has to do with the body. "A voice means this: there is a living person, throat, chest, feelings, who sends into the air this voice, different from all other voices. . . . A voice involves the throat, saliva." When the human voice vibrates, there is someone in flesh and bone who emits it.

Uniqueness is not a characteristic of Man in general, but rather of every human being insofar as he or she lives and breathes. It is worth underscoring again that this corporal root of uniqueness is also perceptible by sight—that is, by an aspect that is immediately visible to whomever looks at the other's face. The sense of hearing that is privileged here by Calvino nonetheless transfers the perception of uniqueness from the corporal surface, from the face, to the internal body. The sense of hearing, characterized as it is by organs that are internalized by highly sensitive passageways in the head, has its natural referent in a voice that also comes from internal passageways: the mouth, the throat, the network of the lungs. The play between vocal emission and acoustic perception necessarily involves the internal organs. It implicates a correspondence with the fleshy cavity that alludes to the deep body, the most bodily part of the body. The impalpability of sonorous vibrations, which is as colorless as the air, comes out of a wet mouth and arises from the red of the flesh. This is also why, as Calvino suggests, the voice is the equivalent of what the unique person has that is most hidden and most genuine. This is not an unreachable treasure, or an ineffable essence, or still less, a sort of secret nucleus of the self; rather, it is a deep vitality of the unique being who takes pleasure in revealing herself through the emission of the voice. This revelation proceeds, precisely, from inside to outside, pushing itself in the air, with concentric circles, toward another's ear.

Importantly, even from a mere physiological point of view, this implies a relation. Taken in by the relationality of the vocal emission, which broadcasts itself to the outside, the other's ear is in fact able to perceive "the pleasure that this voice puts into existing: into existing as voice." "The pleasure of giving a personal form to sound waves," says Calvino, is part of vocal self-revelation. The emission is a kind of vital pleasure [*godimento*], an acoustically perceptible breath, where one models one's own sound revealing it to be unique.

In Calvino's story, this pleasure comes from the song of a woman. In a certain sense, this is a commonplace, or rather a stereotype full of misogynist overtones. One could easily think of the various myths that the western tradition has made of the seductive, carnal, primitive, feminine voice, which goes back at least to the Homeric Sirens, or to the misogynist interpretation of them that the tradition has passed down. The inimitable originality with which Calvino notably rereads the traditional image nevertheless opens the theme of the woman who sings onto some unforeseen perspectives. In contrast to the tradition from which it derives, in the context of Calvino's story, the feminine song does not celebrate the dissolution of the one who hears it into the primitive embrace of a harmonic orgy; rather, it reveals to the listener the vital and unrepeatable uniqueness of every human being.

On the other hand, it is clear that the voice heard by the king is a singing voice. Not only because the song exalts the voice and its potential, but above all because the exclusive attention of the king on the purely vocal, and not on the semantic, finds in the song its most natural place of expression. As Calvino's story puts it, the regal ear has heard this song too many times. And we do not learn its words, which have no importance anyway here. What attracts the king is precisely the "voice as a voice, as it offers itself in song." What is more, the king, won over by the pleasure of giving himself over to sound waves, is "infected by the pleasure of making itself heard" that this voice manifests. So he tries to engage in a duet with the feminine voice that calls him, so that his baritone voice might be with hers "together in the same intention of listening." As might be expected, of course, the unhappy king does not know how to sing. If he knew how to sing, says Calvino (speaking as narrator to the king), then "the man you are or have been or could be, the you that no one knows, would be revealed in that voice." The phonic emission exalted by the song, the voice that sends itself into the air and makes the throat vibrate, has a revelatory function. Or better, more than revealing, it communicates. What it communicates is precisely the true, vital, and perceptible uniqueness of the one who emits it. At stake here is not a closed-circuit communication between one's own voice and one's own ears, but rather a communication of one's own uniqueness that is, at the same time, a relation with another unique existent. It takes at least a duet, a calling and a responding—or, better, a reciprocal intention to listen, one that is already active in the vocal emission, and that reveals and communicates everyone to the other.

In this case, the other is a woman. She is the source, the beginning and the infectious origin of the pleasure and the desire for the song discovered by the king. Calvino thus has fun staging a rigorously heterosexual, operatic duet engaging in one of the most famous stereotypes of western culture. The misogynist aspects of such a scene are well known. Song is more suited for the woman than for the man, above all because it is up to her to represent the sphere of the body as opposed to the more important realm of the spirit. Symptomatically, the symbolic patriarchal order that identifies the masculine with reason and the feminine with the body is precisely an order that privileges the semantic with respect to the vocal. In other words, even the androcentric tradition knows that the voice comes from "the vibration of a throat of flesh" and, precisely because it knows this, it catalogs the voice with the body. This voice becomes secondary, ephemeral, and inessential—reserved for women. Feminized from the start, the vocal aspect of speech and, furthermore, of song appear together as antagonistic elements in a rational, masculine sphere that centers itself, instead, on the semantic. To put it formulaically: woman sings, man thinks.

It is thus understandable why, having reduced politics to a general acoustic order, Calvino performs a truly revolutionary gesture. The king who listens in fact occupies himself only with sounds and totally overlooks the semantic. There is no rational strategy in the power of the king who hears the polyphonic "rumble of death" emit from the realm and trembles at every noise for his own fate. Thus, while it assumes an unlikely acoustic form, politics does not lose its traditional characteristics: signs of death, traps, threats, falsities continue to innervate its logic. This very heritage nevertheless allows Calvino to carry out his revolutionary gesture and to bring it to even more interesting conclusions. Already (unusually) privileged over the semantic, the acoustic sphere doubles itself in the story. On the one hand, there is the confused, untrustworthy, lethal sound of the realm. On the other hand, there is the distinct, revelatory, and vital vocalization that comes from elsewhere, from a place that is precisely outside the political sphere. The fact that this "outside" is inhabited by a woman ends up being a kind of homage to the tradition, and yet it also poses a challenge to it. Indeed, the woman here does not represent the usual primitiveness of the extrapolitical sphere, but rather the genuine truth of a vocal that forces the political to account for itself in ways that it had not foreseen.

The tradition of interpreting sexual difference from the point of view of the semantic thus gets replaced by a perspective that reinterprets this difference from a vocal perspective. Through an obligatory homage to a tradition that wants the woman to be a corporal, singing, and apolitical creature, the revolutionary privileging of the phonic allows Calvino to signify in another way precisely these stereotypically feminine qualities. Indeed, now she appears on the scene in order to attest to the truth of the vocal, which—instead of being abstract like the truths postulated by reason—proclaims simply that every human being is a unique being, and is capable of manifesting this uniqueness with the voice, calling and infecting the other, and enjoying this reciprocal manifestation. In short, she attests to a rather quotidian, familiar truth of life—namely, the uniqueness and the relationality of human beings. In the context of Calvino's story, this truth comes into even sharper relief because it emerges against a background of sheer noise in a realm where the sounds of things and the voices of men have the same, essentially hostile, ontological status.

Indeed, the king, threatened by every sound, is quite alone. His solitude does not have the romantic tinge of the outsider who rebels against the logic of the system; on the contrary, he is at its center as its key component. It thus becomes crucial that the feminine voice of the song, in the act of revealing the uniqueness of the one who emits it, shows at the same time the relational valence of the vocal sphere. Destined for the ear of another, the voice implies a listener—or better, a reciprocity of pleasure. By breaking through the confines of his exclusively acoustic role, the king is in fact inspired to make of himself a source of sonority. Momentarily deaf to the din of the realm, he discovers a new world where human voices communicate to each other first of all their uniqueness. The scene is thus reversed: it is no longer a question of intercepting a sound and decoding or interpreting it, but rather of responding to a unique voice that signifies nothing but itself. There is nothing ulterior behind this voice that would make it into a mere sonorous vehicle, an audible sign.

Discovering that he has a body, that he has one life to live, the listening king sings. But, then, obviously he is no longer king, but rather a human being rooted in his fundamental ontological condition. The simple truth of the vocal makes the crown fall without anyone ever hearing the crash.

Preliminary Outline of the Theme of the Voice; or, Philosophy Closes Its Ears

Every voice "certainly comes from a person, unique, unrepeatable like every person," Calvino assures us. He calls our attention to what we might call a vocal phenomenology of uniqueness. This is an ontology that concerns the incarnate singularity of every existence insofar as she or he manifests her- or himself vocally. Ontology and phenomenology are, of course, just names (perhaps they are too technical, or too indulgent of a certain philosophical idiom) that indicate how the human condition of uniqueness resounds in the register of the voice. Moreover, the voice shows that this condition is essentially relational. The simple truth of the vocal, announced by voices without even the mediation of articulate speech, communicates the elementary givens of existence: uniqueness, relationality, sexual difference, and age—including the "change of voice" that, especially in men, signals the onset of puberty. There would therefore be any number of reasons for making the voice a privileged theme of a speculation on the problem of ontology. But, surprisingly, authoritative precedents for this kind of speculation are lacking.

In the literary and philosophical production of the west, strange as it may seem, Calvino's story is in fact one of the few texts that encourages an investigation into what the voice as such has to offer. This strange state of affairs is even more surprising today, not only if one considers a phenomenon that is obvious to any pair of ears, but above all if one takes into account the remarkable fortune that the theme of voice has found in contemporary discourse. The thematization of the voice that I will propose here begins by taking seriously Calvino's suggestions, while finding in the thought of late modernity a theoretical horizon that is at once promising and disappointing. On the one hand, in the twentieth century (especially in the last decades), the voice became a specific object of study for various currents of thought, which analyzed the vocal sphere from a number of interpretive perspectives. On the other hand, the simple fact of the uniqueness of voices, not to mention the relationality of the vocal sphere, gained very little attention in this wide range of studies. Today, as in the past, the tradition is reticent when it comes to that which is proper to the voice.

Anyone familiar with philosophy cannot help but be suspicious of this reticence. After all, it is a symptom of a problem that has to do with the philosophical affinity for an abstract and bodiless universality, and for the domain of a word that does not come out of any throat of flesh. Calvino helps us to identify the elementary terms of the question. The uniqueness of the voice is an incontrovertible given of experience, technologically proven by digital machines that can trace it; this is not a problem. The problem arises from the obstinate way in which philosophy not only ignores this given, but stands out among the disciplines for the force with which it renders the voice insignificant. The history of the voice's relegation to insignificance is long and complex. I will try, in the pages that follow, to reconstruct and explain this history in some detail. As a start, however, it will be useful to outline some general points.

First, there is a simple but crucial caveat. The philosophical tradition does not only ignore the uniqueness of the voice, but it also ignores uniqueness as such, in whatever mode it manifests itself. The unrepeatable singularity of each human being, the embodied uniqueness that distinguishes each one from every other is, for the universalizing tastes of philosophy, a superfluity. Uniqueness is epistemologically inappropriate. Discouraging as this may seem, this still does not by itself liquidate the thematic importance of the voice. After all, the voice is a central theme for a kind of knowledge that is inaugurated in Greece as the self-clarification of logos; and that after various (but coherent) developments throughout the millennia arrives in the twentieth century vis-à-vis the obsessive theme of language. If what is at stake in the term *logos*—a notoriously equivocal word that means, among other things, "language"—is "speech" [*parola*], then the "voice" also plays a part here. To put it formulaically, speech refers to speakers, and speakers refer to their voice. Plausible as it might seem, however, this is not the road taken by philosophy. Philosophy instead chooses a path that, through precise strategies, avoids getting caught up in the very question of the voice.

The basic strategy, which is the inaugural act of metaphysics, consists in a double gesture whereby speech is separated from speakers and finds its home in thought. Or, put differently, it finds its home in a mental signified of which speech itself, in its sonorous materiality, would be the expression—its acoustic, audible sign. The voice thus gets thematized as the voice in general, a sonorous emission that neglects the vocal uniqueness of the one who emits it. In this way, the voice in general turns into the phonetic component of language as a system of signification. In this semantic and depersonalized form, the voice becomes the specific object of a discipline that—while it takes the modern name *linguistics*—actually goes back at least as far as Plato's *Cratylus*. Over and beyond the acceleration of this trend (which is itself complicated and complex) over the course of the past century, it is in fact possible to trace the theoretical developments that bring modern linguistics to inherit from classical metaphysics a programmatic lack of attention to the uniqueness of the voice. This obviously does not diminish the legitimacy of linguistic studies, but rather testifies to the ways in which forms of knowledge dedicated to the phenomenon of speech are able to focus on the voice as such without ever dealing with the singularity of each voice. In other words, the voice—as it is studied from the perspective of language, and especially from the perspective of language as a system—becomes the general sphere of sonorous articulations where what is not heard is, paradoxically, the uniqueness of the sound. Language insofar as it is a code, whose semantic soul aspires to the universal, renders imperceptible what is proper to the voice. The plural uniqueness of voices does not form the background for the methodological filter of the linguistic ear.

In another totally different quarter, one finds the methodological filter of another modern discipline that focuses its attention explicitly on the voice. Because this discipline is articulated in many ways and mobilizes different categorical horizons—as does linguistics—I shall place it under the general rubric of studies dedicated to orality. These studies have the merit of making a certain theme clear: there is a realm of speech in which the sovereignty of language yields to that of the voice. I am talking, of course, about poetry.

Poets have always known this—and in a certain sense no one has ever know this better than Plato—but the theorization of the phenomenon, the fact that poetry has become the object of a specific kind of research, is recent. The origins of this kind of research in the first decades of the twentieth century go back to the so-called Homeric question, and in particular to the role of epic in oral cultures that do not know writing or that use it only marginally. Indeed, the vast line of research that recuperates, for the theme of the voice, a specific horizon of inquiry gets its impetus precisely from a speculation on the difference between orality and writing—two categories that are destined to be central to twentieth-century thought. Given the importance of Homer for the genesis of this theoretical perspective, the accent falls above all on the centrality of the acoustic sphere in the bard's performance. It is the voice, with its sonorous rhythms, that organizes the words of the epic song. The semantic, not yet subservient to the congealed rules of writing, bends itself to the musicality of the vocal. Above all in epic poetry, but also in all poetry, the realm of sounds thus turns out to be the musical side of language, soliciting bodily pleasure.

This very relationship between vocal pleasure and poetry—foregrounded by studies on oral cultures—becomes a central theme of another type of theoretical approach, but one that is no less important or variegated, and one that calls on contemporary thought to explore the question of the voice. A constellation of perspectives, influenced by psychoanalysis, that valorize the pulsional and presemantic component of the acoustic sphere have taken their place alongside studies on orality. From these perspectives, the voice plays a subversive role with respect to the disciplining codes of language—and in fact turns out not only to organize poetic song but also the poetic text, if not the text in general and therefore writing as such. The voice appears this way, not so much as the medium of communication and oral transmissions, but as the register of an economy of drives that is bound to the rhythms of the body in a way that destabilizes the rational register on which the system of speech is built. These two perspectives—which are, of course, irreducible to two precise schools of thought—are not linked, and in many ways are quite heterogeneous. The former studies orality as it stands in opposition to writing, whereas the other privileges textuality as the realm that has its chief paradigm in writing. What they have in common, nevertheless, is a tendency to "rediscover," in a positive sense, the musical and seductive power of the voice that the metaphysical tradition—starting from Plato's famous hostility toward Homer—has constantly tried to neutralize.

The most significant part of the question lies, again, not only in the fact that these two perspectives share this "rediscovery" (at once antiplatonic and antimetaphysical), but, moreover, in the surprising fact that both perspectives are indifferent to the uniqueness of the voice. Even in those theories that focus on the corporal aspect of the voice—the hot rhythms of its emission, the pleasure of the throat and saliva—the plurality of unique voices still does not emerge as a matter worthy of note. Although it gets linked to deep drives and to the vitality of breath, and although it is seen as subverting or destabilizing the codes of language, the voice still remains a voice in general. Whether in studies on orality or in studies on the vocal nature of the text, there are still no voices that, in communicating themselves, communicate their uniqueness. Rather, there is only voice: a voice that is doubtless rooted in the fleshiness of the body, but a voice of everyone and no one. Unlike linguistics—where the voice becomes the scientific object of a cold analysis that understands it from the perspective of the semantic, in order to then incorporate the voice into a coherent system—here the voice challenges the coherence of that very system. Nevertheless, this attention to the bodily resonances does not open the ear to the vocalic revelation of singular bodies. The musicality of speech, or as Calvino would say, the pleasure of giving one's own form to the sound waves, once again fails to be tuned into the plurality of voices, each one different from the other, that make up the symphony.

The relegation to insignificance that metaphysics reserves for uniqueness therefore continues to function as the unheard background of even those theories that, in principle, seek to use the voice against a writing or a language that is seen as metaphysical. The question before us is therefore, again, even more paradoxical if one takes into account the increasing number of disciplines that take the voice as an object of study. The more that the voice turns out to be a question worthy of inquiry, the more the usual deafness with respect to singular voices appears surprising.

Even those studies that claim to be novel in this regard suffer the same fate, although this time, the specific object of research gets called the *order of the vocal*. This expression was coined by Paul Zumthor, an authoritative medievalist who has broadened the horizons opened by the early studies on orality. Zumthor does not fail to point out, among other things, that "it is strange that, among all our institutional disciplines, there does not yet exist a science of the voice."[2] Attempting to remedy this state of affairs, Zumthor proposes a distinction between orality and vocality: he defines *orality* as "the functioning of the voice as the bearer of language" and *vocality* as "the whole of the activities and values that belong to the voice as such, independently of language."[3] The original aspect of vocality, as a new object of study, therefore concerns an analysis of the voice that avoids the traditional privileging of its relationship with language. It thus opens broad, divergent horizons for understanding the phenomenon of the voice—so broad and divergent, in fact, that the list of disciplines it would comprehend includes, as a start, philosophy, cultural anthropology, the history of music, phonetics, psychology, cybernetics, and ethnology, if not studies on orality and communication.[4] It is precisely the voice as voice, in its multiple manifestations, that orients an investigation that recuperates—but also puts into crisis—the specificity of various canonical disciplines. Significantly, though, even here the uniqueness of the voice remains essentially uninvestigated. Even though this line of research is dedicated to challenging the dominion of language, the voice of vocality insists on presenting itself as a voice in general.

In addition to being extremely interesting, studies dedicated to vocality are above all important because they bring to light a fundamental theoretical bond: namely, the bond between voice and speech. The voice is sound, not speech. But speech constitutes its essential destination. What is therefore at stake in any inquiry into the ontology of the voice—where uniqueness and relationality come to the fore—is a rethinking, without metaphysical prejudices, of this destination. The fundamental prejudice concerns the tendency to totalize this destination so that, outside speech, the voice is nothing but an insignificant leftover. When the register of speech is totalized—for instance, when it is identified with a language system of which the voice would be a mere function—it is indeed inevitable that the vocal emission not headed for speech is nothing but a remainder. Rather than a mere leftover, however, what is really at stake is an originary excess. Put another way, the sphere of the voice is constitutively broader than that of speech: it exceeds it. To reduce this excess to mere meaninglessness—to whatever remains when the voice is not intentioned toward a meaning, defined as the exclusive purview of speech—is one of the chief vices of logocentrism. This vice transforms the excess of the voice into a lack. Indeed, speech becomes more than an essential destination for the voice; it becomes a divider that produces the drastic alternative between an ancillary role for the voice as vocalization of mental signifieds and the notion of the voice as an extraverbal realm of meaningless emissions that are dangerously bodily, if not seductive or quasi-animal. In other words, logocentrism radically denies to the voice a meaning of its own that is not always already destined to speech. It is thus understandable why, as Zumthor points out, the perspective that cuts out for vocality its own autonomous investigation into "the whole of the activities and values that are proper to the voice, independently of language" is crucial. And it is moreover understandable why, between the two roots of western culture—Hebrew and Greek—it is symptomatically the first that nurtures the challenge that a vocal ontology of uniqueness poses to logocentrism.

This challenge—which is essentially the aim of this book—is ambitious but simple. In elementary terms, it consists in thinking of the relationship between voice and speech as one of uniqueness that, although it resounds first of all in the voice that is not speech, also continues to resound in the speech to which the human voice is constitutively destined. The vocal communication of uniqueness, although it inheres exclusively in the register of sound, in fact ends up being essential to that destination. Meaning—or, better, the relationality and the uniqueness of each voice that constitutes the nucleus of this meaning—passes from the acoustic sphere to speech. Precisely because speech is sonorous, to speak to one another is to communicate oneself to others in the plurality of voices. In other words, the act of speaking is relational: what it communicates first and foremost, beyond the specific content that the words communicate, is the acoustic, empirical, material relationality of singular voices.

All that needs to be understood, obviously, is the meaning of the term *speech* [*la parola*]. Because of a complex series of events having to do with the history of metaphysics, in the modern lexicon, *speech* is indeed an ambiguous and equivocal name that often ends up indicating the general idea of the verbal sphere instead of indicating a contingent, contextual sonorous articulation that emits from the mouth of someone and that is destined for the ears of another. The result of all this is the mystification of a phenomenon that is as obvious as it is essential: there is speech because there are speakers. Philosophy's strategic deafness to the plural, reciprocal communication of voices depends precisely on the methodological decision, so to speak, to ignore the elementary materiality of this phenomenon. This method—which is metaphysical in nature, but which also informs various disciplines—consists in thematizing speech while neglecting the vocality of the speakers. The uniqueness of the voice thus goes unnoticed because, methodologically, it does not make a sound. Cut off from the throats of those who emit it, speech undergoes a primary devocalization that leaves it with only the depersonalized sound of a voice in general.

In order to contest the effects of this devocalization, it is thus necessary to adopt another method—a method that takes inspiration from Calvino's story instead of from the texts of the history of philosophy. This method is faithful to the vocal phenomenology of uniqueness, and it consists in listening to speech as it resounds in the plurality of voices who—each time and always addressing themselves to one another—speak. In a certain sense, therefore, this second method functions as a kind of reversal, if not a deconstruction, of the first. It seeks to understand speech from the perspective of the voice instead of from the perspective of language. Speech, understood as speech that emits from someone's mouth, is not simply the verbal sphere of expression; it is also the point of tension between the uniqueness of the voice and the system of language. Privileging either one over the other radically changes the interpretive axes of the theoretical frame. This might seem an easy gesture, or simply a reversal of perspective, but the broader range of contemporary studies on the voice suggests that things are not so simple. Even to thematize the voice as voice—or, if one wants, as "vocality"—does not guarantee any restitution of meaning to the phenomenon of vocal uniqueness. One must have the prudence and the patience to beat down the metaphysical filter that for millennia has blocked our listening. Rather than simply vindicating an independence of the vocal order with respect to language, it is therefore a matter of recording the strategies that allowed the "pole" of language (or, better, its totalization) to neutralize the plurality of voices that constitute the other "pole" of speech. That which is proper to the voice does not lie in pure sound but rather in the relational uniqueness of a vocal emission that, far from contradicting it, announces and brings to its destination the specifically human fact of speech.

In another quarter, there are the writings of Roland Barthes, whose reflections on vocality and textuality have exerted considerable influence on contemporary thought. According to Barthes, what is proper to the voice is what he calls its *grain*. Rather than appertain to breath, the voice concerns "the materiality of the body that springs from the throat, there where the phonic metal is forged."[5] His attention, in short, falls on the oral cavity, the quintessential erotic locus. The grain of the voice has to do above all with the way in which the voice, through the pleasure of sonorous emission, works in language. What interests Barthes is "song" as a primary place of phonic and musical texture from which language grows. Indeed, he underscores that "the voice, which is the bodily aspect of speaking, is situated in the articulation of the body and of discourse," at the point of their exchange.[6] The task of the voice is therefore to be a pathway, or better, a pivotal joint between body and speech. Symptomatically, again, Barthes does not write of a body whose singularity is foregrounded, nor of a voice whose uniqueness is given any importance. Rather, the grain refers to a body of the voice and should be understood as "the way in which the voice lies in the body—or in which the body lies in the voice."[7] But here both body and voice are still presented as general categories. Indeed, in Barthes' writing, the voice and the body are categories of a depersonalized pleasure in which the embodied uniqueness of each existent (something that Barthes never thematizes) is simply dissolved along with the general categories of the subject and the individual. In other words, Barthes encourages us to focus on a vocality that far from being a pure and simple sonority, or a mere bodily remainder, consists in a power relating to speech. And, at the same time, he discourages every perspective that would find in uniqueness and in relationality the fundamental sense of this power.

It is not enough to tune into the sonority, into bodily pleasure, into the song of the flesh, or into the rhythmic drives from which this song flows; this attunement alone will not suffice to pull speech itself from the deadly grip of logocentrism. The metaphysical machine, which methodologically negates the primacy of the voice over speech, should be dismantled by transforming this primacy into an essential destination—and by keeping in mind that the metaphysical strategy that neutralizes the power of the voice is also a strategy in which the spoken exchange of "more than one voice" [*à piu voci*], each one different from the other, remains unheard for millennia. This inability to listen has many pernicious consequences. For example, it makes it so that even those philosophies that value "dialogue" and "communication" remain imprisoned in a linguistic register that ignores the relationality already put in action by the simple reciprocal communication of voices. To thematize the primacy of the voice with respect to speech, in fact, also means opening new directions for a perspective that not only focuses on a primary and radical form of relation that is not yet captured in the order of language, but that is moreover able to specify this relation as a relation among uniquenesses. This, and only this, is the meaning that the vocalic sphere consigns to speech, inasmuch as speech is its most essential destination. And this is a meaning that, through speech, moves from ontology to politics.

PART I

HOW LOGOS LOST ITS VOICE

1.1

The Voice of Jacob

> [T]he word which comes out of the mouth is a sound made
> in the echo of God.
> —Grace Paley, *Later the Same Day*

The primacy of the voice with respect to speech—that is, the inarticulate voice—lies at the origins of many cultures that, in various ways, trace the beginning of the acoustic sphere to a divine presence. As Corrado Bologna notes in a study that provides an extremely broad survey of the theme of vocality, in the Indian tradition of Upanishad "the syllable OOHM, when it is left to vibrate in the airways, is the expression in inarticulate form of that original sonority."[1] The ensemble of breath and voice—both coming from the mouth in the dawning of a newborn life—is also present in Egyptian and Sumerian-Babylonian cosmogonies. We find this also, as a sort of prephilosophical thread, in Greek religion, according to which god is breath and vapor that come out of the crevices of the earth in order to make themselves into speech, through the hoarse voice of the Pythia.[2] It is moreover symptomatic that in the classical era, the Greek word *phone* is applied to both human and animal voice, as well as to any other audible sound. Even in the homeland of logos, this fact shows that acoustic phenomena, in all the variations of their expressions, tend to constitute an autonomous sphere, independent of speech. This confusion of voice and sound, which would be "typical of mystic, archaic thought," is thus also a horizon of meaning that seems to require the vocal to be measured first of all against the whole realm of sounds instead of depending right away on the system of speech.[3] Still, this is not the best way to understand the primacy of the voice in the Greek tradition, certainly not in the philosophical tradition from which logos emerges.

On the other hand, the same cannot be said for the Hebrew tradition, from which we have many significant indications. According to the Bible, God's power—which manifests itself to the people of Israel through creation and revelation—finds its expression in breath, *ruah*, and in the voice, *qol*. The term *ruah* indicates above all breath—the living breath of God breathed into the mouth of Adam—or, rather, that same divine breath that exhales into the chaos before naming the elements that flow from his breath. The Greek renders this term as *pneuma*; in Latin it becomes *spiritus*. As it comes from God, *ruah* also manifests itself wind, breeze, storm, and, above all, as a creative force. God creates with the breath of his mouth," recites Psalm 33. This breath is the same spirit *ruah*, that blows the waters at the beginning of Genesis. Its characters are similar to that of *qol*, the Hebrew term that gets translated by the Septuagint version as *phone*. Significantly, besides indicating the voice, also indicates the acoustic effect of the wind and storms, and above all hunder. *Qol* is similar in its power and its modes of manifestation to *ruah* but is distinguished by way of sound. Just as happens with the Greek word *phone*, *qol* refers to the acoustic sphere and refers to everything that is perceptible by the ear. Not unlike Psalm 33, which attributes creation to the *ruah*, which comes out of God's mouth, in Psalm 29 we find that Yahweh's *qol* is powerful, fearful as it thunders over the water as the creator's voice. There is, in short, a notable affinity between *ruah* and *qol*, between breath and voice—or, to use the Septuagint translation, between *pneuma* and *phone*. Both refer to the mouth of God, and both evoke the essential bond between voice and breath, a bond that in the Hebrew Bible is at once pneumatic, sonorous self-revelation and creation. *Ruah* and *Qol*—which are sources of an inspiring and vocal communication between God and the world, and human beings—belong in the Hebrew tradition to a fundamental sphere of meaning that comes *before* speech.

As is well known, the thesis of creation through speech—a pervasive commonplace in western culture—suffers from the Christian rereading of the Old Testament. For ancient Israel, neither creation nor self-revelation come from the speech of God but rather from his breath and from his voice. Even when it is explicitly voice, *qol*, the divine power pertains to a sphere that distinguishes itself from speech and is independent of it: a pure vocal, indifferent to the semantic function of language, which takes various forms of sonorous manifestation. With respect to the creation through Yahweh's *qol* that is evoked in Psalm 29, the story that opens Genesis in fact reflects a later conception. The scansion of the six days and the eschatological rest on the seventh appear, as Franz Rosenzweig puts it, not as a revelation but as "the exemplarity of divine creation for human beings."[4]

The story describes creation as a verbal event of God. He utters a word that brings into being what was said: "God said, 'let there be light.' And there was light" (Genesis 1:3). The verb "to say" is, in the Hebrew text, *amar*, a verb that indicates speaking as a pronounced and expressed signification, as the communication of a content.[5] This verb was in common use, both in ordinary and in theological language, and can be found in many passages in the Bible, where it gets used primarily in the case of a communication that presupposes a listener and, often, a response. Anyway, the difference in semantic valence between *amar* and *qol* should be clear. Whereas *amar* indicates speech, or a verbal event whose acoustic aspect is a function of the communicative expression of a content, *qol* indicates the pure acoustic phenomenon that leaves every verbal content aside.

For the most ancient phase of the Hebrew religion, God is voice, or also breath, not speech. Speech, according to the ritual formula "word of God," is what God becomes through the prophets who lend him their mouths, in such a way that the divine *qol* is made articulate language, or the language of Israel. The prophet "does not make God speak, but, at the moment in which he opens his mouth, God speaks."[6] The word of God thus makes itself "perceptible in the *medium* of human language."[7] In this language the most essential element is, as Gershom Scholem indicates, "the sound that is at the base of every language, the voice that gives them form, that forges it by elaborating its sonorous material." In other words, it is a question of the presence in language of "something that is not only sign, signified and expressed"; that is, "something unexpressed that reverberates behind every expression."[8] From this voice that reverberates but is not sign—if anything, its sign is articulate speech—springs the kabbalistic tradition that privileges writing as the realm of the sign. The original horizon is, however, precisely that of a transcendent, divine voice that generates and exceeds speech—and whose reverberation still makes itself heard in languages and constitutes the unexpressed side of speech. As Walter Benjamin puts it, "God breathes his breath into man: this is at once life and mind and language."[9]

It is generally believed that the essential function of speech is to communicate a given content. Benjamin ironically calls this the "bourgeois conception of language," according to which "the means of communica-

tion is the word, its object factual, and its addressee a human being."[10]
Speech, in short, would have the job of designating and transmitting a
content. Of course, this is quite different from the idea of communication
that can be traced back in the Hebrew tradition. This idea affirms that
speakers communicate themselves to one another, in the voice of God,
which reverberates in the sound of their language. The reverberation of the
divine *qol* in articulate speech is in fact the originary communication that
makes communicable every further act of communication. In this sense, it
is indicative that Hebrew writing, modeled on biblical writing, uses a con-
sonant alphabet that omits the vowels. The vocal sound of speech, which
is identical to the breath of life—*qol* and *ruah*—does not pass to the visible, mute order of writing. Starting in the sixth century, before the Ma-
soretic writing of the Torah annotates the vowels with diacritic signs, it is
the reader who has to lend "his voice, his phonic organ to the text."[11] If it
is indeed true that Hebrew civilization, more than any other, can be defined as a culture of writing—in spite of the fact that "for Judaism the oral
doctrine is more ancient and more sacred than the written one"—it is also
true that this writing, when one takes into account the vowel, shows a crucial resistance to the regime of signs.[12] The sound of the vowels must be
added by the one who reads aloud, or rather by the one who reenunciates
the prophetic work. It is sound and breath, as they reverberate in the word,
which is in the closest relation with the transcendence of God. Indeed, one
of the most significant differences between the Hebrew and the Christian
traditions has precisely to do with this aspect. In the Hebrew tradition, the
sacred Word is first of all a sonorous event, a fact that is confirmed in the
very name of the Bible: *miqra*, or "reading, proclamation" (from the verb
qara, "to call, to proclaim, to declare"—present also in the term *Koran*). In
the Christian tradition, on the other hand, "the Word is crystallized in
writing, as it becomes *graphè/graphai*, namely Writing/Writings, or *Biblia*,
the plural for the Greek *biblion* [book]."[13] Typically, the difference is reflected also in the reading of the sacred text, which for the Jews is done
aloud with a rhythmic undulation of the body that underscores the musical sonority of the Word, whereas for the Christians it is silent and immobile.[14] Muslims, too, read the Koran aloud, undulating the body back and
forth; as Rusmir Mahmutcehajic says, "the voice confirms the Word: to
speak is our way of seeking the voice at the Beginning."[15]

The fact that, for the Jews, it is forbidden to pronounce God's Name
only confirms the centrality of the acoustic. The Name that can be *recalled*,

but not *proffered*, indeed represents, for the Jews, the "abyssal and inexorable character" of the transcendent God.[16] In writing, this Name takes the form of the so-called tetragram, but it also appears in one of two consonants and in one of three consonants. The most interesting of these is the biconsonant form, or as Rosenzweig calls it, the bigram. In fact, the bigram *Jah*—which can be traced back to a group of names for God that recall cultic invocations—corresponds "to one of those originary grids from which the language must have had its origins: speech at the original place of the encounter . . . pure vocative prior to any possibility of other cases of declension."[17] Insofar as it is pure vocative, *Jah* is therefore also a pure vocal—an "originary cry," voice before speech. "The proper name of God, unlike all other proper names, not only had to have been at the beginning, but must always remain."[18] And in effect, in the joyous sound of the *Hallelu-Jah*, it still remains.

There is in the Bible a famous story that, by itself, would suffice to refute the deaf strategy of logocentrism. The primacy of the voice with respect to speech receives, in the story, a particular torsion that makes evident not only the uniqueness of the voice, but also its crucial asymmetry with respect to the order of speech. The story tells how the voice of Jacob, in spite of his deceitful words, could not fool his father.

The story is well known (Genesis 27). Old and blind, and feeling that he is close to death, Isaac calls his firstborn son Esau in order to give him his blessing. Esau must go hunting for some game and prepare a delicious meal for his father, so that Isaac can bless his son before he dies. Obediently, Esau goes off to hunt. Rebecca, who is party to everything, takes advantage of Esau's absence in order to play a trick on Isaac. She invites the younger son, Jacob, to take his brother's place and steal the paternal blessing. She herself will prepare a sumptuous meal of goat meat, of which Isaac is quite fond. There remains one problem. Esau is hirsute, whereas Jacob's skin is smooth. "My father might touch me and realize that I'm taking advantage of him, and he will lay on me a curse instead of a blessing," worries Jacob. However, Rebecca finds a solution for this problem as well: Jacob will wear one of Esau's shirts and will cover his arms and neck with the goat's skin. The trick works. Pretending to be his brother, Jacob presents himself to his father and says: "I am Esau, your firstborn son." Of course, as Jacob had predicted, Isaac wants to touch him. Having verified his son by touch, Isaac still shows his uncertainty: "The voice [*qol*] is the voice of

Jacob, but the arm is the arm of Esau." Jacob persists in the lie and repeats to his father that he is, in fact, Esau. In the end, with the help of the olfactory, the trick works. Isaac smells the odor of Esau's shirt and, taking Jacob for his firstborn son, gives him his blessing.

The story teaches a number of things, but what is interesting from our perspective is the confrontation of the acoustic sphere and that of touch and smell. From a certain point of view, the latter prevail—inasmuch as they convince Isaac that he should trust his sense of touch and smell rather than his own ears. On the other hand, the story shows that, unlike the touchable surface of the body and its smell, the voice plays no trick. The voice—always unique and recognizable as such—cannot be disguised. If it is true that the lie organized by Rebecca and Jacob is part of God's plan, it is also true that the voice appears here as the only element that is extraneous to the lie. Artifice cannot capture the voice: "The voice is the voice of Jacob." Indeed, this is why Isaac doubts his son's word and resorts to the sense of touch. When Esau, who arrives too late, tells his father "I am your firstborn son Esau," Isaac in fact has no need for recourse to touch. The speech that says "I am Esau" is, in this case, indubitable. It is almost a redundancy, or a superfluous confirmation, of the voice of Esau.

The story also teaches us the difference between the register of the voice and the register of speech. For Isaac, who is blind and cannot see his sons' faces, the problem is to recognize them, or to identify their uniqueness. The voice should therefore suffice. And, in fact, it is enough: "The voice is the voice of Jacob"; Isaac is not mistaken. What makes the voice insufficient here is precisely the contradiction of the speech that it brings: "I am Esau," says the voice of Jacob. What he says contradicts the voice that says it. In fact, two exemplary modes of uniqueness come into confrontation here: the voice and the proper name. The proper name, unlike common names, does not designate a category of things but names the uniqueness of the one who bears the name. The proper name is in fact, first of all, the name of the call to which, in biblical language, one responds, "here I am." What is paradoxical, therefore, is the trickery of Jacob's speech that pretends to respond to the convocation of his brother. The voice nevertheless unmasks him.

The voice indeed does not mask, but rather unmasks the speech that masks it. Speech can play tricks. The voice, whatever it says, communicates the uniqueness of the one who emits it, and can be recognized by those to whom one speaks. But it is not being recognizable that renders the voice unique. On the contrary, every voice is unique, and because it is unique, once it is known it can be recognized. Not by chance, in the Hebrew tradition, the vocal sphere in which the voice of God reverberates is also the sphere in which each human being manifests his uniqueness. Breathing into their mouths, God creates unique beings—just as their voices, in which His voice reverberates, reveal them to be unique.

Thus, in the final analysis, we could conclude that in the story of Jacob, God's plan is manifested in the single element of the story that resists falsification. "The voice is the voice of Jacob." Jacob, whose voice is known by both God and Isaac, obtains the blessing.

1.2

"Saying," Instead of the "Said"

> There is an ancient Talmudic text that has always impressed me: God is absolutely extraordinary. In order to stamp coins, States use a mould. With a single mould they make many piece, all alike. God, with the mould of his image, is able to create a dissimilar multitude: of "I's," all one of a kind.
> —Emmanuel Levinas

Greek texts are "experts in species and genres," writes Emmanuel Levinas, whereas the Bible teaches inimitable singularity, the uniqueness of each soul.[1] Levinas is talking about the Hebrew Bible: the explicit source of an ethics that he roots in the uniqueness of the other's face, as a principle of radical responsibility for the other. Indeed, the Hebrew matrix of certain contemporary thinkers who, in various ways, attack the metaphysical tradition in the name of uniqueness is quite remarkable—Rosenzweig, Buber, and Arendt, for example. In the confrontation of the two roots of the west, Greek and Hebrew, the theme of uniqueness turns out to be decisive. Individuated as products of logos, the universalizing arrogance of anonymous categories like Man, subject, individual is unmasked.

Surprisingly, this attack rarely leads to the question of the voice—at least, not directly or explicitly. Instead, the everyday dialogue of an *I* and a *you* is called on by these twentieth-century thinkers in order to challenge the logos of the metaphysicians. The unique existent thus ends up having a say in the matter, but it is still not heard as a voice. Strange as it may seem, even those thinkers who rely on the Hebrew matrix have trouble recognizing the subversive potential of the voice in their critiques of language.

Language, according to Levinas, "in its expressive function, addresses others and invokes them."[2] The common plane of speech—what the in-

terlocutors communicate to one another through language—is different
from the plane of the interlocutors themselves. This difference has, for Levinas, the status of a transcendence. In other words, while the speaker is invoked by speech—or implicated by the fact that there is speech—the
speaker is not a function of the sphere of speech. He is, for the interlocutor, the one who is in front of him: a unique being whose uniqueness transcends speech and the verbal system of signification. This "being in front
of" is defined by Levinas as the face of the other—an expression that designates the irreducible uniqueness of every human being as a face that regards me; indeed, as the "face of the one who regards *me* par excellence."[3]
The horizon is therefore visual. The face of the other is "this dear piece of
flesh with forehead, nose, eyes, mouth," which is "neither sign which tends
toward a signified, nor a mask that hides it."[4] There is therefore nothing to
reveal. The unique human is already here, in the face. He, she, is in proximity, in front of me, face to face. The face of the other signifies itself, before and beyond every system of signification. Or, as Levinas says, the face
of the other speaks to me.

The visual and the verbal thus penetrate one another and are confused with one another. In the complex work of Levinas it is, however, un-
doubtedly the former that plays the fundamental role. His radical ethics,
which postulates the responsibility of each one for the other, is an ethics
based on vision—the ordinary, material, unavoidable vision of the other's
face. It is, however, symptomatic that when he deals with speech—as in
the case of the transcendence of the interlocutor—Levinas cannot help
sliding from speech itself to the vision of the face, and precisely to a face
that, in turn, as Levinas often says, speaks. Obviously, the point is not to
highlight a contradiction in Levinas' text; nor is it to insist on a rigid distinction between the vocal and the visual. Rather, the point is to reflect on
the surprising tendency of Levinas to proceed from the question of speech
not to the voice, but to resolve speech in the face.

If I may be picky for a moment, it seems to me that the move Levinas makes in founding the uniqueness of the interlocutor in the showing
of his face is rather illogical. After all, the face of the other is, by definition,
unique and therefore it does not matter if the one who shows his face engages in interlocution or not. In interlocution it is instead precisely the
voice that transcends the plane of speech and manifests the uniqueness of
the other. After all, I can speak in the dark to someone who is not in front
of me. Calvino's king, confined to his throne, does not see the face of the

woman who sings. Nor does Isaac, who is blind, see the face of his sons. In the realm of speech, it is not the face of the other, but rather his or her voice that constitutes the proper of uniqueness. And this voice, like the face but perhaps more so, is "neither sign which tends toward a signified, nor a mask that hides it." Bound to a verbal system of signification—or, better, to logos—the voice is perfectly suited to the role of signifying the "human fact" of uniqueness before and beyond this system. And it is perhaps thanks to this prelogic self-signification of the vocal that one can say that the face speaks.

This speaking face is, for Levinas, the "speech of God, and word in the human face . . . already language before the word, originary language."[5] The visible nature of this language, which is decidedly unvocal, is clarified by Levinas when he calls it an "unheard language, language of the un-said. Writing"[6]—not voice, therefore, but writing: divine revelation, word of God, in the face of the other as text, or rather, the word of God in the face of the one next to me—who is, symptomatically, trace. In the Judaism of Levinas, the centrality of writing therefore prevails over that of the voice. And in this case, it is a writing that signifies not because of its specific content, because of its Said, but rather because it is the visible trace of an absolute transcendence that makes itself proximate in the proximity of the other's face.

Elsewhere, as he continues his critique of metaphysical logocentrism, Levinas explicitly invites us to distinguish between Saying (*le Dire*) and the Said (*le Dit*). This move is paradoxical. Saying is in fact understood by Levinas as "anterior to verbal signs, anterior to linguistic systems and to semantic reflections—preface to languages."[7] Again, this is not the phonetic aspect of speech, not a voice that reverberates. Rather, Saying is here—at least, in its simplest meaning—the act of speaking, the event by which human beings speak to each other one by one, without regard for what they say. This Saying is distinguished by Levinas from a Said that is, at the same time, that which they say to one another and that which the entire knowledge of the west says. But the Said is above all the system that organizes speech. The Said is therefore the logos of the Greeks, or rather the principle on which the metaphysical tradition that "subordinates the human to the anonymous games of being" is founded.[8] In any case, this is the polemic objective of the distinction between Saying and the Said in Levinas' text.

From its Greek origins, philosophy has always focused on the Said—indeed, a Said that is assumed as an autonomous reality, independent of the proximity of the interlocutors in the event of Saying. Philosophy's exclusive interest in the Said corresponds to the central role of a logos understood as an intelligible order that represents, expresses, signifies, designates, duplicates, and organizes the objective order of beings. As it develops in different forms over the centuries, the logocentric tradition of metaphysics continues to insist on *what* is Said and never asks after *who* is Saying. The tradition judges the "words of a language in front of a mouth that opens, coming from the one who speaks" to be inessential.[9] In order to recuperate the reality of this mouth, Levinas claims, "it is necessary to return from the Said to Saying," and precisely to a Saying that "remains elsewhere, or goes beyond, the Said."[10] The aim is nevertheless not simply liberating ourselves from the system of signification in order to fall back on the meaningless, the irrational, or the nonsensical. Rather, the aim is to recuperate the "very significance of signification."[11] It is a question, in other words, of leading the realm of meaning back to the given of the uniqueness of speakers; or, better, to their proximity that makes them responsible for one another. Levinas' text therefore poses a crucial question, even if only in passing. This question asks: who speaks?

"The *who* of *saying* is not simply a grammatical necessity (in the propositional sense that every verb implies a subject)," says Levinas in a note. Neither is it "a retrocession in the face of language's paradox which would be a Saying of no one, which would be a language that speaks and would disappear into the air."[12] It is therefore necessary to abandon the old metaphysical tendency to thematize language by claiming that it speaks on its own, in an anonymous form of a Saying that poses itself as separate from, and indifferent to, the one who actually speaks. "The *who* of Saying does not separate itself from the very act of speaking," says Levinas.[13] Every act of speaking is thus from the start the relation of unique beings that address themselves to one another. They reciprocally expose themselves to one another, in proximity; they invoke one another and communicate themselves to one another. Or, better, they do not only communicate something, some content, some intention, some knowledge, or even less, a language. Rather they simply communicate, in the act of speaking, the radical proximity of their reciprocal communication. This reciprocal communication in Saying, which is anterior to every organized form of speech, is precisely the condition of every communication. It is the communicability of the communicable, or the significance of signification. As a radical sign of communicability, the significance announced by the who of saying precedes, generates, and exceeds verbal communication. "Saying signifies without stopping in the Said, it does not start from an I, it is not reducible to the revelation of a consciousness."[14] Who speaks, as a unique being, is above all open to the uniqueness of another; he or she has nothing in common with the sovereign, self-mastering subject of the philosophical tradition. Leaving aside all pretenses of the autonomous "I," Saying is above all "the supreme passivity of the exposition to Others"—proximity as the eminent form of relation.[15]

Even beyond the explicit citations and indirect references, in Levinas' discourse, there is a Hebrew breath that blows over the surface of his lexicon, further unsettling its syntax. The term *saying* itself attests to this in Levinas' usage—insofar as it draws on and opposes itself to its ordinary lexical sphere, namely the realm of speech and language. Indeed, it might seem a bit extravagant that, for Levinas, this Saying is neither intentional nor conscious. It is a Saying that does not say, does not transmit or communicate any content; a Saying that is anterior and indifferent to the Said. We might ask: why, in order to tell us what he wanted to tell us, did Levinas not take recourse instead in the theme of the voice?

For as the Hebrew tradition itself teaches, the voice in fact maintains a relation—of distinction, anteriority, and excess—with speech, in a way that seems perfectly adapted to the role that Levinas calls on Saying to express. It is certainly not a stretch to indicate in the voice a communication of oneself, a physical proximity of the one to the other, as such prior to any consideration of what is said. In the voice both uniqueness and relation—indeed, uniqueness as relation—manifest themselves acoustically without even taking account of what is Said. The voice, which is embodied in the plurality of voices, always puts forward first of all the *who* of saying. As a faithful testimony to the uniqueness of the one who emits it (as Calvino says) "from a throat of flesh," the voice not only dethrones the "subject" of traditional metaphysics, but it renders this subject ridiculous. From this perspective, the whole task of contrasting Saying and the Said suddenly seems like an awful lot of work—if for no other reason than pure philology.

It is therefore hardly surprising that, in the development of Levinas' text, Saying gets further and further away from the range of its ordinary meaning in order to get closer to the theme of the voice. The first step, as one might expect, is in the direction of the body—or, better, of sensation. Levinas in fact emphasizes that Saying finds precise correspondences with the human fact of sensation—an emblematic experience where "the material is the place itself of the for-the-other." Or, rather, it is the proximity of the other "who is hungry and who eats, who has skin and, thus, is susceptible to *giving* the bread from his own mouth or laying bare his own skin."[16] There is an essential bond between Saying [*Dire*] and Giving [*Donner*], which shows up in a "Saying that is proximity, contact, obligation without end—a Saying still indifferent to the said and saying itself in *giving*."[17] The emphasis thus falls again on proximity, a proximity that is understood as the communication of oneself to another quite beyond any content. All the more in sensation, the human fact [*le fait humain*] is a self-communication precisely because it consists in a communication of oneself to another that precedes and exceeds the linguistic system of communication.

In Levinas' text, Saying finally approaches the theme of the voice through a decisive step: namely, his focus on the theme of respiration. Nothing more than the act of breathing is able to testify to the proximity of human beings to one another; nothing else better confirms their communication as a reciprocal exposure that precedes any initiative. Breathing. For breathing is not subject to a decision, but is rather involuntary and passive—it is a profound communication of oneself, an exchange in which one inhales the air that the other exhales. The proximity of the other in breath, is "the fission of the subject, beyond the lungs, to the very nucleus of the 'I,' to what is indivisible in the individual."[18] This phenomenon, which arises from an absolute proximity that belies any isolation of human beings and confirms the ethic of the for-the-other, is given an emblematic name by Levinas: *pneumatism*. Thus, the ancient *ruah* finally makes its appearance in the Levinasian problematic of Saying, through the Septuagint translation of that term with *pneuma*. Unlike the link between *ruah* and *qol*, however, Levinas remains with a pneumatism that continues to put off involvement with the voice. Levinas' explicit attention falls totally on the breath. Levinas does not focus on the acoustic aspect of breathing, but rather on the fact that breathing alludes to a reciprocal contamination that opens everyone to the other in the vital act of respiration itself. What is significant, therefore, is that Levinas here poses, with respect to breath, the very same interrogative that the metaphysical Greek tradition poses, often, with respect to the voice. In fact, he asks himself whether "the diachrony of inspiration and expiration, separated by an instant that appertains neither to one nor the other," is not perhaps animality. And he goes one step further: "Would perhaps animality be the opening to a beyond essence?"[19] In much the same way, the Greek philosophers—who were bothered by a *phone* that was shared by animals and men—took care to emphasize that in man this *phone* is a *phone semantike*, a "signifying voice," while the animal's is not. The further Levinas gets from the Said, the more that animality gets closer. Breath and voice, as the ancient philosophers knew all too well, are risky themes.

And yet, this is not the answer that Levinas provides regarding the relative risk of the human regression toward the animal. He in fact hypothesizes that animality, our sister in respiration, "is still short of breath of the soul."[20] Breath thus introduces the theme of the soul that, like *ruah*, belongs to the semantic family of respiration: in Latin, *anima*, in Greek *anemos*; or else, *psyche* from the verb *psycho*, "to breathe"; or even *pneuma* itself. The soul of the animal [*l'anima dell'animale*], which is too short of breath, is contrasted by Levinas not only with the long breath of the human being, but above all with the human capacity for a long, last, extreme expiration without return. With this move, breath—which is already proof of the proximity of the other—experiences, both at the beginning and at the end, at birth and at its death, the proximity of God dying in His mouth. Levinas in fact recounts that "the sages of Israel say in a parable that Moses had died kissing God. To die by order of God is, in Hebrew, 'in the mouth of God' (Deuteronomy 34.5). The absolute expiration—by kissing God—is death by order of God, in passivity and obedience, in the inspiration towards the Other for the other."[21]

Breath thus ends up focusing on a long, last expiration. The pneumatic proximity, which yet again founds the ethic of the one for the other, has at its center a dying figure. This is, of course, in perfect symmetry with the centrality of the other's face that, for Levinas, coincides above all with the very mortality of the other: "as if this invisible death which hides behind the face of the other were *my* affair, as if this death 'regarded me.'"[22] And in fact, Levinas strongly maintains that it does regard me; this is precisely the ethics that Levinas proposes as the task of thinking after Auschwitz, an ethics that is called to respond to the death of the other. The fact remains that breath, *ruah*—in spite of the fact that it invokes birth, and indeed creation itself—ends up, in Levinas' account, being brought back to death. Levinas' attention on the dying breath lets the sonority of the newborn's first breath, first cry pass unheard. He does not hear the acoustic, inarticulate, fragile yet undeniable revelation that invokes responsibility for a proximate newcomer, for an existence that is beginning.

1.3

The Devocalization of Logos

> If someone hears a sign that is unknown to him, for example the sound of a word of whose meaning he is ignorant, he desires to know it; that is, he desires to know what idea this sound evokes. . . . But it is necessary that he already know that it is a sign, that the word is not an empty sound, but a sound that signifies something.
> —Augustine, *De Trinitate*

In the metaphysical tradition, according to Levinas, "*logos* as discourse is completely confused with *logos* as reason."[1] He thus synthesizes the two poles that make *logos* the most important, and yet the most ambiguous, term in philosophy. Often a synonym for what we call "language," the term oscillates between "discourse" and "reason," between the realm of speech and the realm of thought. It comprehends and confuses them both.

The etymological matrix is well known. The word *logos* derives from the verb *legein*. From ancient Greek, the verb means both "speaking" and "gathering," "binding," "joining." This is hardly surprising, because the one who speaks joins words to one another, one after the other, gathering them in his discourse. Nor is it strange that, precisely for this reason, *legein* also means "to count" and "to recount." In its ordinary meaning, logos refers to the activity of the one who speaks, of the one who links nouns to verbs and to other parts of speech. Logos consists essentially in a joining together of words. Indeed, philosophy focuses its attention precisely on this joining together, which links and gathers according to determinate rules. And this attention, again, comes at the cost of focusing on the acoustic aspect of speech. Philosophical logocentrism is in fact interested above all in the order that rules the "joining," or rather in language as a system of signification.

Aristotle says in the *Poetics* that logos is *phone semantike*, signifying voice.[2] The argument is of the highest importance because it evokes the famous formula of the *zoon logon echon* that defines man in the *Politics*.[3] According to the current translation, this formula is rendered as "rational animal," but to the letter it means "the living creature who has *logos*." Rather than a "rational" animal, therefore, the definition names a "speaking" animal. Having logos distinguishes man from the other living creatures, or from the other animals. Like men, animals have voices; but these voices are different from the human voice. They are inferior to it because they are not *signifying* voices. In the *Politics*, Aristotle is quite specific on this point. He emphasizes that only in man is the voice signifying, *semantike*. With the other animals, the voice is instead a "sign" [*semeion*] of pain or pleasure, a cry or a yelp. The voice as prior to speech or independent of speech is therefore simply an animal voice—an *a-logic* and *a-semantic* phonation. And yet, even in the animal, it is already "sign" or *semeion*, almost as if the voice could be nothing but a sign, nothing but the function of a nonvocal reality. Or, better, it is almost as if the realm of the *phone* could only be measured from the realm of that which the voice is bound to signify or, at least, to sign.

Indeed, this is where the peculiarity of the philosophical approach to the voice differs crucially from that of the Hebrew Bible. Unlike the *qol*, the *phone* of the philosophers alludes neither to an originary communication nor to the revelatory or creating power of a pure vocal that is divine precisely because it precedes and generates the semantic register of speech. In the Greece of the philosophers, there is no space for reflection on the voice as voice, no room for the reverberation of language as the unexpressed within expression. If anything, in language there reverberates only the mute order of thought. The *phone* of the metaphysicians is inextricably bound to signification or to signing. Without this bond, the voice is an empty sound because it is emptied of its semantic function. The sense of the voice is entirely bound up with the role of vocalizing concepts, so that whatever is left over is an insignificant remain, an excess that is disturbingly close to animality. As a specific object of interest for philosophy, the human voice is grasped within a system of signification that subordinates speech to the concept; that is, that subordinates verbal signification to mental signifieds. Because man possesses this system—because he speaks, as Aristotle puts it, his voice is *semantike*. In the case of other animals, meanwhile, the voice is limited to signing certain affectations, passions, or anxieties. As long as the voice "signs," it stands for, and depends on, something else.

In logos it is therefore the semantic that counts. Logos—at least within the Aristotelian definition—is *phone* (substantive) *semantike* (adjective). Despite the grammar, the fundamental role falls to the semantic; and, precisely, to a semantic founded on the priority of the order of signifieds with respect to the signifiers. To the voice, therefore, goes the service role—it makes signifieds audible, it provides an acoustic robe for the mental work of the concept. And this explains, among other things, why the translation of *zoon logon echon* with "rational animal" is a rather perspicacious error. For this translation is limited to that part of the logos that is not the vocal aspect, but the nexus of speech and signifieds. In other words, the translation emphasizes only the silent activity of the mind that, respecting the order of these signifieds, "gathers" them and "links" them together. Understanding logos as speech and understanding it as reason thus becomes more than ambiguous; it becomes more or less indifferent. Of course, in spite of this translation, what really differentiates thought from speech is *phone*. But this voice has already been reduced to an exterior sign, to a secondary, instrumental factor that is, as happens in Plato's discourse, superfluous.

By capturing the *phone* in the system of signification, philosophy not only makes a primacy of the voice with respect to speech all but inconceivable; it also refuses to concede to the vocal any value that would be independent of the semantic. Reduced to an acoustic signifier, the voice depends on the signified. This dependence is not only obvious, it is decisive, for it captures the voice in a complex system that subordinates the acoustic sphere to the realm of sight. As in the Platonism of Augustine (see the epigraph for this chapter), sound evokes the idea; the order of the signified appertains to the realm of the eye. This is expressed in Greek by terms such as *noema* and *idea*. What we call "signified" is, in fact, for metaphysics an object of thought that is characterized by visibility and clarity. The problem here is not only the relation between the realm of thought and that of speech, nor is it simply the usual metaphysical privileging of thought over speech. Rather, at stake is the fundamental gesture that locates the principle of the system of signification, of the signified, in the visual sphere.

Greek philosophy understands thought—and therefore the entire realm of truth that lies in its purview—in terms of vision. The *noema* and the *idea* are basically mental images. As Hannah Arendt points out, they result from the capacity of thought to present (or to represent) to the mind the desensitized and generalized images of physical objects as they are perceived by the bodily eye.[4] This explains why the invisible God of the Hebrews corresponds to the ineffable truth of philosophers. "The invisibility of truth in the Hebrew religion is as axiomatic as its ineffability is for Greek philosophy."[5] Truth in Greek is *aletheia*—a term that literally means that which is not hidden by any shadow and is therefore resplendent in the full light of day. Rather than concerning man, or the "subject," *aletheia* refers to the realm of objects, "The unwavering heart of well-rounded truth" as Parmenides expressed it; or the luminous and perfectly visible ideas of Plato that found philosophy as science.[6] Science is, in Greek, *episteme*. Here too, a bit of etymology cannot hurt. The term expresses "the incontrovertible necessity of that which stands firm." The Latin *scientia* instead means "seeing clearly after having sought to perceive."[7]

This metaphysical predilection for vision certainly does not originate with philosophy. The conviction that sight is the noblest sense characterizes the whole of Greek culture. Already in Homer, a blind poet who specializes in vocal performance, *seeing* [*idein*] signifies knowing as well—as, for example, when the Sirens alert Odysseus to their omniscience by telling him "we know [*idmen*] all." Plato's *ideai*—a term that means "the visible"—belongs to this same etymological family. Likewise, the lexicon relating to thinking [*noein*] shows that the faculty of thought [*nous*] is, already in Homer's poems, constructed through an analogy to the faculty of sight. This most transparent example, however, is *theoria*—from *theorein*, "to contemplate." According to Bruno Snell, the verb accentuates "the faculty of the eye as it apprehends an object."[8] In this way, the object acquires a primary role in *theoria* and thus justifies the platonic conceptualization of the objectiveness of the signifieds. Both "ideas" and "theory" go on, in any case, to become essential parts of the philosophical vocabulary, and of western science, in modern languages. It would be easy to continue this list of philosophical terms that show how the Greeks in general, and philosophy in particular, held the sphere of vision in the highest esteem.[9] The visual metaphor, which characterizes the truth of the metaphysical tradition, has its roots in a privileging of vision that is shared by Greek culture as a whole. Philosophy, as a metaphysics of presence—in spite of what Jacques Derrida maintains—owes its origins to the realm of the eye.[10]

"Eyes are better witnesses than ears," declares Heraclitus. In an essay inspired by phenomenology, Hans Jonas compares the sense of sight to the sense of hearing. He notes that hearing is characterized by the evanescence and the dynamic nature of perceptible sounds: "what sound immediately reveals is not an object but a dynamic event in the place of an object."[11] One hears barking, not a dog. The existence of the dog and of every durable thing that can be inferred by its perceptible sound is, as such, extraneous to the sonorous event. Sight, in contrast, perceives every object that is in front of the onlooker—objects that are characterized by a certain permanence in space and time. They are stable, lasting, present. Moreover, sight perceives more objects simultaneously and sees them as distinct from one another, in their discrete difference. Hearing, however, is bound to temporality and perceives distinct sounds only in their dynamic succession: melody is not generated by a sequence; it is a sequence. When sounds are juxtaposed, as in polyphony, it is difficult to distinguish them—far more difficult, in any case, than in the spatial realm because "space itself is a principle of distinction and of a simultaneous plurality of objects."[12] In short, sounds are dynamic events, not static qualities, and thus they are transient by nature. What characterizes sounds is not being but becoming.

Another crucial difference, noted by Jonas, concerns the position of the subject. The hearer is completely exposed to sonorous events, which come from an exterior that the hearer does not fully control. Unless one is warned in advance by Circe, it is impossible to close one's ears as Odysseus' companions did in order not to hear the Sirens. Our ears are always open, even when we sleep. With respect to sounds, therefore, we are in a position of passivity. They can strike us without our being able to foresee or control them. Hearing consigns us to the world and its contingency. Sight, on the other hand, suggests the active position of a subject, for not only can this subject open and close his eyes whenever he wants, but he is not affected by the objects of his vision. Objects do not look at him and, above all, they do not require him to look. If I look at the countryside, "it is present to me without my having to be thrown into its presence."[13] Sight permits a position of autonomy that is at once active and detached. The world is there, it is visible, but it is up to us to look or not. The visible world is not a world that interrupts, interferes, or surprises everywhere with its sounds; it is, rather, a stable, immobile, objective world that lies in front of us. This guarantees the reality of being and thus the status of truth as presence.

Jonas' essay is interesting in many respects, first of all because it shows how *theoria* structures not only its lexicon, but its entire categorical apparatus, on the sphere of vision. The visual metaphor, in other words, is not simply an illustration; rather, it constitutes the entire metaphysical system. In the development of his analysis, however, Jonas' own work seems bound to this very system. For in his analysis, both hearing and seeing are examined in relation to things or animals—while the ordinary situation of human beings looking at each other or speaking to each other gets neglected. Indeed, Jonas centers his investigation of hearing on the examples of barking dogs or musical sounds, whereas his analysis of seeing describes primarily the contemplation of inanimate objects or a gaze that looks out over the countryside. He therefore avoids the human voice and thus does not ask after the problems of uniqueness or relationality. The same goes for his analysis of sight, where the objects he chooses as his examples have absolutely no relation to the observer. The end result is thus an interpretive analysis that—precisely because it takes metaphysics as its focus—convincingly lays bare the peculiar static, unrelational videocentrism on which metaphysics is founded.

The entire philosophical lexicon in fact finds its base in the objectivity and presence of things, which is guaranteed by this detached gaze. This starts above all with Plato, who uses the term *theoria* to mean "the contemplation of real, lasting, immobile things" whose truth lies in being visible, in being ideas. The decisive element is, of course, presence. This presence refers to both the spatial dimension that is typical of the object that lies in front of the onlooker, and to the temporal dimension of a simultaneous "now" that is eternalized by the contemplator. The only reason that hearing does not occupy a more fundamental place in this conceptual structure is that sounds are perceived in succession rather than simultaneously: "sounds exist in a sequence, where each "now" disappears into the past as soon as it happens."[14] The simultaneous gaze on things that are here, now, in the present and among beings who are present, confers on the things themselves a certain permanence in being. The tree that I am looking at persists while I look at it. Transferring the experience of the bodily eye to that of the mind, the metaphysician simply eternalizes the autocircuit between this permanence of the object and the "now" of the gaze. Frozen in an immobile presence, mental images thus end up constituting the spectacle preferred by philosophers.

Along these lines, Hannah Arendt reminds us that, according to Pythagorean doctrine, life is a festival to which the best people come as spectators [*theatai*].[15] The *theoria* of the philosophers and the passion for viewing spectacles share the same lexical root. Even the Olympic gods love the spectacle of the world. In the Homeric epics, they watch what happens from above and, at times, go down to earth to offer themselves as a portentous spectacle for the mortals, who repay them with an astonished stare. The life of the philosopher, for the Pythagoreans as for Plato, is the best life precisely because it falls within the category of spectacles. The objects of the philosophical spectacle are not, however, tangible things, persons, events, or even portentous apparitions but are instead the ideas contemplated by the mind. Eternalized in the now of their presence, they confer the divine privilege of this eternity on the contemplator. Envied by mortal creatures, the gods who enjoy the spectacle of the world are immortal. But the philosopher imitates them and surpasses them by conquering an extended present, the fruit of immaterial visions, which suggests that the sphere of thought is eternal. Eternity, understood as a dimension immune to the movement of temporality, thus becomes the mark of truth.

The event that confers a spectacular mark on truth occurs within the platonic doctrine of ideas, but it originates in the attitude of the Ionic philosophers. Struck by the totality of existing things that offer themselves to their gaze, or rather by a *physis* that presents itself as an all, they inaugurate the spectacular and prelogocentric phase of philosophy. Before Heraclitus and Parmenides, philosophers are not concerned with logos. Astonished, they admire the multiform totality of nature and they attempt to give a single name to its principle: water, *apeiron*, air, atoms. This astonishment still leaves traces in the work of Plato and the young Aristotle, where they refer to the capacity for wonder [*thaumazein*] as the experience that gives birth to philosophy.[16] For those who know how to view it, the spectacle of the world is a beautiful order, a *kosmos*, that captures one's attention and provokes wonder. The beginning of philosophizing, therefore, seems to have been constituted by this awestruck gaze. And for Plato, this is also its end.

The vision of the *ideai*, entrusted to the faculty of *nous*, is indeed the origin and the end of dialectic as a movement of the self-clarification of logos. As Plato declares in the *Seventh Letter*, the dialectic method that proceeds by question and answer, submitting the interlocutor's words to verification, aims precisely toward the noetic vision of an idea that, as a signified, is already at the origin of the semantic function of words and of the logos that joins [*legein*] them.[17] Thus, the apparently paradoxical problem of a metaphysics that is at once videocentric and logocentric—namely, the problem of a system in which the visual character of thought must continually grapple with the "obvious" connection between logos and the acoustic sphere. Although it is hard to give the term a univocal definition, *logos* does allude to speech and involves vocalization. Not by chance does Aristotle define it as *phone semantike*. Although it is true that logos is generally reduced to a phonic signification, the voice still seems to anchor logos to a horizon in which there are mouths and ears, rather than eyes and gazes.

At least, it would seem.

The history of metaphysics should in fact finally be told as the strange history of the devocalization of logos. As the Neoplatonist philosopher Plotinus puts it, the final end of philosophy is a silent contemplation that at last takes its leave of logos and refuses to offer even a single word.[18] Metaphysics has always dreamed of a videocentric order of pure signifieds. Verbal signification is, from its perspective, a hindrance—especially when it unfolds acoustically in vocal speech. Even Parmenides, early on, had condemned "language [*glossa*] that makes hearing deaf by its echoes."[19] As Maria Zambrano says, when philosophy emerges as a new type of knowledge, "step by step, the being of 'things that are' will come to appear as a figure, as a *morphe*, as an *eidos*, but without a voice. . . . Revelation will be a function of sight. It will be a seeing. But not a hearing. And this in spite of dialogue."[20] In an antiacoustic sense, Plato's system is exemplary, in spite of his recourse to dialogue, for Plato makes the signifieds of words and the ideas contemplated by the eye of the soul coincide with one another. Every time that we, in speaking and conversing, say that something is beautiful—declares the philosopher—our words necessarily imply a signified that corresponds to the idea of the beautiful as such. Not only is this idea visible to thought, but it comes ontologically and logically before the name that is proffered, a name that is simply the idea's acoustic sign, its signifying vocalization. As Levinas puts it, "the world of signifieds precedes, for Plato, the language and culture which express it; it is indifferent to the system of signs which can be devised to express it."[21] Analogous to this is the genetic function of the signifieds—or the ideas—with respect to every thing that exists or happens in the ordinary world. Indeed, Plato's doctrine of ideas gets accepted in all of its metaphysical audacity. Objects of a noetic vision—present to this vision and therefore true and real—the ideas belong at once to the order of verbal signifieds and to the order of original, stable, and eternal forms, of which empirical things are imperfect copies.

Beyond the idea of the good, the just, and the beautiful, there is also the idea of the dog, or the bed, or even of a hair. They are thinkable or contemplatable by the faculty of *nous*—and they lie as much at the origin of what is sayable as they do at the origin of the existing thing. The name "dog," for example, and the dog who really barks at the market of Athens both depend on the idea of the dog. Alone in being true and real, the ideas constitute the origin of both verbal language and the empirical world.

1.4

The Voice of the Soul

> The idealistic world is not created by speech, but rather by thought. . . .
> And, since this first step is decisive for every successive step, it follows that
> this diffidence with regard to language and its apparent "accord" with
> thought remains a permanent inheritance of idealism—one which pushes it
> ever closer to a "pure" logic, extraneous to language.
> —Franz Rosenzweig, *The Star of Redemption*

It has been said that the entire history of philosophy is nothing but a
series of footnotes to Plato. If this is true, it is rather strange that Plato's
readers have rarely taken the trouble to reflect on the phenomenon of the
devocalization of logos, which follows from its reduction to the visual as
the guarantor of truth as presence. Put simply, this problem could also be
described as a subordination of speaking to thinking that projects onto
speech itself the visual mark of thought. The result is the firm belief that
the more speech loses its phonic component and consists in a pure chain of
signifieds, the closer it gets to the realm of truth. The voice thus becomes
the limit of speech—its imperfection, its dead weight. The voice becomes
not only the reason for truth's ineffability, but also the acoustic filter that
impedes the realm of signifieds from presenting itself to the noetic gaze.

This is not simply a privileging of sight or the subordination of
speaking to thinking, but rather a precise strategy of devocalizing logos
that relegates the voice to the status of those things that philosophy deems
unworthy of attention. That which *each* voice as voice signifies—namely,
the uniqueness and the relationality that the vocal manifests—does not
even get proposed as a matter for reflection. Stripped of a voice that then
gets reduced to a secondary role as the vocalization of signifieds, logos is

thus taken over by sight and gravitates increasingly toward the universal. Given that it is nevertheless linked to the realm of the sayable—although this link becomes ever more bothersome—logos concerns itself with saying, but not with the human world of singular voices that, in speaking, communicate the speakers to one another. Rather, this Saying becomes an abstract, anonymous logos—a code, a system. Chained to speech, but indifferent to the vocal, reciprocal communication of the speakers themselves, logos ends up moving toward a realm of mute, visible, present signifieds that come to constitute its origin and its fulfillment. In a certain sense, therefore, the process of self-clarification for logos, which makes up the history of metaphysics, is also a process of the self-negation of logos, for in being devocalized, logos is forced to coincide as much as possible with the silence of thought.

Of course, this coincidence—which is nothing but a metaphysical dream—is always imperfect. Even the aspect that is privileged by philosophy—namely, logos as a joining together of words—stands in uneasy contrast to the essential principles of videocentric thought. This joining together, after all, manifests characteristics that are quite different from the simultaneity and presence that are guaranteed by metaphysical vision. Theorein implies the duration of discrete objects, which are immobilized in the eternal present of the "now"; *legein*, however, requires a sequence, or a chain that is developed temporally. Indeed, this is how another decisive term of the philosophical lexicon finds its place—namely, *reason*. United with thought rather than speech (notwithstanding the assonance of *ratio* and *oratio*) in the philosopher's imaginary, reason has the advantage of being more mobile, more disposed to passing from one signified to another. Reason is, so to speak, a mental activity that supplements and makes up for the ecstatic immobility of contemplative thought.

This problem, which is present in the whole history of philosophy under the rubric of the contrast between reason and intellect, appears in Plato's text in the form of a double version of the status of thought. At times, thought is understood as "a silent discourse of the soul with itself" that thus maintains the character of joining together or sequence that is found in *legein*. Other times, thought is understood as a static, panoramic, and simultaneous vision of the order of signifieds. The capture of logos in the sphere of thought—its devocalization—ends up being reflected in the problem of the doubling of thought itself into a discursive form and a contemplative form. It is almost as if there were a "minor" metaphysics, still bound to the movement of discoursing, which does not succeed in dissolving itself fully into the "major" metaphysics that is instead dedicated to the immobility of contemplation.

A famous passage from the *Sophist* is emblematic here. It affirms that thought and logos are the same thing: "one is the dialogue [*dialogos*] without voice that the soul makes with itself, and this is why we call it thought [*dianoia*]," whereas the other corresponds "to the flux of the soul that comes out of the mouth together with the voice."[1] It is worth recalling that this is neither an innocent metaphorical game nor a simple exchange "of equals" in which thought appears as devocalized logos and logos appears as vocalized thought. The movement goes from the soul to the mouth: the silent *dia-logos* of the soul with itself—which is thought—flows outward through the mouth and takes a voice, or is vocalized.

The soul in question here, the *psyche*, is that superior part of the soul that has purely intellectual functions. It is, precisely, the seat of thought, a mental activity that Plato calls both *noein* and *dianoein*. In the passage cited above, the choice of the term *dianoia* is evidently dictated by the easy play on the term *dialogue*: *dia-noein* corresponds to *dia-logos*. This means that there is a *dia-logos*, identical to *dia-noein*, that consists of a silent operation of the soul that regards the joining together of ideas. When this operation comes out of the mouth and is vocalized, the *dia-logos* loses—so to speak—the *dia* and becomes *logos* in the ordinary sense of the term. Plato does not maintain that logos, as it internalizes itself in the soul, loses its voice. He maintains exactly the contrary: it is the mute logos of the soul with itself that, in being externalized, is vocalized. Spoken discourse is a sonorization of "thought discourse." The latter—insofar as it joins together, gathers, and discourses—constitutes an activity of thought that is distinguishable from the ecstatic immobility of thought itself, from contemplation or *theoria*. Its task resembles the work of "reason" more than the work of contemplation. With respect to the spectacle of ideas that is reserved for the "major" metaphysics of the *nous*, the silent logos of the soul with itself alludes, again, to a "minor" metaphysics.

Of course, understanding the platonic logos as "reason" or "rationality" would resolve a lot of problems. Indeed, most translators of Plato's *Republic* inevitably render the part of the soul that is apt for thinking—the part that Plato, in the *Republic*, calls *logistikon*—with the expression "rational soul." When it is a question of logos and the terms that refer to it, the problems in the translation are symptomatically a direct result of the irresistible platonic tendency to devocalize it and to make it conform to the videocentric sphere of thought. Thought itself, which is disturbed by a logos that cannot totally erase its legitimate relation to speech, thus ends up having to duplicate itself. While stripping it of the plurality of voices, the devocalization of logos cannot stop certain constitutive characteristics of speech from continuing to disturb the videocentric and contemplative horizon into which logos has been transferred. In other words, because it is constitutively extraneous to the noetic sphere of vision that characterizes it, logos gets its revenge by continuing to blow a disturbing breeze. Carried by the improbable wind of thought toward the heights of its visions, metaphysics in fact has no air for its flight. It knows neither breath nor sigh nor suspiration. A subtle breeze is enough to upset it.

Ideally, as Plato suggests and Plotinus confirms, the fulfillment of the metaphysical system is a contemplative, immobile, and perpetual state that admits no discoursing—not even the silent discoursing of the soul with itself. In its perfection, metaphysics has no need for a logos that proceeds by joining together nouns and verbs, or with a logos that discourses while time passes. The pure and silent spectacle of a totality frozen in eternity is its end and its principle. Even language—or logos understood as a verbal system of signification—ends up presenting itself as a superfluous attribute of the human condition. The philosopher makes no secrets of his desire to remain forever in the realm of truth that contemplative thought discloses to him. From his point of view, language is thus bound first of all to conform to thought, to correspond to it and to reflect its order. Because it is bodily, the *phone* inevitably threatens the metaphysical instance of this conformity. The voice—and this is, finally, the point—disturbs philosophy. And this is true even leaving aside for the moment the question of the uniqueness of each human being that the voice announces to the ear. The metaphysician is proud of his desensitized visions, and turns out to be, without exception, the deafest of the deaf.

This deafness with respect to the voice as such nevertheless does not prevent there from being, within the dialogue of the soul with itself—what I am calling "minor" metaphysics—"a pronounced discourse [*logos eiremenos*], not however addressed to another and with the voice, but in silence addressed to itself."[2] The platonic insistence on this metaphoric register, which describes the soul as discoursing and as listening to itself, "interrogating itself and responding to itself by itself," is of extreme importance for the history of philosophy.[3] Not only does it anticipate, far in advance, the figure of consciousness; but above all it entrusts to the future fortunes of this figure the typical theoretical frame that depends on the soliloquy of an *I* whose disembodied ear concentrates on its own mute voice. Egocentric and without external interlocutors, the philosophical theater of consciousness has no sounds, and yet within this theater, everything happens according to the rules of the acoustic sphere. The evidence of this is ubiquitous; I will limit myself to only a few citations. Giovanni Gentile, for example, declares that "we speak to others because we speak first of all to ourselves. And so to speak, the first ears that listen to us are not the ears of others but our own. Even speaking inside ourselves, without breaking the silence with the voice, we think without pronouncing words."[4] In another quarter, Jacques Derrida's analysis of the phenomenological account of consciousness assigns to the Husserlian "ego" the criterion of a speaker who "hears himself speak."[5] The more serious side of this problem, however, does not lie in the metaphorical identification of thinking with speaking or in the interiorization of dialogue, but rather in the conviction that this interior discoursing is the condition of possibility for speaking to others.

In the theater of consciousness, the natural relationality of the vocal—the acoustic relationality that speech itself, insofar as it is sonorous, confirms—is preemptively neutralized in favor of a silent and internal voice that produces a self-referential type of relation, an ego-logical relation between the self and itself. The price for the elimination of the physicality of the voice is thus, first of all, the elimination of the other, or, better, of others. Already announced in platonic metaphysics, the silent dialogue of the soul with itself is not only a monologue; it is a soliloquy that—while it metaphorizes itself on the voice—neutralizes the relational status of the voice and thus of speech in general. The soul, as Plato ends up suggesting, can do without the bodily *phone* and contents itself with a metaphorical voice. And from this point on, the soul obstinately speaks with a voice that does not reverberate. When its interior discourse comes out of the mouth and is vocalized, it thus finds itself confronted with a verbal interlocution that spoils the mute and disembodied perfection of the solipsistic colloquium. It must register the fact that, beneath the silent firmament of the ideas, there are human beings in flesh and bone who are particular, contingent, and finite. It must renounce the metaphysical dream that stands ready to sacrifice the vocality of speech in order not to have to worry about the existence of others.

1.5

The Strange Case of the Antimetaphysician Ireneo Funes

> Locke, in the Seventeenth century, postulated (and rejected) an impossible language in which each individual thing, each stone, each bird and each branch, would have its own name. Funes once projected an analogous language, but discarded it because it seemed too general to him, too ambiguous.
> —Jorge Luis Borges, "Funes the Memorious"

Following a conviction already expressed by Nietzsche in the nineteenth century, many of the most significant thinkers of the twentieth century share the opinion that metaphysics is inaugurated with Plato, and that it is now time to liquidate it, or at least to go beyond. The most formidable attack that the twentieth century has mounted on the metaphysical tradition, however, does not come from a philosopher—analytical, postmodern, or other. Rather, it comes from Ireneo Funes, a fictitious character in a story by Borges. Funes' story is a strange one. Paralyzed by an accident while horseback riding and finally killed by congestion of the lungs, Funes is only a poor Uruguayan farmer. But he has a prodigious gift: his perception and his memory are infallible. In fact, they are so prodigious and infallible that, in order not to lose sight of Funes' critique of metaphysics, we should deal with them separately. For now, we will limit ourselves to the matter of Funes' perception. In the context of the story, this means the human capacity to see the things of the world. And—in order to make clear how far it is from the spirit of Plato's text—the world itself is understood in the story as that whose reality and truth are not doubted by the perceiver.

As the narrator of Borges' text says, "We, at one glance, can perceive three glasses on a table; Funes, all the leaves and tendrils and fruits that make up a grape vine."[1] But this is not enough. Funes saw sharply all the drops of foam raised by an oar or, one by one, the hairs on the mane of a pony. "In the overloaded world of Funes there were only details, almost immediate." The necessarily generalizing function of language thus seemed to him incomprehensible. "It was difficult for him to comprehend that the generic symbol *dog* embraces so many unlike individuals of diverse size and form." But, obviously, his instinctive critique of language went even further. Not only did he denounce the unforgiveable reduction of different examples of the canine species to a single substantive, but "it bothered him that the dog at three-fourteen (seen from the side) should have the same name as the dog at three-fifteen (seen from the front)."

The gaze of Funes, in short, not only grasped the uniqueness of each existent, but even the active becoming—typical of living things—that continually transforms every thing. He discerned "the tranquil advances of corruption, of decay, of fatigue." He was "the solitary and lucid spectator of a multiform, instantaneous and almost intolerably precise world." In short, he perceived the mobile plurality of the contingent, held in the unrepeatability of the moment. In the absolutely real world of which Funes was the spectator, nothing was, or appeared as, another. The human habit of fixing many similar things, or even the same thing, in a single name that is always the same seemed to Funes incomprehensible and bizarre. Nothing in fact was, for him, the same. Nothing justified the use of the name as a generic signifier. To his eyes, the world consisted of an unrepeatable and infinite series of innumerable difference—or, better, fragments of a flux that becomes fixed in the instant of their appearing.

In a certain sense, Ireneo Funes was therefore a forerunner of postmodernism or poststructuralism. However, this farmer turned out to be far more radical than anyone in the academy. For Funes in fact had an absolute confidence in the reality of the multiple and unfolding things that he perceived. The perception of the immediately given was, for him, immediately true. As far as he was concerned, there was nothing beyond whatever offered itself to his perception. He paid no attention to the linguistic turn of the twentieth century and therefore did not attribute the sense or nonsense of the world to language. He did just the opposite. For Funes—from the point of view of the physical reality of the world as he perceived it—it was precisely language that made no sense.

After all, language generalizes, universalizes, and erases differences. It proceeds by resemblances and abstractions, reducing the multiplicity of things to a series of names, continually iterated as the same. Reduced to empirical referents by language, all four-legged creatures who bark become "dog." All bunches—so different in color, odor, shape, and flavor—become "grapes." All drops of seawater, raised by an oar, become "foam." In short, language reduces the many to one, or rather it says the one of the many. And this coincides exactly with the problem that lies at the center of Plato's metaphysics—namely, the problem of the idea. In fact, Ireneo Funes was totally incapable "of general ideas of the Platonic sort." (And thus, as the narrator reasonably suspects, he is incapable of thought.)

Funes is indeed strange. The passage from names to ideas exceeds his abilities, rendering him the most audacious empiricist and the most radical of antimetaphysicians. He gets blocked precisely where Plato establishes metaphysics; in fact, on closer inspection, he stops even sooner. He stops on the threshold of a language whose falsity and inconsistency he denounces, because nothing in language is how it really is. Moreover, if measured on the drastically antimetaphysical criteria of Funes, whether or not Funes stops short of language does not really matter. What matters, rather, is the capacity of the Uruguayan farmer to show how metaphysics owes a greater debt to the generalizing function of names than Plato would like to admit. The *reductio ad unum* of multiplicity that the name performs, the classifying effect of language, facilitates the platonic aim of devocalizing speech and transforming the generality of the name into the universality of the idea. As Funes intuits with a certain dismay, the universality of the signified is already implicated by the simple application of a single name to a multiplicity of particular cases.

There is therefore a certain wisdom in the strange case of the antimetaphysician Ireneo Funes. Not only is he on the side of the variable spectacle of the world, against the generalizing effect of language, but he embodies the excess of sensible perception that is capable of enjoying this spectacle in every detail. Just as the platonic theory of the ideas embodies the excess of the abstractive work of language, extreme empiricism and extreme idealism thus confront one another. Incapable of understanding the reasons for language, Funes resists the abstraction of sonorous signification that Plato instead devocalizes and makes dependent on the autonomous and videocentric reality of the mute signified. Funes and Plato are, moreover, perfect adversaries. Both work in the field of vision and attribute the status of truth to what they see. Both judge to be real that which—in the

time of an absolute present that is shared by the instant and eternity—
shows itself to the gaze, except Funes sees with the eyes of the body, rendered extraordinarily acute by his strange nature, whereas Plato sees with
the eyes of the mind, rendered extraordinarily acute by the exercise of
thought. Symptomatically, in any case, the vision of both is superhuman.
One grasps the multiform spectacle of the world in a hyperrealistic way.
The other contemplates the spectacle of otherwordly ideas whose absolute
reality makes this world unreal.

This also explains why, unlike Funes, Plato takes an ungrateful attitude toward visual perception. For the philosopher, the eyes of the body
play tricks—they see nothing but shadows, simulacra, imperfect and material copies of the ideas. Or, better, they see nothing but appearances—
whereas thought is able to see being. This is, of course, the famous theory
of the two worlds: the false world that is grasped by the eye of the body,
and the real world of luminous ides contemplated by the eye of the soul.
The bodily organ itself, which allows the experience of vision to become a
paradigm for what is true and real, thus gets cataloged among the human
faculties that produce illusions. There is a certain paradoxical strangeness
in all this. "I saw it with my own eyes," goes the popular proverb that emphasizes the immediate access to reality that sight guarantees. If the
proverb were not obvious, plausible, or experienced by everyone every day,
then the metaphor that transfers the principles of physical vision to intellectual vision would not work. Nevertheless, Plato transfers the veracity of
the bodily eye to the immaterial sphere of thought—and then accuses the
eye itself of producing a realm of tricks, shadows, and illusions.

Plato is not just talking about the optical illusion of the stick in the
water that seems bent. On the contrary, what is at stake if anything is the
question of a stick out of water that appears straight—and yet it can never
be as perfectly straight as the idea of straightness. According to Plato, empirical vision is always illusory, tricky, and imprecise, not so much because
the eyes of the body see badly, but because the things of the ordinary world
are mutable and contingent. For Plato, what makes the gray dog (seen at
profile at three-fifteen in the afternoon) an object that plays tricks on the
eyes is the fact that the dog is alive—and thus particular, subject to
change, in the process of becoming. As Funes intuits perfectly, a dog of
flesh and bone is never the same, and what is more, this dog is different
from all other dogs; it is not the other dogs, even as it continues to be a
dog. Without letting himself be confused by the metamorphosizing effects

of time, Funes contents himself with the immediate, instantaneous certainty of his visions. Plato, on the other hand, eternalizes the instantaneity of vision, transferring and fixing it into an immobile duration that withdraws from the contingency of this world. Thus frozen in the eternal present of an immobile contemplation, the idea of the dog radiates a universal and fixed dog-ness. It is always the same, admitting no spatial or temporal change.

The visual mark of the metaphysics of presence, inaugurated by Plato, is constituted precisely through the repudiation of the ordinary sight from which it emerges. This explains why, although it constitutes the visible par excellence—as its very name testifies—the idea is invisible to the eyes of the body. Moreover, this capacity to evoke the invisible also regards language in general. As Funes understood, the name "dog" does not necessarily imply that there are dogs in view, even if it does not exclude this possibility. Philosophical thought's habit of occupying itself with (empirically) invisible objects is, in fact, structural and constitutive. Whoever thinks "dog" sees only the mental image, not the four-footed creature that is there in front of him. To think means "to have present *in front of* (and not only *in*) the mind what is physically absent."[2] It can thus be supposed that one of the reasons for the platonic tendency to reduce the sphere of language to that of thought is the fact that both share a kind of invisibility. As a result, "thought" is a vision of pure signifieds that are finally freed from verbal signifiers, and thus from speech as such. The "objectual" theory of the signified produced by Platonism in fact ends up postulating "the existence of a true being of thoughts independently of their being thought and therefore embodied-expressed in language."[3]

If human beings had all dreamed the metaphysical dream of Plato, language could in fact be done away with. If, on the other hand, everyone had the vision of Funes—or, perhaps, if they had not lost it—language would never even have been born. Funes risks never arriving at language; Plato risks never returning to it. This is precisely the tragedy of metaphysics, onto which Borges' story sheds some light. The world as it is—living and unrepeatable—is distant from the language that says it. Just as the platonic ideas are distant from the multiplicity of the things of the world. From Funes' point of view, the perfect language would be that which assigns a unique name to the instantaneous uniqueness of every thing. In short, it would be the sonorous copy of a multiple and restless becoming—the human vocalization of its infinite differences, a sort of polyphony of the world in a human voice. Typically, the metaphysical mind of Plato inaugurates the eternal and futile philosophical search for a perfect language where the name, instead of adhering to the unstable particularity of the thing, corresponds to the fixed, universal idea.

The fact remains that for both Plato and Funes human language is basically equivocal, imperfect, false. For as much as they look in different directions, both are too enamored of their visions to really care for speech. Both the most rigorous of ancient metaphysicians and the most radical of his contemporary critics therefore seem to opt for muteness. The *zoon logon echon*, understood as a speaking animal, ends up being superfluous to both of their perspectives. Neither has much use for the *phone*.

1.6

The Voice of Language

> The fact that language is an ordered ensemble inspires one to seek, in the formal system of language, the form of a "logic" that would be intrinsic to the mind, and thus external and anterior to language.
> —Emile Benveniste, *Problems of General Linguistics*

When Greek philosophy takes the *phone* into consideration—much in the same way as modern linguistics—it understands it to be the acoustic component of language. It is a matter of an anonymous, virtual voice, one that does not concern itself with the reality of the speakers and that abstracts itself from the unmistakable uniqueness of those who emit it. The voice is the sonorous material of logos, understood as a system of signification. By means of the terminology of modern linguistics, we could say more precisely that the voice belongs to phonology and not simply to phonetics.[1] In the linguistic system, the phonemes combine to create morphemes—that is, the smallest given units of significance that in turn combine to create ever more complex units. In this horizon, the prejudicial question thus consists in reducing the expressive potential of the *phone* to discrete elements, or letters.

Aristotle says in the *Poetics* that the sounds emitted by the vocal apparatus of man are all different, just like every letter of the alphabet is different from every other. Classifying them, he defines them as indivisible sounds, and he specifies that "they differ according to the shape or region of the mouth, according to whether or not they are aspirated, whether they are long or short; or, further, according to whether they have an acute, grave or intermediate accent."[2] Uniting these indivisible sounds makes syllables; and assembling syllables leads to nouns and verbs. This is the point

at which the semantic intervenes. Although the phonetic elements—
namely, the letters and syllables—that compose the nouns and verbs are
insignificant [*asemoi*], the verbs and nouns that result from this composition are finally *phone semantike*. As a composition of nouns and verbs,
therefore, *phone semantike* is logos.[3]

A similar theory can be found in Plato's texts, which go even further
in emphasizing this anonymous character of the *phone*. As Socrates says in
the *Philebus*, "the voice [*phone*] that comes out of my mouth is one and infinite [*apeiros*] and multiple; it is the voice of everyone and each one."[4]
Considered in general, the voice is "one"—that is, it appertains to a single
category, namely, a category of sounds emitted by the mouth of each and
every one. It appertains, in short, to the human capacity for phonation. Although this phonation is presented as variegated, it nevertheless also presents itself as indeterminate [*apeiron*]. And this indeterminacy applies not
only to the strict sense of the term *phone* as the human voice, but also to
the broader sense of *phone* as acoustically perceptible sound in general.
Socrates in fact notes that the problem raised here also concerns the art of
music. Whether through singing or through playing an instrument, music
makes some order out of the vast sea of sound because it distinguishes
acute tones from grave tones and defines the intervals between them. Both
the musical doctrine of harmony and the order of alphabetic script deal
with an analysis of sounds in order to distinguish them from one another
through opposition and difference. These are, in other words, two analogous ways of ordering the infinite multiplicity of sonorous emissions. As far
as language is concerned, the undertaking meets with some success. The
reduction of sounds emitted from the mouth to simple, "indivisible" elements [*stoicheia*]—elements that are in turn regrouped into vowels and
consonants—owes its origins, according to Socrates, to the Egyptian god
Theuth, who was the first to recognize the number of letters in the infinity
of the voice.[5] Without this divine operation, the voice would not lend itself
to the process of signifying—or rather, it would not be able to constitute
the phonetic component of logos.

There is a platonic text that, half-serious and half-joking, discusses
the origins of names: the *Cratylus*. The investigation begins with an elementary observation that Plato learned from Socrates. When one speaks—
and all the more when one speaks of speech—speech is already there. Language precedes the one who speaks, or who discourses about language.

Even if the name comes second in the ontological hierarchy that Plato founds on the idea, language—in this case Greek—is always the point of departure, the obligatory means of every investigation into the process of signification. This investigation, in the *Cratylus*, begins with names and asks what level of correctness [*orthotes*] names possess with respect to things. The problem is apparently quite simple: is there a reason why we call a dog by the name "dog"? Is there a necessary link between the phonemes of the word *dog* and the dog itself?

The investigation is clarified when the protagonists of the platonic dialogue—among them Socrates, in decidedly platonic clothes—decide to take up the problem of the origin of names. They discuss the thesis according to which there is a natural, and thus necessary, relation between name and thing; and they discuss the thesis that postulates that this relation is conventional or arbitrary. The real turning point of the dialogue, however, comes when Socrates advances the hypothesis that language owes its origins to a primitive work of nomination carried out by "ancient givers of names." These name-givers—who Plato calls *nomothetes*, usually a term reserved for legislators or law-givers, but here used to designate those who establish the significance and usage of names—quickly turn out to be divine figures, "rarely found among human beings."[6] The speakers, in short, do not create their language; they find it already made. They can therefore attempt to discover its laws, its criteria. As Socrates suggests, however, it is best to proceed with caution, without getting lost in endless etymologies and keeping in mind the historical contamination and development of the language. Still, although difficult, the undertaking has a firm ground that is quickly established: the correctness of the name lies in its relation to the idea, and not in its relation to empirical things. The "dog" is a sign of the idea of the dog, and not of the dog in flesh and bone. Precisely because they are divine, the ancient legislator–name-givers could not avoid such an elementary, inescapable truth. It is thus hypothesized that in order to assemble the phonetic material in precise combinations that would render the *ousia* of each thing that is named, the legislator–name-givers completed their work while watching the ideas.

This hypothesis introduces into the history of philosophy a theme that has become classic and has never really disappeared: namely, the notion of a universal, univocal, and perfectly transparent language. In its platonic version, this language finds its universality in the postulated universality of the ideas, which command the system of phonation. It is an ideal, original, and primeval language—a language made by divine legislators. Indeed, the language that Socrates and his interlocutors themselves are speaking is a mere residual of this divine language, one that is late, confused, and untrustworthy. And this is precisely the problem. The actual language that Socrates speaks has lost the correctness [*orthotes*] of the link between name and idea that is present in the ideal language. If this is the situation of the language that we speak, then there is no hope that the study of names can make known to us the essence [*ousia*] of every named thing. Trusting names in order to come to know the ideas is an absurd operation. As the final pages of the *Cratylus* suggest, it is better to leave aside names entirely and occupy oneself with the ideas. Nothing is, of course, more platonically obvious, just as nothing could be more Socratically improbable.

According to Plato, good philosophers share with the divine legislator–name-givers a very important aptitude. Both know how to look at the essence of things, at *ousia*, at the idea. Names, all things considered, are useless, if not downright harmful for whoever approaches the true knowledge of what is. The loss of the ideal language thus ends up reinforcing the platonic ideal of a mute logos, spoken by the silent voice of the soul and constituted by the pure signifieds that can be contemplated by the mind's eye.

In the course of the discussion, among fantastic etymologies and a good dose of irony, the investigation into the criteria followed by the divine legislator–name-givers leads to an interesting observation. Socrates hypothesizes that their work was anything but easy. For their work involves, in the first place, an accurate analysis of phonetic emission. They had to distinguish between sound in its vocal, aphonetic, and mute elements and then articulate them in letters, syllables, names, and every other part of speech. Only then could they arrive at the final assemblage that coincides with logos, with language.[7] So far, none of this is much different from what can be found in many other passages from Plato's work, not to mention that of Aristotle. There is, however, a particularity here that goes straight to the heart of platonic metaphysics—namely, that the most important aspect of the work of the divine legislator–name-givers consists in the use of phonetic material in order to imitate the essence of things. This is moreover, according to Socrates, what painters do when they imitate things through the use of color. The divine name-giver, like the painter, is an imitator [*mimetes*].

This is an unfriendly analogy. In fact, according to Plato, not only do painters have the fault of imitating empirical things because they are ignorant of the ideas, but the very activity of artistic imitation is among those activities that the philosopher vehemently condemns in all of his writings. His thesis regarding the name as mimesis of the idea—its vocal image— functions as a kind of indirect devaluation of the language made by the divine legislator–name-givers. Socrates even jokes about this when he says that imitating a dog using the voice does not require one to start barking.

The real question, however, is something else. The real problem lies with the platonic analogy of the status of imitation with the status of the sign. Socrates notes that a statue that perfectly imitates Cratylus would no longer be the image [*eikon*] of Cratylus, but another Cratylus altogether. If a copy is going to be a copy, it must distinguish itself from the original on which it depends. This goes for the name as well. The same thing happens when the letters of the name are figured as the phonetic imprint [*typos*] of the idea, or as the idea's revelation [*deloma*].[8] In closing the dialogue, in short, Socrates orients the investigation into names toward the essential question of the sign. The sign is not something that stands by itself; rather, it depends on that of which it is a sign, the original. Put in platonic terms, whether it is imitation, copy, image, imprint, or revelation, the name always depends on the idea. The signifier always depends on the signified, which is its original and its reason for being—the *primum* from which the entire process of signification follows. Thus, it is enough—and this is, again, Plato's point—to turn oneself directly to the ideas, overlooking names. However one looks at it, logos for Plato is noetic, visual, and mute. Freed from the acoustic materiality of speech, this pure semantic—which is the privileged object of *theoria*—occupies the place of origin and rules over the phonetic.

Among its many fantastic etymologies, the *Cratylus* contains one particular series that is relevant here. It is suggested in the dialogue that logos means "every thing" [*to pan*], or the "all." Like the god Pan—a hybrid creature with a human face and the body of a goat—logos is double: true and false, divine and earthly. It resides in heaven and it resides here below.[9] This duplicity of logos, which plays on the dichotomy divine/human and true/false, emphasizes its two sides. The first is the way in which logos coincides with the mute, visible order of the ideas contemplated by pure thought. The second is the way in which logos coincides with language, with sonorous names that implicate the ideas and depend on them. In a certain sense, thinking and speaking are therefore two components of logos, arranged in hierarchical order. The ambiguity is constitutive and irremediable. Like the god Pan, logos is a two-form monster.

Just as it is crucial for the so-called destiny of metaphysics, the platonic speculation on logos brings to light the basic problems on which modern linguistics works and is based. The way in which Plato presents the relation between the name and the idea can in fact be traced to the linguistic sign of Saussure as the association of a signifier (acoustic image) and a signified (concept). Like Saussure, Plato focuses his analysis on this association and does not concede any role to the referent. He takes under consideration the relation that the name "dog" has with the idea-dog; and he maintains that the flesh-and-bone dog is secondary because it plays no active role in the process of signification. Indeed, this exclusion of the referent is precisely what distinguishes the platonic theory of language from that of Aristotle.

In Aristotle, we in fact find an investigation of language that—to put it in modern terms—moves closer to the triadic structure of the sign elaborated by Pierce, the so-called semiotic triangle that, alongside the signifier and the signified, admits the referent.[10] Aristotle's reflection appears on the first page of *De Interpretatione*, which "opens with a formula destined to remain for centuries as the *incipit* of every theory of the signified."[11] It reads:

The sounds of the voice [*ta en te phone*] are symbols [*sumbola*] of the affectations of the soul, and written letters [*graphomena*] are symbols of the sounds of the voice. In the same way, since written letters are not the same for all men, so too not all sounds are alike. Sounds and letters are above all signs [*semeia*] of the affectations of the soul, which, however, *are* the same for everyone and which constitute the images of things [*pragmata*] that are likewise the same for everyone.[12]

Put simply, using the example of the dog, this passage from Aristotle produces the following thesis. The various specimens of the canine race, placed in the role of the referent, are the same the world over (Funes would, of course, disagree)—and therefore, they provoke in the soul the same mental image of the dog, a signified with a universal valence. The name "dog," which is its acoustic signifier, is, however, not at all universal because it varies from one language to another. The same must be said for the graphic signifier—the name "dog" as it is written—because this written sign depends on the acoustic signifier. In the "semantic triangle" of Aristotle, unlike what happens in Plato's text, the referent seems to play an important role. When this is brought to bear on the definition of logos as *phone semantike*, the problem of the diversity of languages casts an unfavorable shadow on the *phone*. Variable and conventional, the sounds of the voice are contrasted with the universality of mental images. In other words, the phonetic signifier signifies because it is in relation with a universal signified; it is its sign [*semeion*], or, better, its symbol [*sumbolon*].

Although the term *semeion*, as it is used by Aristotle, refers to the notion of the sign as a simple indicator (the animal's voice is, as we read in the *Politics*, a *semeion* of pain or pleasure), the term *sumbolon* seems instead to refer to a somewhat more interesting and complex relation. In Greece, the *sumbolon* is first of all an object (a ring, a coin) that is split into two parts, both of which can serve for a future recognition when the two fragments will be brought together. This means that neither of the two parts can be privileged over the other. The symbol consists of both and functions through their shared relation. The passage from *De Interpretatione* could therefore suggest that between the mental signified and the acoustic signifier, there is a certain kind of parity. In other words, the universality of the semantic and the particularity of the phonetic are presented by Aristotle as two parts of the same medal. The same could be said of the relation between the sound of the voice and the written letters that are its symbols. A "symbolic" series of correspondences links the concept to the name, and then to its written form. The *sumbolon* thus puts the function of the *sun* ["with"] in evidence. The Aristotelian theory of the sign implies a series of connections.

In the complex horizon of the Greek reflections on language—that is, in the horizon that intends logos as the joining together of words—the theme of connection cannot but be decisive. Indeed, the "connective" valence of language gets organized as a complex structure.

Reflecting on the notion of "structure," Benveniste says that modern linguistics "teaches the predominance of the system over the elements."[13] The phonemes, the morphemes, and the words are "linguistic entities that admit two types of relation: between elements of the same level and elements of different levels."[14] In other words, the relation between the letters that form our nouns and verbs cannot be isolated from the relation between nouns and verbs that form the sentence. Both depend on language as a complex structure in which each element receives its raison d'être from the totality that it works to compose. Plato's and Aristotle's insistence on the various connections in which logos consists in fact anticipates a frame of this sort. For them, logos is above all a question of connections, linkages or joints. These joints concern the discrete elements of each level (letters, nouns, verbs, and so on) as much as the relation between one level and another (like the one between the acoustic signifier and the mental signified).

In this sense, an interesting thesis is illustrated by a passage in Plato's

Sophist. The specific object of inquiry here is logos itself—or, more precisely, the role of the *phone* in the process that, beginning with the letters of the alphabet, joins sounds together to form syllables, and how these syllables in turn join together to form words and, finally, entire sentences. On this point, Plato and Aristotle are in agreement. In the *Sophist*, however, Plato insists especially on the fact that the joining together [*harmottein*] of letters that form words does not happen by chance but rather through the vowels "which are not like the other letters, but are a link [*desmos*] which runs throughout all the letters."[15] The verb *harmottein* here is the same one that leads to the substantive "harmony" [*harmonia*]. In the ordinary language of the Greeks, this term designates the work of the carpenter when he joins two pieces of wood, uniting the one and the other in the appropriate way—that is, in the right way. The sort of joint that unites letters to form syllables, and that then unites syllables to form words is therefore a "right" joining [*una giusta congiunzione*]. Sonorous emissions are articulated according to an order that admits some combinations and excludes others. Logos respects and emphasizes this combinatorial task of harmonious, right joinings.

In its minimal and essential form, according to Plato, logos in fact consists in the joining [*sunploke*] of a noun and a verb, the elementary type of sentence. For example: "man knows."[16] Neither a series of nouns put in a row without a verb, nor a sequence of verbs without a noun can be called logos. "The name of *logos* is given to this intertwining [*plegma*] precisely because it is a joining [*legein*] and not just a naming [*onomazein*]."[17] My translation, which renders *legein* with "joining" instead of "speaking," obviously does not do justice to the bivalent structure of the Greek verb that Plato is exploiting. In fact, for Plato, "speaking" and "joining" are the same thing. In the platonic context, however, what counts is the right joining of words of which logos consists. The principle of this "harmonious" joining regards not only the combinatorial level of the *phone*, or the linking of nouns and verbs, but, as might be expected of Plato, it arrives at these levels from a superior level—namely, that of the ideas.

Precisely in the *Sophist*, in the very same pages that reflect on language as a system of "harmonious" joining, there appears the oft-cited sentence that defines logos as a silent discourse of the soul with itself. Before coming out of the mouth and acquiring voice, logos lies in the dianoetic part of the soul—that is, in thought. It is here in this mute seat that the principle of "harmonious" joining finds its originary place. Nothing is in fact more harmonious than ideas that are connected with "right" links in the totality of the intelligible order that the soul's eye contemplates. The criteria of the right joining—no matter the level of logos to which the problem of joining in the "right" way gets applied—is rooted in the order of ideas. Nouns and verbs, which are generated by the harmonious joining of letters and syllables, are in fact defined in the *Sophist* as phonetic revealers [*deloma*] of that which is: *ousia*, or the idea.[18] When logos, which is originally in the soul, comes out of the mouth and is vocalized, this logos also determines even the modes of this vocalization. Not only is the *phone* limited to giving sound to signifieds, but it also receives from the visible order of signifieds the very rules of its sonorous labor.

Harmottein is therefore the basic principle of the entire system. This system, constructed on the analogy of its levels, has at its center the ideas. As the realm of pure signifieds that are joined in the right way, the level of ideas constitutes an originary model that the inferior levels receive and repeat. Two intertwined axes of relation, or of correspondence, are thus created. One axis is that which allows the idea to reveal itself in the name "dog," which in its phonetic combination reveals (as a *deloma* of the idea) the substance of the idea. The other axis is that which derives from the supreme principle, which joins the ideas to one another, both the combinatorial criteria of the phoneme "dog" and the criteria of any other combination of whatever level. Put simply, the originary, harmonious relation between the ideas founds the relational principle that is at work in every level of logos, understood—as in Benveniste—as a structure in which each element receives its raison d'être from the ensemble that it composes.

1.7

When Thinking Was Done
with the Lungs . . .

> For the ancients, the voice is generated by the alchemy of internal fluids, it
> coagulates in the vital organs, in the heart and diaphragm; in the seat of the
> *thumos*, which is force, energy, ire, and impulsive instinct (its etymology is
> the same as *fumus*: and in Dante smoke rises from the chest when the pas-
> sions pulsate).
> —Corrado Bologna, *Flatus vocis*

The devocalization of logos inaugurated by Plato, in addition to es-
tablishing the ontological primacy of speech over thought, above all tends
to liberate speech from the corporeality of breath and the voice. Rooted as
it is in the organs of respiration and phonation, speech in fact alludes to
the vicissitudes of the body where the humors of the passions boil. As Plato
suggests, thought lies instead in the noblest position of the head and, more
precisely, in that divine part of the marrow that constitutes the brain. For
the philosopher, the centrality of thinking thus ends up reorienting the
physiological imaginary concerning speech. When it is forced to take into
account the fact that speech is situated in the body, metaphysics tends to
locate speech in the mouth, not far from the head, without going into
much detail about the workings of respiration. The subordinated role of
the voice as the vocalizing of signifiers again takes precedence. Firmly set-
tled in the brain, thought decides the physiology of speech.

Yet it seems that, before the advent of metaphysics, it was more natural to believe that thought was a product of the lungs. In a study that
crosses philosophy with anthropology, R. B. Onians argues that this was
the opinion shared by the most ancient phase of a number of cultures.

With respect to "a primordial individuation of the importance of speech for thought," he argues, there was an obvious association of words "with the breath with which they are emitted."[1] In the Homeric poems, for example, "thinking" tends to get defined as a "speaking" whose seat is in the corporal organs that extend from the area of the breast to the mouth. The reasoning for this is quite simple: thought is linked to speech, and speech is linked to the voice and to breath. For the most ancient Greeks, this breath has its principal source in the blueish-blackish organs [the *phrenes*]—that is, the lungs—which contain an aeriform substance that Homer calls *thumos*. "Spirit"—as the exhalation of blood that, according to the physiology of the time, is concentrated in the lungs and in the heart—or *thumos* evokes not only the emotions but also the intellectual functions, or thought. As Empedocles says, the heart is "nourished in a sea of churning blood where what men call thought is found—for the blood about the heart is thought for men."[2] Strange as it may seem, prior to the triumph of metaphysics, the Greeks were thus convinced that thinking was done with the lungs, not the brain. According to Onians, this belief was so spontaneous that it can be found in the archaic phase of other cultures as well. The affinity between thought and speech—or, better, the derivation of the first from the second—situates the mind and the intellectual activities in the respiratory apparatus and in the organs of phonation. It is, so to speak, the *phone* that decides the physiology of thought. By the same token, beating one's breast, the deep chest of breath from which the voice emerges, is "a direct gesture of the conscious 'I.'"[3] This is indeed how Odysseus behaves, at the court of the Phaechians, before speaking and telling his story, almost as if to suggest that, beyond thought, memory resides in the aria of the heartstrings as well.

According to Onians (who, although he may not be the most accredited philologist, is full of brilliant intuitions), archaic cultures are therefore in agreement on the matter of finding consciousness and thought in the natural essence of the breast, in the blood and vapor that it exhales; namely, breath. Thought derives from speech, and speech is found first of all in the organs of phonation—and also, as we will see, in the organs of alimentation—which have their source in the gaseous chemistry of the lungs. These vehicles of sonorous air guarantee communication. Through the voice, breath comes out of the *thumos* of the speaker in the form of discourses that are received by listeners in their own *thumos*, thus enriching their own knowledge. Words "pass from lungs to lungs, from one mind to another."[4] To speak and to think consist of a vocalized, aeriform effusion: "the mind, thoughts, and consciousness are breath that can be exhaled."[5] For the physiology of the ancients, the ears are in fact furnished with conduits that link them to the mouth and thus to the lungs. As the proverb goes, sometimes we drink the words of others.

The Homeric poems tell us that the gods whisper to men and inspire in them not just emotions, but also propositions, intentions, thoughts. The entire gamut of human experience, which refers to the most ancient precursor of the "conscious I"—as Onians calls it—has an aeriform character and is rooted in the lungs. This is true not only for *thumos*, which Plato himself links to the churning spirits of the passions that are situated around the heartstrings, but also for *nous*—a highly decisive term for metaphysics that, according to Plato, denotes a pure intelligence dedicated to the contemplation of the ideas. If one believes Onians, it in fact seems that the term *nous*—in a manner that is in keeping with the pulmonary source of thought—is originally related to a family of words that indicate the nose, *noos*, rather than the faculty of sight.

So we are in the realm of respiratory functions. However, the olfactory power of the nose, and the taste buds of the mouth, transfer the seat of thought into the zone of alimentary functions. Onians—overlooking, in this case, the Homeric language that links knowledge to sight through the verb *idein*—turns his attention to Latin culture in order to point out a curious link between knowledge and tasting [*gustare*]. For speakers of Italian, this link is hardly surprising because the Latin *sapere* is used to designate an operation of the mind, as well as for a pleasing aroma. (As Dante says, in good Florentine, "il pane altrui *sa* di sale.") Obviously, the nose too is evoked here because the verb *sapere* refers "not only to the juices that are absorbed in the act of tasting, but also to its exhalation or breath, and thus to odor, absorbed by the nostrils in the act of breathing."[6] Breathing and digestion, nose and mouth, are rendered indistinguishable, leading to the spontaneous identification of thinking with speaking.

According to Onians, this archaic imaginary in fact proceeds through a series of associations that, for a premetaphysical mentality, are rather obvious. Thinking recalls speech, and speech recalls the various physiological functions—situated between the mouth, nose, and breast—that regard respiration and alimentation.

Even from a scientific perspective, this state of affairs is not as strange as it may seem. As a respected contemporary ear, nose, and throat specialist notes, speaking in fact lacks "an organ physiologically appointed for that effect . . . because we are furnished with a digestive apparatus and a respiratory apparatus; but nothing was given to us that is aimed towards language."[7] Thus, although man is generally defined as a speaking animal, he must rely on systems made for other vital necessities in order to reach speech. He must, as it were, distort their natural functions. In the process of becoming *homo*, "a first grouping—of digestive apparatuses; namely, lips, mouth, palate, tongue, teeth—and a second grouping—of respiratory apparatuses; namely, larynx, nasal cavities, lungs, diaphragm—come together for acoustic purposes."[8] Speaking, which is first of all a labor of phonation, is rooted in the labyrinths of the body for modern science as well. In the final analysis, the strangeness of the ancient account depends on a single factor: the links that bind thought to speech and thus anchor it in the breast.

In Plato's view, by contrast, thought lies in the head. At least in this sense, Plato anticipates a scientific framework that is more familiar to us. Obviously, it is indisputable that one thinks with the brain and not with the lungs. From a scientific point of view, Homer and the other representatives of the ancient world are incorrect. From a more general point of view, however, it is interesting to note how this curious adventure of the physiological imaginary narrated by Onians resonates with the advent of metaphysics and the devocalization of the logos. In the scientifically correct move from the lungs to the head, it is not only the seat of thought that is at stake, but also, and above all, the sovereignty of thought with respect to speech. The belief that speaking depends on thinking takes the place of the belief that thinking derives from speech.

This substitution is decisive because, besides configuring itself as a prevalence of the head over the lungs, it moves the measure of the human being from the physicality of the body to the impalpability of the mind. Whereas before, thought was a coproduct of the vital functions of respiration and alimentation, it now comes first and is not produced by the body. As Plato says, thought lies in the brain—in the marrow of the encephalon—but it is not an effect of the brain, because the gray matter is not at all its cause.[9] Thought, or the activity of the noetic soul (as it moves from the lungs to the head) gains autonomy from every corporeal cause and thus earns its metaphysical status.

In keeping with the liquidation of the *phone*—which gets reduced to an auxiliary role that is basically superfluous or in any case inadequate with respect to the realm of truth—thought itself is characterized by metaphysics as a mute activity. Isolated from the organs of phonation, the soft material of the brain, where thought makes its home, is in fact mute. For the Greeks, this material is the primary seat of the *psyche*, or the soul. The soul can also have other parts that lie elsewhere in the body, but it is substantially situated in the head as its natural casket. According to Plato, this is a *psyche* with specific intellectual functions and thus, as Onians puts it, belongs to the mind. This identification of the *psyche* with the mind, which passes on with some success into the philosophical tradition, had very few counterparts in the culture previously. In the archaic period, *psyche* denoted a substance with procreative functions totally deprived of intellectual functions. Thought lay in the lungs, not in the head. To think is to speak, and to speak is to breathe. If in the *psyche* there is no breath, then there is also no voice, and thus, there is no thought.

And yet the *psyche*—from the verb *psycho*, "to breathe"—could not but sound to a Greek ear like a phenomenon linked to the emission of air. As already indicated, the same could be said for the Latin term that corresponds to it: *anima*—from the Greek *anemos*, "wind," "breath." However, according to Onians, in these cases, "air" is not the air that passes through the lungs in the act of respiration, but rather a breath that comes out of the sexual organs of the man in the act of procreation. As if by a pneumatic mechanism activated by excitation, the seed is blown out of the penis. This seed emerges from the cerebral material that, like sperm, is soft and viscous. Thus, there emerges a natural link to the brain and to the head. For the physiology of ancient Greece, the content of the cranial box is simply procreative sperm that, as it passes through the bony tube of the dorsal spine, reaches the penis and gets blown by it toward the outside. Faithful to its etymology, like the Latin *anima*, the *psyche* thus finds its most obvious meaning. It is precisely a vital spirit that generates by breathing.[10]

Plato knows this archaic meaning of the *psyche*, and in the *Timaeus*, he gives it credence—not without a certain bit of fun. He in fact says that the gods, who shaped the human body, made a conduit "in order to receive the marrow [*muelon*] that runs from the head along the dorsal spine, what we have called sperm [*sperma*]; and this marrow, because it is animated [*empsuchos*] and breathing [*anapnoen*], provokes a vital desire for emission in that part where it breathes, and thus provokes the desire for procreation."[11] Also in the *Timaeus*, however, it is said that only that invisible part that is dedicated to intelligence [*nous*] can rigorously be called *psyche*.[12]

This is, of course, the noetic soul that the gods surround with gray matter, but that is not the same thing as the brain and is itself totally immaterial. The soul is eternal, bodiless, and does not breathe. Much closer to a "mind" than a spermatic marrow, it is this soul that is identified with the work of thought.

Plato is therefore perfectly in line with the belief of the time when he sustains that the *psyche* has its seat in the head. As he no doubt knows, according to this belief, the *psyche* does not think but rather inseminates, procreates. And, still in keeping with this belief, "the soul reveals itself to be the part of man destined to survive death."[13] As the seat of life rather than the seat of consciousness or thought, the preplatonic *psyche* is a vital *breath* that is capable of generating new lives and of surviving the death of the body. In the last analysis, the turnabout that Plato performs does not consist in locating the *psyche* in the head, but rather in changing its function—namely, in identifying with the mind that which had been identified with the lungs. The result is a conception that appears much more familiar to us.

From a philosophical point of view, although this move obviously places Plato much closer to the modern scientific framework, it ends up being interesting precisely for the archaic implications that it still conserves. In addition to lending credence to the old doctrine of "breath" as it relates to the mechanism of procreation, the philosopher in fact recuperates a spermatic function for the new model of the *psyche* as well, which he has come to identify with the mind. This happens above all in the well-known platonic scenario that presents Socrates as midwife. Aided by the maieutic arts of the teacher, we read in the *Symposium*, the young are able to "deliver" the true logoi with which their souls are pregnant.[14] Likewise, in the *Phaedrus*, Plato affirms that logos passes from one soul to another, generating a series of descendants and brothers that are all legitimate children.[15]

And it is useful to remember that, behind the platonic Socrates, there is the figure of the historical Socrates who intends philosophizing as speaking, rather than as thinking or contemplating.

1.8

Some Irresistible (and Somewhat Dangerous)
Flute Playing

> He refused to play the flute, considering it a contemptible instrument
> unworthy of free men.
> —Plutarch, *Life of Alcibiades*

Socrates is "unlike any other man, of the past or the present, and this must provoke our amazement [*thaumastos*]," declares Alcibiades in the *Symposium*.[1] Hardly one to meditate on the uniqueness of each human being, Plato nevertheless registers—with an amazement reserved for awestruck spectators—the exceptionality of Socrates. He is unlike any other; he is anomalous, incomparable. He is distinguished from others in clear and evident ways. Contrary to his usual habits, in the *Symposium* Plato also spins for Socrates a sort of biographical narration; he tells of an episode of Socrates' life. This tale is put in the mouth of Alcibiades, one of the young Athenians beloved by Socrates (among whose number one finds Plato as well). Indeed, this biographical homage to Socrates' uniqueness has to do with this experience of love. In the *Symposium*, in fact, *eros* is discussed—above all, in the context of the erotic rapport between the adult man (the lover, the *erastes*) and the young boy (the loved, the *eromenos*). This refers, of course, to pederast homosexuality as a model of cultural and political formation in the Greek aristocracy. In the scenic fiction of the dialogue, the game is subtle. The enamored Alcibiades speaks for himself, but he also speaks for the author: "the *Symposium*'s portrait of Alcibiades is in some sense Plato's own self-portrait."[2]

Alcibiades is not among those who participate in the banquet at

Agathon's house. He arrives late, all of a sudden, drunk and yelling loudly: "the voice [*phone*] of Alcibiades was heard."³ Closed in a room, before even seeing him, the others recognize him by his voice. The text goes no further with the theme of vocal uniqueness. Yet signs of an unsettling sonority are disseminated in the text with great skill. Drunk with wine, Alcibiades makes a huge racket; he is in the grips of a bacchic frenzy, the Dionysian inebriation that is linked to the orgiastic rhythm of the flute. In keeping with this rhythm, Alcibiades stumbles his way into the room "half-carried by the flute-girl."⁴ In fact, the entire discourse that Plato puts in his mouth centers on flutes and flute players.

Alcibiades tells the story of Marsyas, the arrogant satyr who is the protagonist of a cruel myth. Marsyas was a champion of the art of the flute [*aulos*], who challenged Apollo and his cithara. Marsyas was convinced that the flute produced an irresistible and extremely sweet melody that was superior to that of string instruments. But he was wrong. The myth in fact tells us that Apollo won the competition, and as punishment, Marsyas was flayed alive. His skin was torn off while his mouth, no longer intent on blowing into the flute, emitted tremendous cries of pain. Thus Marsyas learned, at great expense, that one should not challenge the gods. But he also learned that the wind instruments are a prolongation of the mouth and that they are too similar to the voice. Besides the fact that they swell the cheeks and deform the face, they require breath and thus impede the flutist from speaking. In other words, the flute lets itself, dangerously, represent the *phone* in the double sense of the term: voice and sound. Whoever plays it renounces speech and evokes a world in which the acoustic sphere and expressions of corporeality predominate. It is the world of the Dionysian dithyramb, where the flute modulates rhythms that accompany an orgiastic dance. Nothing is further from the videocentric comportment of the philosophical logos. And yet Alcibiades' thesis is that Socrates, the great teacher of Plato, is similar to none other than Marsyas.

In order to demonstrate this thesis, Alcibiades refers to the mythological figurines of Silenus. First, what is at stake is the strange combination of ugliness and beauty in Socrates. After all, Socrates' face and body are ugly. In this sense, he is like the statuettes of Silenus that are made by the Athenian artisans. For as Alcibiades recalls, these figurines are miniature Silenuses that play the pipe or flute. They have a secret, however: "if the statuette is split in two, on the inside it shows that it's full of tiny images of the gods."⁵ Socrates, too, is like this: ugly outside and divinely beautiful inside. His ugly body is the superficial casing of a soul that is resplendent with beauty. And this suggests, moreover, that the exterior aspect is only skin-deep, only a matter of skin. In order to see the interior beauty of Socrates, it is necessary, so to speak, to skin him. Marsyas himself underwent just such an experience.

Alcibiades in fact goes on to declare that Socrates is an even more amazing [*thaumasioteros*] flute player [*auletes*] than Marsyas. Like all good flute players, Marsyas initiated his listeners into the Dionysian experience of the divine; "through his instruments he enchanted men with the power of the mouth."[6] And yet, without instruments and with bare words alone [*psilois logois*], Socrates does exactly the same thing. His logoi produce the same effect as the flute. They enchant, and they subdue. Alcibiades knows this well, for when he listens to Socrates' discourses, he feels heart flutter in his breast, and he becomes a slave to what he hears: "these are the sensations that I, like many others, feel as the effect of the melody of this satyr flutist."[7] Among these listeners, of course, is Plato as well. The only choice—says Alcibiades—is thus to flee from Socrates, "as from the Sirens, stopping my ears."[8] Because of his wild and frenetic life, Alcibiades freed himself from the enchantment of the Socratic logoi; he chose to spend his energies elsewhere. So too, although in a different way, did Plato.

In the refined architecture of Plato's text, Alcibiades not only functions as the double face of himself and Plato, but also as the one from whom Plato comes to distinguish himself. Alcibiades—who is beautiful, famous, and charming—is an ambiguous figure on whom hangs, among other things, an accusation of sacrilege.[9] His lifestyle, well known to the Athenians, is opposed to that of Plato. In this sense, the message of the dialogue is clear: the true Socratic legacy falls to Plato, not Alcibiades. In fact, Alcibiades turned his back on Socrates; he stopped his ears in order to extract himself from the teaching of the Socratic logoi. On the other hand Plato, his legitimate heir, stayed to listen—all the while worrying about how to eliminate precisely the enchanting aspect of this listening. Plato, in other words, found his own way to stop his ears—namely, through the devocalizing of logos. Plato in fact concurs with Alcibiades on the necessity of freeing oneself from the irresistible flute playing of Socrates, the particular talent that Socrates has for making discourses that "bite like a viper."[10] In contrast to Plato, Socrates does not write; he speaks. Logos comes out of his mouth and effectively enters the ears of his interlocutors. The comparison with the flute is therefore hardly coincidental. Just as Marsyas puts the flute to his mouth and produces a sound that bewitches his listeners, so too Socrates makes his own mouth into a flute from which come bewitching discourses.

This is not pure *phone*, voice and sound. Given that Socrates speaks, it is of course *phone semantike*. And yet what is at stake is not (at least not explicitly) the contraposition of speech and writing. At stake, rather, is the seductive effect that Socratic speech shares with the acoustic—or, more precisely, the musical. Indeed, according to Plato, the flute represents the very worst of the musical sphere. For music does not solicit the noetic part of the soul, but rather stimulates the passions and the instincts. As the true instrument of Dionysus, music leads to a loss of judgment. Flaying Marsyas alive was an act of justice—indeed, a divine one. The enchanters, all the more if they are flute players, are punished. Plato is totally convinced of the justness of this punishment. In order to flay Socrates, his beloved teacher, he thus decides to mimic himself under the mask of Alcibiades. The operation is ambiguous and complex, but it revolves around the quite ingenious notion of the artificial statuettes of Silenus. It is in fact these curious containers, with their logic of *inside* and *outside*, shell and substance, that make sense of the platonic flaying of Socrates. Poor Marsyas did not have, under his skin, any reality that was more beautiful or authentic. Socrates, on the other hand, does. And, moreover, the Socratic logoi have such a reality, once their sonorous skin has been peeled away.

As Alcibiades affirms toward the end of the dialogue—emphasizing the importance of a crucial theme that we have not yet addressed—not only Socrates but "also his logoi are very similar to the statuettes that open up."[11] On the outside, they seem banal and ridiculous, because Socrates speaks of donkeys, blacksmiths, shoemakers, and such. But when they open up, one discovers that these discourses are divine because they have inside them *nous* and the images of virtue.[12] The rhetorical surface of the Socratic logoi is ugly, but the content is beautiful. Alcibiades stops here. His drunken discourse has reached its end. The whole of platonic philosophy, however, without a drop of wine in its veins, goes well beyond this. It devocalizes logos. It cuts off its sonorous skin and founds in its place an order rooted in the videocentric and noetic sphere of thought. It makes of speech an acoustic shell of the idea. If this were not the real strategy, if this were not the doctrine that hides beneath the textual surface of the *Symposium*, nothing that Alcibiades says about flutes and flute players would make any sense. It is hardly necessary to insist on the flute in order to exemplify the enchanting and hypnotic effect of Socrates, which is here figured as the bite of the viper and elsewhere compared to the sting of the ray. Nor is it necessary to paint Socrates as a flute player in order to underscore that Alcibiades is inebriated. On the other hand, as the *Symposium* itself says, Socrates drinks generously, but never gets drunk. He is immune to the bacchic. He is a sober flute player who does not participate in the dithyrambic orgy.

The centrality of the flute, synecdoche of Silenus, in the final pages of the *Symposium* thus serves to construct a scene that illustrates and above all justifies the transformation of the Socratic logoi into the metaphysical logos of Plato. Socrates' discourses, like the statuettes of Silenus, have two sides: the exterior, ugly side that is only a surface that hides the divinity, and the beauty that lies inside. The inside is more valuable than the outside, which becomes secondary and thus can be eliminated, or flayed. In platonic terms, this means that in the logoi, or, better, in logos, the beautiful and divine inside is the order of signifieds, the ideas contemplated by *nous*—whereas the superficial outside, the mere shell, corresponds to verbal expression, to audible speech as acoustic signifier. The *Cratylus*, which compares logos to the god Pan, evokes an analogous position, corroborated by the fact that Pan plays the pipe; he belongs to the world of wind instruments, to the acoustic prosthesis of the mouth. As I already mentioned, Pan is called on because of his duplicity; he has both a human and goatlike semblance, he is divine and earthly, true and false.[13] So, too, is logos—it is both thought and language. The Silenic statuettes from the *Symposium* explain the importance of this reference to the two-sided Pan. Because they have an inside and an outside, the statuettes serve to illustrate the fundamental metaphysical notion of *being* and *appearing*. Underneath Socratic speech—the very sonorous, audible speech that comes out of his mouth—there is a devocalized logos whose reality is truer, more originary, and thus, more divine.

The strategy of this devocalization has, in the *Symposium*, many subtle levels. It is not in fact said that Socrates' discourses are ugly, as his face certainly is, but rather that they can *seem* ugly because he talks about ridiculous and banal things. The voice therefore, at least on the argumentative level, has nothing to do with it. And yet the voice returns in an oblique and obsessive manner in the continual allusions to the flutelike nature of Socratic logoi. Mouth and sound are thus foregrounded and play the crucial role of evoking the seductive power of the acoustic sphere. This power is, in the flute, peculiarly negative, invasive, disturbing. It is, again, worth noting that Plato does not like the flute at all. And yet in the *Symposium*, the negative judgment on the flute ends up being ambiguously overturned. By recalling the enchanting effect of the flute through the statuettes of Silenus, which represent *inside* and *outside*, Plato is able to silence the flute and, by the very same token, valorize it.

In the platonic construction, the flute playing can be explained on two levels. One is the superficial level, where speech resounds and the acoustic sphere is in play—voice, mouth, and ears that get stopped in order not to hear the Sirens. The other, more important level is the internal realm, situated in the soul and in thought. In the second case, it is a question of a flute playing that no longer shares anything with the world of Dionysus or musical possession. By moving its listeners, this flute playing evokes the agitation of pregnant souls, which Socrates-the-midwife helps to give birth to true discourses. The young Plato has in fact had an experience of this kind, before orienting his soul toward a contemplation of a perfectly immobile and solitary truth. As the object of the noetic eye, truth itself, which illuminates the order of ideas, is for the metaphysician the supreme seduction. Indeed, it is the supreme paralysis.

This order, as the harmonious, right joining of ideas that are grasped by a simultaneous vision, in fact corresponds to the logos that is the dream of what we were calling major metaphysics. There are no more flutes, nor voices, nor sounds; only a perfect noetic ecstasy. The minor metaphysics instead proclaims the priority, with respect to vocalized discourse, of the "silent dialogue of the soul with itself." Symptomatically, both betray the spirit of Socratic confutation. Socrates' logoi are in fact always vocalized discourses, addressed to an interlocutor who participates in the discussion, according to the dialectic method of questioning and answering. Moreover, rather than undergo the experience of the soul that dialogues with itself, Socrates is often solicited by a voice that commands him not to take certain actions.[14] No matter how large the temptation to read here a metaphor for consciousness, this is not an interior voice, nor is it a voice of the soul. It is the voice of the *daimon*, a divine, external, and imperative voice that neither develops arguments nor proceeds in a dialectical mode but rather commands. The fact that it is only audible to Socrates does not signal its general muteness, but rather signals the singular uniqueness that is part of the Greek meaning of *daimon*.[15] Socrates hears a divine voice, addressed only to him, and he obeys its command. In this sense too, he continues to bear witness to an auditory mentality and to an oral register. The video-centric enchantment of metaphysics, the noetic flute playing of the *inside*, is an inheritance that Plato does not receive from Socrates.

As children know, there are many tales that recount the magical power of flute playing. Among these is an old fairy tale, put into verse by Robert Browning.[16] The city of Hamelin, goes the story, was infested by rats. The city council, headed by the mayor, debated the problem but did nothing about it. The politicians' vain discussions did nothing to drive away the communal ills. Along came a tall and thin stranger, however, who proposed to liberate Hamelin in exchange for one thousand guilders. His rat-killing weapon was his pipe. Putting the instrument to his mouth, he walked the city streets of Hamelin, followed by thousands of rats who danced to the sound of the irresistible melody. The strange procession went all the way to the river Weser, where the rats plunged into the water and died. The city, which was happy to be free at last, sounded the bells to celebrate. The mayor of Hamelin, thinking with the typical astuteness of the politician, still refused to give to their liberator the thousand guilders he had promised. This was, of course, a fatal error. The story in fact tells that the stranger, playing a different melody of only three notes, turned his enchanting power on the children of the city. They followed him to a deep cave in the mountains and, together with the Pied Piper, disappeared forever.

At once angelic and demonic, the Pied Piper of Hamelin is both good and evil. Of course, he teaches a lesson to the foolish governors of the city. However, even to the most detached interpreter of the tale, a lesson that is accomplished through the disappearance of the city's children seems a bit excessive. There must be another explanation. Perhaps the fable simply wants to suggest that the sound of the flute, bewitching as it is, only seduces animals and children, not just because irrational creatures are more sensitive to music, but because the music produces in the listeners a state of enchantment that makes them regress to infancy or animality. That it is a flute—and not, for example, the lyre of Orpheus—seems significant. As a wind instrument, the flute is a substitute for the voice, one that impedes the one who puts it to his mouth from speaking or singing words. As the inarticulate voice of the infant or the animal, the sound of the flute in a certain sense *precedes* speech. It precedes it not only in the development of a human life or in the genealogy of the species, but above all because it does not need speech; it renders speech useless, or superfluous with respect to the acoustic pleasure. The fable in fact teaches that sound is more powerful than speech. Speech, especially that of the politicians of Hamelin who talk without saying anything, does not enchant or produce a state of irresistible ecstasy; if anything, it rouses the masses and crowds. In this sense, it is symptomatic that the illustrations in the children's book for this fable—like those that can be seen in the signs of shops and pubs in the actual city of Hamelin—depict the piper followed by mice or children in a long line. The magic of the flute does not move the masses, but rather arranges its followers in an ordered line while they proceed in dance step. Naked speech could not do this—although Socratic flute playing would be a prodigious exception.

Refigured by Plato in the *Symposium*, Socrates the flute player, follower of Dionysus, does not attract the attention of the young Nietzsche. For the German philosopher, who tends to identify the protagonist of the platonic dialogues with Platonism, Socrates is instead "Dionysus' chief opponent, the new Orpheus."[17] This sentence appears in the context of Nietzsche's famous thesis that describes the origin of philosophy as a victory of the Apollonian over the Dionysian. This is not simply the triumph of the cithara over the flute, but rather the triumph of visionary reason over musical experience. Letting Dionysus preside over the acoustic sphere, Nietzsche understands Apollo above all as the god of figurative art, and thus of the eye and vision, of beautiful and luminous appearance, of form. The essential Platonism of philosophy has its roots precisely in this privileging of form, which organizes the videocentric logic of thought. Starting with an already Platonized Socrates who, rather than embodying the bewitching song of the flute, gets placed on the side of the cithara, philosophy announces itself as Apollonian contemplation of the ideas and, at the same time, as dialectic. Videocentrism and logocentrism coincide in metaphysical knowledge, which opposes itself to the enchanting flute playing of Dionysus.

According to Nietzsche, the result is the annihilation of those Dionysian impulses that liberate men from the "chains of individuality," producing a total forgetting of the self.[18] The culmination of Dionysian intoxication consists in an alienation of the self, in a dispossessing of the individual, in an enthusiastic ecstasy. Indeed, this is the ecstatic experience described by Alcibiades in the *Symposium* when he refers to the flute playing of Socrates. And the *Symposium*'s Socrates—even if one leaves aside the problem of the "historical" Socrates—testifies to the fact that the relation between Plato and the Dionysian is much more complex than the young Nietzsche is prepared to admit. While he condemns the flute, or the acoustic sphere in general, Plato in fact seems hesitant to fully renounce its enchanting effect. In other words, he does not attack the forgetting of the self that comes from the Dionysian but rather the acoustic, bodily solicitations that provoke this forgetting. Plato asks the power of Dionysus—the god of dispossessing ecstasy—for a *contemplative* ecstasy. For Plato, what is needed is to flay Socratic flute playing, to tear off its sonorous shell, in order to go *inside*—where the *nous*, the eye of the soul, shows itself as the true protagonist of this enchantment. Immobile and perfect, the metaphysical dream is static and ecstatic. At the culmination of its vision, what we would call the "subject" annihilates itself in the totality of the spectacle. If the bodily ear is replaced by the noetic eye, the effect of the flute becomes the effect of the idea.

Amending the Nietzschean perspective, the philosopher Giorgio Colli notes that the figure of Dionysus does not stand in contrast to the videocentric dream of platonic metaphysics. Colli is here thinking of Dionysius' link to the Elusian mysteries. The initiation into these mysteries culminated "in an *epopteia*, in a mystic vision of beatitude and purification, which in some sense can be called knowledge."[19] This knowledge, centered on vision, was ineffable. It was attained through a complex ritual and a subterranean descent into the *other* world, which culminated in the supreme vision of an unsayable truth. In the myth of the cave, Plato—alluding explicitly to this scenario—in fact inverts this descent into a gradual, ritual, path of ascent toward the supreme vision of the Good. This vision is also ineffable, as is any idea insofar as it belongs the visible sphere of *nous* rather than the verbal sphere of logos. Even more interesting, from the point of view of the platonic imaginary, is the mirroring that appears in the myth of Dionysus. Looking at his reflection, the god in fact sees reflected not himself but rather the world. Thus, as Colli suggests, "this world, the men and the things of this world, have no reality as such; they are only a vision seen by the god."[20] The echo of platonic metaphysics here is, again, quite evident. For Plato—a lover of mirrors, reflections, replications, doubles—the ordinary world has no reality in itself; rather, it is a copy of the otherworldly order of ideas.

However, Colli is able to read in platonic philosophy a crucial Apollonian influence as well. He places alongside a Dionysius (who presides over the sphere of vision) an Apollo (who looks after the sphere of logos). As the god of divination and the oracular sentence, Apollo in fact inspires words that are then joined to one another according to enigmatic formulae. This joining is fundamental, according to Colli. It is not a question of indistinct words or of hidden allusions, but rather of precise precepts like the famous "know thyself."[21] The Pythia proffers these words—indeed, her body functions as a vocal transmission of the vapors, the god's breath, which rise up from the depths of the earth. What Apollo says is a message that must be interpreted. His enigmatic form is not, however, an exception within the Greek mentality. The enigma, which often gets characterized by banal utterances like that of the Sphinx, is the verbal expression of the divine—an expression that challenges the ordinary use of speech. Moreover the enigma is often lethal, as the arch of Apollo demonstrates: its challenge contains a destructive power. It is an arrow that is shot, from a certain distance, with precision and with intent to wound. From the divine perspective of the Apollonian, logos is thus not a transparent representation, a simple communication, or a silence. Rather, it alludes to the ambiguity of the semantic as a deadly game.

As Colli reminds us, there is an ancient legend that suggests that Homer died because he did not know how to resolve a silly riddle about lice. On arriving on the island of Ios, the blind poet asked some fishermen if they had caught anything, and they, who were delousing themselves on the beach, responded, "All that we caught, we left behind, and we carry away all that we did not catch." Embarrassed at not having solved the riddle, Homer died. The legend shows the remarkable contrast between the deadliness and the banality of the enigma. Indeed, precisely because it is ordinary the sphere of verbal signification is the plane on which the god plays his cruelest game. In the prephilosophical epoch, the divine power shows itself through an unfathomable combination of words that challenge human beings on their own "specific" terrain. The animals who have logos, as Aristotle will call them, still—in the archaic epoch—play the god's cruel game, caught in the constitutive ambiguity of logos itself.

With the advent of the era of philosophers, the divine aura that characterizes the enigma dissolves. Significantly, this is not a simple liquidation of the enigma; rather, it is a reductive understanding of this enigma that makes it into a mere "contradictory discourse." As it gets reduced to the terrain of human dispute, logos (which joins contradictory utterances) becomes the verbal playing field for experts who take its joints apart and put it back together with their expertise. The method goes something like this: two contradictory theses are taken; one is shown true while the other is shown false. The game soon gets out of control and—*voilà*—the sophistic and the heuristic arts are born. These arts demonstrate to an audience that the contradictory theses are both true and false.

This is not all, however, for the Socratic type of dialectic is also born—namely, confutation. This dialectic is a discourse between two interlocutors that assumes a thesis and proceeds through questions and answers in order to demonstrate how the thesis leads to a contradictory result. Like the ancient enigma, Socratic dialectic is thus characterized by a destructive tendency. The perfect interlocutor, who plays the role of the interrogator, seems to enjoy his eventual victory throughout, but he delays it through digressions in order to prolong the pleasure. "The cruelty of the Sphinx becomes here a mediated, disguised cruelty, but in this sense more Apollonian as well."[22] In this case too, logos is in fact the protagonist of a challenge in which the conqueror strikes methodically and unhurriedly from afar. If logos were transparent, simply representational, univocal in its capacity to say things, then the dialectic undertaking would not function. Like the ancient enigma, dialectic counts on the constitutive ambiguity of logos.

In Colli's view, the Socratic logoi that enchant, or paralyze, the interlocutor are thus Apollonian. Socrates' discourse, deprived of its flute-playing effects, is above all a cruel game that wounds like an arrow aimed at the right spot. Equally destructive is Plato's dialectic—which turns out to be Dionysian because it aims toward the purity of the noetic vision. Surprisingly, therefore, with the advent of videocentric metaphysics, the Apollonian—the enigmatic sphere of speech—is subjected to the ecstatic frenzy of vision.

1.9

The Rhapsodic Voice; or, Ion's Specialty

> When the oral culture in Greece began to transform itself into a culture of
> writing, speech slowly ceased to be an echo and became an artifact.
> —Ida Travi, *L'aspetto orale della poesia*

The ancient legend according to which Homer died because he did
not know how to solve the riddle about the lice is not just a bizarre aberra-
tion; it has a grain of historical truth. The semantic register of speech,
which is privileged by the enigma, is constitutively foreign to the great
Greek poet. He is an expert in the vocal register, a champion of sonorous
speech, a flute player without *aulos*. Plato knows this, of course. And it is
known with philological precision by modern studies as well that, starting
from a rereading of Homer, discover the world of orality as distinct from
that of writing. The origin of these studies goes back notoriously to the reflections of Milman Parry in the first decades of the twentieth century.
Parry elaborates the principal categories in reference to the so-called
Homeric question.[1] And since the 1960s, a rich vein of research, extending
from literary studies to anthropology, has joined other modern disciplines
devoted to the study of language in concentrating attention on oral cultures. For the most part, these are understood as cultures of "orality" insofar as they are characterized by the absence, or the marginality, of writing—as distinct from cultures in which writing plays a fundamental role.

Given that we live in a culture of writing (of printing and electronic
media), as Walter Ong notes, it is not easy to have a precise sense of what
exactly an exclusively oral tradition is. Like the majority of scholars working within the tradition inaugurated by Milman Parry, Ong agrees that the
Homeric *epos* is an oral culture. The term *epos* has "the same Proto–Indo-

European root, *wekw-*, as the Latin word *vox* and its English equivalent 'voice,' and thus is grounded firmly in the vocal."[2] *Epos* pertains to the acoustic sphere. The poetic performance of the rhapsode is a vocal expression: "virtually every distinctive feature of Homeric poetry is due to the economy enforced on it by oral methods of composition."[3] Homer works with the voice, which obeys the natural laws of sound. Inscribed in the internal body even before it reaches the ear, this law is rhythmical, like breath or the heartbeat. Situated in the right hemisphere of the brain, it makes itself manifest in speech through the regulation of accents, the number of longs and shorts, the modulations, assonances, and silences.[4] This goes for language in general and for poetry in particular. But it goes most of all for Homer and for all the storytellers who work in a primarily oral culture where composition, communication, and transmission are exclusively entrusted to vocalized speech.

Composed like music—indeed, sung and accompanied by the cithara—the Homeric verses find their home in a method in which the choice of words is determined by their metric value rather than their meaning. The vocal commands the semantic. The sound of speech is more important than its *vouloir-dire*. By the same token, the function of the "formula"—"a group of words regularly used in the same metric conditions in order to express a given essential idea"—is indebted to the acoustic sphere.[5] Homer often repeats the same formulas, recombining them, opposing them. This formulaic structure weaves together the exigencies of sound and the work of memory. Indeed, memory is obviously fundamental in a tradition where the words that are pronounced cannot count on the permanence of the written text because they consist of evanescent sounds. The prodigious mnemonic technique of Homer is based on a memory system that is rooted in the laws of the acoustic sphere. As both schoolchildren and music lovers alike know well, prose is difficult to memorize, whereas poetry, especially if it has the form of a canto, is more easily memorized. In other words, the epic "song" is entrusted to mnemonic modulations of a sonorous nature that determine the very syntax of the verse.

In this way, Plato's notorious hostility toward Homer, which might appear on the surface to be absurd or obsessive, can be explained. Defining the Homeric art as a paralysis of thought, the philosopher attacks it in all of his works and, symptomatically, never forgets to link his critique of the content of epic to a critique of its vocality, or to a critique of the musicality that pertains to the rhapsode's performance. Plato does not condemn what Homer says and also the musical form in which he says it; rather, he condemns epic as a totality that is made of the interweaving of musical form and narrative content. "Plato attacks the very form and substance of the poetized statement, its images, its rhythms, its choice of poetic language."[6] He intuits perfectly that the acoustic element—the power of the voice, the charm of song and sounds, the bodily enjoyment of the ear—are integral to the narrative fabric that organizes the "Homeric encyclopedia." To liquidate Homer means, for Plato, to neutralize at once the world of the tale and the seductive, bodily, and enchanting effect of the *phone*.

The most famous interpretation of this battle between the philosopher and the epic poet is provided by Eric Havelock. He characterizes this battle in terms of the historical transition from orality to writing. In the passage from Homer to Plato, the centrality of the ear gets replaced by the eye. The technology of writing in fact produces a specific mental structure, which corresponds to a model of thought that owes its organizing matrix to the sphere of the eye, not the ear. Having heretofore been a sonorous event, speech becomes an image and makes itself available to a visual organization that positions it in discourse according to a spatial, linear, analytical, and permanent process. The typical paratactic structure of *epos* gets substituted by a hypotactic structure that joins words in a causal, ordered, and controllable chain. No longer held in the evanescent, concrete, and socializing flux of primary orality, language itself changes. The syntactic context changes and new words get added. The most noted aspect of this evolution is the fact that adjectives, through a process of abstraction and conceptualization, become substantives: the beautiful Elena gets transformed into the "beautiful as such," the "beautiful itself," the idea of the beautiful. As Bruno Snell notes, the article plays an important role in this as well; "the article is capable of making a substantive out of an adjective or a verb—and these substantives, in the field of philosophy and science, serve as the stable objects of our thinking."[7] In the transition from the centrality of the ear to that of the eye, there thus emerges a thought that is capable of capturing sonorous events and of freezing them as abstract and universal images, characterized by objectivity, stability, and presence, and organized in a coherent system. In other words, a science, or a knowledge, is born, what the Greeks called *episteme*, founded in *theoria*.

The antiacoustic and videocentric mark of platonic thought, and hence of western philosophy, is therefore confirmed by studies that investigate the difference between oral and literate cultures. It is not simply a matter of sustaining that metaphysics is a direct product of writing, but rather of emphasizing how metaphysics is totally in keeping with a practice of writing that "tyrannically locks [words] into a visual field forever."[8] In this way, words not only lend themselves to be analyzed from a critical distance, but they end up assuming an impersonal and objective authority very similar to the characters that distinguish both the universality of the idea and the concept. What is certain is that by entrusting itself to writing, philosophy can afford to turn its attention exclusively on sight in a way that renders the vocal aspect of speech secondary or superfluous. Proof for this can be found in the contrast between Homer's blindness and the "acute vision" of the philosopher that Plato illustrates in the *Republic*. Facilitated by the function of the eye as well as by the silence that characterizes the technique of writing, the philosopher has time to reflect on the faculty of vision and to take full advantage of its characteristics. After all, the written names are there, in front of him—present, immobile, permanent. Like the idea, the written name has a fixity of its own. Likewise present and visible is the joining together of names and verbs into phrases—the work of harmonious joinings typical of logos assumes a linear, organized form. Removed from the dynamic flux of the vocal, and consigned to the fixity of the written sign, language becomes an object of observation.

Alphabetic writing, like that of the Greeks, consists substantially in a muting of speech. Substituting the acoustic sphere with a visual map, the written sign translates sound and eliminates it. Reading aloud has, in this sense, the task of restitution. Unlike the Hebrew tradition, in Greek writing, there are no sounds that resist the regime of signs. The alphabet comprehends consonants and vowels alike. There is no autonomous sphere conceded to the voice, which vowels [*vocali*] invoke in their very name. The devocalization is complete. Every sound that can be pronounced passes into writing and is frozen in it, offering itself in a lasting way to the eye.

It is well known that Plato, in the texts written by his hand, judged writing negatively as a dead letter and the inanimate copy of speech.[9] As most interpreters emphasize, this attitude is somewhat paradoxical, for unlike his teacher Socrates, Plato does not philosophize orally through dialogue but rather writes philosophical dialogues. Symptomatically, however, the true paradox is more complex. In Plato's work, the critique of writing takes place alongside the condemnation of poetry, the form of orality par excellence. The philosopher obviously understands very well that this is not spoken speech but rather a song where the musicality of the voice dominates speech, forcing the poet and the audience into "an absolute, emotional coparticipation through inebriation and pleasure."[10] In his effort to rescue speech from the mortal effects of writing, Plato thus takes care to place speech well within a secure domain from which it rules over the voice and its pleasurable effects. In other words, Plato has two critical targets when he seeks to defend speech: writing and the poetic voice. If the first takes life away from speech, then the second gives to speech a body that is too carnal. It thus seems that speech must avoid the danger of falling into the frozen register of graphic signs, and at the same time, it must avoid the danger of conceding too much to the intemperance of the acoustic realm. In the historical transition from orality to writing, Plato takes the side of an orality that is stripped of its originary connotations and already depends on the antivocal effect of writing.

Indeed, the philosopher does not condemn writing because it silences the voice, but because he regards it as a second-grade copy with respect to speech as a copy of the idea. For Plato, at the origin, and as origin, lies the idea; that is, the mental signified contemplated with the eyes of the soul. The name "that comes out of the mouth together with the voice" comes second and is its acoustic signifier.[11] The written name comes third, as a graphic signifier of an acoustic signifier, or as a copy of a copy that is twice removed from the original. Apart from the idea that functions as origin, everything else, including the voice, is a sign. The explicit, and apparently paradoxical, condemnation of writing is thus quite close to an implicit valuation of writing as the "natural" model of the realm of signs and of every investigation that focuses on signs. Indeed, a culture of primary orality lacks perforce the elements that allow the voice to be thought of as an acoustic material governed by the system of signification. A discipline like linguistics—which Plato and Aristotle inaugurate by anticipating its unfolding—presupposes writing. In fact, all scientific knowledge presupposes writing. Linguistics, however, has the direct aim of swallowing the *phone* within the sphere of the sign.

The unfolding of this history, complex as it is, nevertheless has a more or less coherent development. Indebted to, and encouraged by, the practice of writing, the platonic devocalization of logos results in a reduction of the *phone* to the acoustic sign of the idea. It thus becomes the general voice of language, subsumed under a videocentric logic of the signified and controlled by the system of signification. Spoken speech, which Plato prefers to writing, pertains to the register of signs generated by writing; and it is the acoustic sign of an idea that exalts, as does writing, the role of the eye. One can thus understand why the platonic attack on writing can be accompanied by a far more detailed and obsessive attack on the rhapsodic voice. Plato fears the voice of acoustic pleasure, the voice that is rhythm and breath, the voice that escapes the control of the videocentric system of language. He fears, in short, the corporeal realm of the vocal.

Reflecting on epic, Havelock is able to identify the true subject of the platonic critique. The musicality and the repetition of assonances, he says, entice the ear: the listeners' "ear-drums are bombarded simultaneously by two disparate sets of sounds organized in concordant rhythm—the metrical speech and the instrumental melody."[12] Through "a mobilization of the resources of the unconscious to assist the conscious," there is produced in the listeners a series of "reflexes of the sexual or digestive apparatus [that are] highly sensual and are closely linked with the physical pleasures."[13] In short, the hearer feels pleasure and distension while being hypnotized by the simultaneous effect of voice and rhythm. With a different lexicon, Plato too underscores that through a multiform imitation of the irrational parts of the soul, Homer "nurtures and waters the passions and establishes them as rulers in us when they ought to wither and be ruled."[14] Homer is an imitator, an illusionist, a conjurer of appearances who seduces above all "those who love sounds [philekooi]."[15]

Havelock and Plato both agree on what lends epic its strength. It is the rhythmic matrix of pleasure, the delight of the acoustic sphere that follows the rhythms of the body, which makes the rhapsode's voice powerful. And yet neither Havelock nor Plato thematizes this vocal emission as the sonorous manifestation of an embodied uniqueness. Rather than being brought back to its bodily origins, the voice remains for them a voice in general. The uniqueness of the voice remains uninvestigated. That each voice, as Calvino says, is not only the vibration of "a throat of flesh," but also something that comes certainly from a unique, unrepeatable person is a given that never becomes a philosophical point of reflection. Even Homer, who concentrates on the seductive power of his voice and on the portentous performance of the bards in general, shows the same disinterest for this theme. In fact, it is probably this surprising silence on the part of Homer that impedes the more recent studies on orality from pushing their inquiry beyond a celebration of the poetic voice in order to reflect on the uniqueness of the voice. The exemplarity of Homer, which is constitutive of their discipline, ends up trapping these studies in a problematic and limited horizon—namely, in the distinction and contraposition between writing and orality.

Thus Havelock, along with a whole line of research on orality, misses not only the theme of the plurality of voices, but also the importance of certain platonic passages that seem to denounce its unsettling effect. In this sense, Plato ends up revealing that his negligence of vocal uniqueness is the fruit of a reticent strategy. The passages in question appear in an incomplete text that revolves around a bizarre argument: the *Ion*. Indeed, the text takes up the problem of the rhapsodic art, still in vogue in the time of Plato.[16]

The *Ion* is a brief dialogue; it is ambiguous and extraordinary.[17] Its aim is apparently to demonstrate that both rhapsodes and poets peddle an illusory knowledge that not only lacks the true form of *episteme* but can hardly even be called a *techne*. They do not know what they are talking about, and they are not even capable of defining what the rhapsodic art consists in. The general frame therefore seems reducible to the usual platonic arguments that devalue epic. However, beyond that background, the dialogue announces from the start a sort of peculiarity that pushes it toward even stranger digressions. Indeed, thanks to its very anomalous nature, the text ends up saying more about the theme of the voice than perhaps its author would have wanted to say. This is the thesis suggested by the philosopher Jean-Luc Nancy, according to which the plurality of voices emerges in the dialogue as a sort of enigma that is embedded in the text's ironic strangeness.[18]

"Greetings, celebrated Ion!" exclaims Socrates at the beginning of the dialogue. Ion is a very successful rhapsode who has just won one of the contests for rhapsodes that are held in Greek cities. Yet he has a peculiarity all his own. Unlike the other rhapsodes, who can recite a vast repertory, Ion knows how to perform and speak the verses of only one poet: Homer. With Homer, he gets excited and gives the performance his all. When he hears other poets performed, on the other hand, he gets bored and sleepy. His personal taste is as evident as it is inexplicable.[19] A special and exclusive attraction links him to Homer. The strange case of Ion thus makes the entire dialogue an investigation focused on a sort of mystery, which can be exemplified with a series of questions. If it is true, as many interpreters maintain, that Plato is here attacking rhapsodes in order to get the poets, then why Ion? Why a special rhapsode who is different from all the others, given that the criticism of the general illusionary nature of poets could work quite well, or even better, if Socrates' interlocutor were a normal rhapsode? After all, is not Homer—if this is the point—usually part of the normal rhapsode's repertory?

The mystery allows Plato to digress, to go beyond the general critique of the inconsistency of epic's knowledge, in order to finally concentrate his attention on poetic vocality. This digression leads to the famous passages on the Muse where the enchanting effect [*incantamento*] of the rhapsodic performance becomes, in explicit terms, a chaining [*incatenamento*].

The Muse—says Socrates in the *Ion*—has the same force as a magnet. Like a magnet that "not only attracts iron rings but transmits to them the power to attract other rings," so too the divine power [*theia dynamis*] of the Muse is transmitted to the poets and then to the rhapsodes.[20] In the poetic chain, each ring leans toward the other by the force of an irresistible attraction. The *theia dynamis* is, however, not only this power that attracts and links. It is also, at the same time, a condition of *enthusiasm* that is transmitted from one ring to another. Possessed by the divine power, the poet is literally *en theos*, in god. He is outside of himself, in a state of passivity that helps him to receive and transmit to the rhapsode that which the Muse gives him. Just as the iron rings that lean toward the magnet are magnetized, so too the rings of the poetic chain that lean toward the Muse become divine. The phenomenon of attraction is also a phenomenon of divinization. A gift, something different from the pure power of attraction, a divine mania, passes from the Muse to the poet and to the rhapsode until it finally reaches the audience.

The comparison with the magnet only goes so far, however—namely, up to the point at which Plato adds a modification to the "scientific" frame of magnetism in order to justify his interest in the strange specialty of the rhapsode for whom the dialogue is named. The *theia dynamus*, specifies Socrates, is not transmitted through various rings as a simple and undifferentiated power, as happens in the natural phenomenon of magnetism. Rather, this power is transmitted in the form of a *theia moira*—that is, already from the start it is transmitted in such a way that each one shares his part [*moira*] of the *theia dynamus*. The divine power transmits itself, from one ring to another, in differentiated and singular skills. In the poetic chain the poet's transmission is a distribution of different parts. The term *moira* in fact indicates the part that comes through a sharing or distribution [*spartizione*]. For example, in Homer's language, *moira* touches each hero in the distribution of the spoils after the battle. Likewise, in different cases, *moira* indicates something like fate [*sorte*], or the part of a divine share that assigns to each human being his destiny. An analogous distribution of parts is at work in the poetic chain. Addressing Ion directly, Socrates in fact affirms that "not the art, but rather a divine distribution [*theia moira*] induces one to sing and say many beautiful things, as you do with Homer: everyone is good at composing only that toward which the Muse pushes him."[21]

As Socrates then makes clear, this is a distribution that concerns first of all the single poetic genres. One poet is given dithyrambs, another iambs, and so forth. The *moira* that befell Homer is of course epic; this explains why Homer sings in hexameters, but not why Ion recites only Homer. The point is that the divine distribution of the Muse does involve the poetic genres, but it is first directed to the single poets and then to the rhapsodes. Each one, on account of this divine partition of poetic material, takes part in and performs his allotted task in the world of poetry. Thus, it is not at all strange that Ion has an exclusive task involving a single poet and that he is divinely adept only in regard to Homer. This exclusive task is precisely his *moira*, his sharing, his part, his lot in the poetic chain. The divine attraction/partition, passing through Homer, is extended to Ion, a rhapsode who is in fact so good at his art that he wins all the competitions in which he participates.

According to an image in the *Ion*, which Plato takes from the poetic tradition, the power that comes from the Muse was a gift made from the honey of the divine gardens that the poet transports and transmits in making [*poiein*] verses.[22] This is why he is a poet, *poietes*. In the sweet rhythm of the verses, his voice puts in words the honey [*mele*] of the Muse. In the etymological game that Socrates proposes here, this goes first of all for the lyric poet, the *melopoion*. But beyond the etymological game, it goes for every type of poet who makes verses. The gift of the Muse, the divine nectar, is in the rhythmic sound. The metaphor suggests that poetizing has to do with the physicality of a sound that pleasingly strikes the ear, just as honey delights the palate. The Muse thus proffers to the poets verses that attract and seduce by the timbre of their sound. Similarly, in the *Republic*, we read that the great natural enchantment of poetry comes from meter, rhyme, and harmony.[23] The metaphor of honey has a precise sense: it is not the case that verses attract and seduce because of the sound, beyond their content. This is not the point of the *Ion*. The point is rather a logos whose phonetic, rhythmic, and musical substance is as sweet as honey and passes from the speaker to the listener as a sonorous flux of irresistible delight. There is obviously a content, a tale. But it is above all the acoustic aspect that manifests the divinity and the pleasing effect of the song. In Homeric orality, the vocal has a preponderant and dangerous role. At the center of epic lies the question of the voice. Homer is not simply a narrator of stories. As he receives these stories from the Muse, he puts them into a voice and sings them.

In this respect, Plato seems in the *Ion* to adhere faithfully to the representation that epic gives of itself. What passes through the first ring of the poetic chain is a divine logos that acquires sonorous materiality in the voice of the poet. Socrates' insistence on this passage from divine logos to the voice of the poet is evident. It is the Muse who speaks through the voice of the poets that she possesses. She takes from them their judgment, so that they are out of their senses, and she uses them as her transmitters—"so that we who hear them should know that *they* are not the ones who speak those verses that are of such high value, for their sense is not in them; the god himself is the one who speaks, and he gives voice through them to us."[24] In Greek, this passage reads, *O theos autos esti o legon*: "god himself is the speaker," proclaims Socrates. Through the poets, the god *phthengetai pros hemas*: he makes himself heard vocally, emits a sound that the listeners [*oi akountes*] can hear. Insofar as he puts into voice, or carries in his voice the logos of the Muse, the poet can thus be considered the messenger of the god.

Poets are the messengers of the gods [*hermenes erisimo ton theon*], Socrates goes on to say.[25] It could even be said, according to the usual translation, that poets are the interpreters of the gods. But the verb *hermeneuein* does not really mean "to interpret." As Nancy emphasizes, citing Heidegger, the verb means above all "to carry a message," or "to announce."[26] The poet's song is an announcement of things of which he is the messenger. The very concept of a message carried in voice implies at the very least three players: the source, the transmitter, and the receiver. In the *Ion*, however, it is a game involving four players. In epic poetry, between the poet and the audience, the rhapsode intervenes. As the voice of the poet's voice, or the messenger of the god's messenger, the rhapsode is the second ring in this vocal transmission.[27] At the beginning is the Muse, at the end is the audience. In the middle lies the poet's, and the rhapsode's, voices.

Epic is a matter of musical voices. As is well known, it is only in a later tradition that poets are called *poietes*. In Homeric Greek, the poet is a singer [*aoidos*] whose song [*aoide*] is his voice [*aude*]. Poetry is a song and the song is a vocalization.[28] The poet vocalizes a song that in turn produces enchantment [*epaoide*]. Symptomatically, without this shifting of the name of the poet from *aoidos* to *poietes*, Plato could not play out his critique. In fact, only insofar as the poet enters the sphere of making [*poiein*] can he be placed among the artisans and measured by the standards of their arts of fabrication [*techne*]. But the poet does not make; he sings.

Obviously he sings words, but in such a way that underneath the words—as Marcel Proust might say—the "aria of the song, which in each one is different from all the others" becomes perceptible. It is, in fact, probable that the solution proposed by Plato's *Ion* is the following. The divine distribution [*spartizione*] of poetic genres is understood as a distribution of singular songs: each poet receives the aria of his song. In other words, not only does lyric have a musicality that is different from epic, but within both genres, each poet has his own song, his own acoustically perceptible expressive style. If this were not the case, the curious specialty of Ion could not be understood. For he does not love epic in general, but rather the aria of the Homeric song. The peculiarity of Homer—what makes him a poet that the attuned ear can distinguish from all others—is the modulation of the song, the specificity of rhythmic texture and his musicality. Thus, through the strange case of the rhapsode Ion, Plato comes to thematize the uniqueness of each poet as a vocalizer of a certain specific and singular melody, of an inimitable style that is his voice.

It is perhaps worth pointing out here that, in the language of literary criticism, *voice* is today a technical term that indicates the peculiarity of the style of a poet, or more generally, of an author. This use is interesting above all for the way in which it recalls a vocal uniqueness that is implicitly understood to be removed from the acoustic sphere: "the fact that there are no two human voices that are absolutely identical makes it so that in literature 'voice' becomes the general equivalent of expressive difference, losing all reference to orality."[29] In this lexical context, the "voice" of an author—while it implicates as something *given* the uniqueness of each voice—corresponds nevertheless to a stylistic idiom or to the aria of a song that can only be heard mentally—for instance, the very aria that Proust perceives when he reads. In other words, the uniqueness of each voice becomes the presupposition for the specificity of an authorial "voice" in a written text. The functioning of the metaphor requires that the voice, in its perceptible sonority, be unique, but the metaphor itself transforms the fact of such uniqueness into the peculiarity of a style consigned to writing. If, among the various aspects of this style, there is also a musical aria, then the figurative authorial voice might once again move closer to the acoustic voice.

Just as literary criticism will end up doing, Plato's *Ion* is interested in the plurality of the sung arias, and not in the singular voices of those who sing them. Rather than push toward a reflection on a vocal ontology of uniqueness, the philosopher meditates on an aesthetic of the sung performance. But Nancy's reading of this—which focuses on the passage concerning poetic magnetism—seems to recuperate for us from the *Ion* the theme of vocal uniqueness. For Nancy, in fact, it is always unique voices that interpret the parts assigned to them by the divine *moira*. And it is obviously the Muse herself who speaks through these voices—which means, according to Nancy, that the divine is that which is shared or distributed in the voices [*la partage des voix*]. It is the original, divine *sharing of voices* that is given in the singular voices of the poets and rhapsodes.[30] Symptomatically, even Nancy does not pay attention to the materiality of the acoustic sphere. The natural phenomenon of the uniqueness of each voice, the simple given that the voice of each one is different from every other, lends a tacit support to Nancy's interpretive thesis—but it does not become an explicit object of reflection in his text. Indeed, Nancy is not concerned with a vocal ontology of uniqueness, but rather with a hermeneutics of "sharing" that focuses on logos.[31] The curious specialty of Ion thus finds a plausible explanation. Even in the most "repetitive" ring of the poetic chain—that of the rhapsode—logos gives itself in a singular voice. The poetic chain is always divided in a plurality of voices; indeed, it is the divine voice that divides itself originarily in its constitutive plurality.

Among all of the works of Plato, the *Ion* is certainly an ambiguous and anomalous text. Nancy's reading of it nicely forces it toward platonically incongruous, and metaphysically disruptive, horizons of meaning. In this reading, the "sharing of voices" moves from the poetic logos to logos as such. In other words, according to Nancy, what is shared and distributed in the plurality, beyond the words sung by the poets and rhapsodes, is logos itself. Thus a theoretical space is opened—even if it is, unfortunately, not developed—for the theme of the relation between vocal uniqueness and speech. At the same time, Nancy seems to leave aside the question of Plato's agon with poetic song. Indeed, we should remember that what is crucial is the essential link—that Plato himself obliquely notes—between the uniqueness of the song and the uniqueness of the voice. The *Ion* seems to intuit this link, but it ends up focusing on it as an escape route rather than as a stimulus for further reflection. What remains, in the fragments of a textual game that is perhaps willfully left incomplete, is thus the intuition that vocal uniqueness is announced, originally, in the play of rhythm and resonance. Moreover, there is the no less important intuition that speech, far from being a copy of the idea, is rather first of all given to the aria of a song that delights the mouth and ears. The singular voices into which, according to Nancy's reading, logos is distributed are in fact thematized by Plato above all for their sonorous timbre. For Plato, these voices belong to an acoustic sphere of pleasure—over and beyond, or before, any separation between vocal expression and the content of what these voices say.

Without acoustic pleasure, without the relation between the enjoyment of mouths and ears, the uniqueness of the voice risks becoming an abstract, disembodied category. The voice is unique and the voice sings. Plato seems to intuit that these two aspects cannot be distinguished from one another. The world of epic signals for him the pleasure of giving a proper sonorous form to speech—and it makes of speech itself, above all, a song.

PART II

WOMEN WHO SING

2.1

"Sing to Me, O Muse"

> The herald came, guiding the faithful singer; he was much loved by the Muse. But as she gave him one gift, she took away another. She reft him of his sight, but she gave him the sweet singing art.
> —Homer, *Odyssey*, book 8

In the poetic chain, which Plato's *Ion* describes with great skill, the Muse has a fundamental role. She is the source of the message, the origin of the vocal transmission, the wellspring of the phonetic *mania*. Her voice is nevertheless inaudible to common mortals. For their ears, she is mute. The audience gains access to her song only through the voice of the poet, and thus the rhapsode. The mute, divine song makes itself sonorous in the human voice. For the audience, the poet is the audible form of the inaudible inspiration; it is the sonorous voice of the mute Muse.

Invoked by Homer, the divine Muse sings [*aeode*] or even recounts [*eipe*]. She sings to the poet what she has seen. Just as happens with Ireneo Funes, nothing escapes the prodigious sight of the goddess. This is why the poet invokes the Muses:

> Sing to me now, you Muses who hold the halls of Olympus!
> You are goddesses, you are everywhere, you know all things—
> All we hear is the distant ring of glory, we know nothing—
> Who were the captains of Achaea? Who were the kings?[1]

The immortal Muse *sees*, or rather *knows*, because she is present. She sees what happens on the Trojan battlefield, the actions of the humans and gods, the events that together form the fabric of single stories from which the whole story of the *Iliad* results. She is an eyewitness with acute vision and a panoramic gaze; she sees the stories that result from the actions of the heroes *and* she sees them in the actuality of their happening. As the daughter of Mnemosyne, she conserves a detailed recollection in her infallible memory. She knows all the names of those who fought at Troy, she knows everything—fact, action, and word—in detail. This is precisely the truth [*aletheia*] of the Muse that Hesiod mentions: a completeness of vision and memory that omits no detail.[2] The coincidence in the Muse of a complete vision of the events and a perfect memory of these events confers to the story an objective status of reality and truth. The story is true because what happened took place precisely like this and not otherwise, down to the smallest detail, in the direct presence of the Muse, who sees them happen and conserves their memory.

In a time that extends to infinity, she could therefore narrate everything to men, if such a tale were humanly audible. But it is not. Such a synoptic and detailed tale would in fact be an absolute tale that perfectly corresponds to the objectivity of the story, to its truth. In short, it would be a tale in which it would take ten years to narrate ten years of the Trojan War. Human ears would not be able to tolerate it. This explains the function of the poet as a vocal medium. His privileged relationship with the Muse consists in a superhuman power to hear the absolute tale and to make it into a story, one that is necessarily partial and incomplete, but humanly audible.

Not all of the story narrated by the absolute tale of the Muse passes into the tale of the poet. He can only summarize with veracity the principal thread of events, the most eminent heroes, the most visible characters, reducing all the others to a background multitude. For example, of the multitude of Achaean and Trojan soldiers, only a few are named. The Muse is at once the figure who confers to the story an extreme realism, and the one who signals the impossibility of the human tale ever perfectly coinciding with the reality of the story that it recounts. As Homer says:

> The mass of troops I could never tally, never name,
> Not even if I had ten tongues and ten mouths
> A tireless voice and the heart inside me bronze
> Never unless you Muses of Olympus, daughters of Zeus
> Whose shield is rolling thunder, sing, sing in memory
> All who gathered under Troy.[3]

The Muse has a fundamental function in Homeric "poetics." As an eyewitness and source of the tale, she represents first of all the necessary connection between history and tale—but also their distinction. Her tale is absolute because it corresponds perfectly to the story that gets told, but it is not reducible to this telling. For her tale has a reality that comes from the real events of history [*la storia*]. As Hannah Arendt would say, the story has no author.[4] The Muse herself is not the author but simply the one who tells the story because she was present at its happening. In the divine horizon that guarantees the story's reality, the story thus comes ontologically and logically before the tale. And by the same token, Homer has access to this reality only through the Muse's tale. As a special ear for a divine voice, the poet does not tell what he has seen—he is, after all, blind—but rather that which the Muse has told him. As Gilles Deleuze notes, in the human world, the telling of stories does not consist in "communicating what was seen, but rather what was heard."[5] The absolute tale, which the Muse tells to the poet, alludes to this hidden oral source of every tale. The emblematic blindness of Homer only serves to emphasize this allusion.

Homeric epic is a narrating song; the sphere of the *phone* is wedded to that of narration. In fact, there are three ideal narrative functions that the Muse synthesizes: eyewitness testimony, a perfect memory, and an absolute tale. Although not divine, Homer proudly points out how such narrative functions pass from the Muse to the human poet in a way that constitutes the very heart of epic. The absolute tale corresponds to the partial tale of the poet; the mnemonic techniques of the poets correspond to the daughter of Mnemosyne; the presence of the seeing Muse corresponds to the "wisdom" of the blind and absent poet.[6] Through the Muse, the blind poet "sees" and "makes seen" the story that he recounts to his listeners. The initial passage from the visual to the acoustic, which in a certain sense is what the Muse brings about, is thus reversed in the work of the poet. The poetic song resuscitates visions; the voice recuperates the visible horizon that guarantees the reality of the story.

This is not, however, an exclusively visual horizon. The realism of the story is essentially guaranteed by the presence of the Muse at the events in question: she not only sees but also hears. The story—like all stories—is made of a world of things, faces, names, actions, and discourses. And it is also made of sounds and noises, like the clash of arms or the pounding of the horses' hooves. In other words, something more than pure seeing takes place in the Muse's testimony: it is acoustic as well as ocular. She not only sees the actions of those who are at Troy, but she also hears their words, their discourses. By conserving the story in a sort of eternal actuality, the daughter of Mnemosyne also conserves the discourses that are proffered in her presence; in fact, ideally, she conserves the sound of the unmistakable timbre of the various voices. It is as if, in her divine memory, there still resounded the singular voices of Hector, Achilles, Helen, and all those who acted at Troy—each one speaking in his or her unique voice. Because Homer has only his voice—which is equally unique—he can do nothing but imitate these voices. So, too, do all the other rhapsodes who recite the Homeric poems. When the epic reports the direct discourse of Agamemnon, the voice is not that of the hero but of the poet or rhapsode. Although it can be imitated, the uniqueness of each voice resists the art of the tale: the narrative fiction cannot capture it. The vocal message transmits the story, but not the voice. The words—the words of the singular heroes—can be repeated infinitely as long as they are retained by a good memory; but this repeatability stands in marked contrast to the unrepeatability of the voices.

As a curious story narrated by Thomas Bernhard suggests, the inimitability of voices has an intrinsic and inviolable limit—namely, the uniqueness of the voice of the imitator. The story tells of a famous imitator of voices who toured the whole of Europe. He is a gifted imitator, but he has a limit that the audiences quickly discover. "We could also make requests, and the voice imitator took pains to fulfill all of them. But when we proposed that he close the program by imitating his own voice, he told us that he could not."[7]

As Plato's *Republic* tells us, in the ideal city that is constructed and ruled by philosophers, there is no place for the Muse's song.[8] This is curious, given the fact that it is the philosopher himself who will come to occupy the privileged place that the poet had reserved for the Muse. In a sense, the Muse's gaze—which takes as its object true and real things—is quite similar to that of the contemplator of ideas. Just like the Muse, with whom he shares the trustworthy power of the eye, the philosopher sees and knows. But there is, of course, a notable difference. With a panoramic gaze from on high, the Muse looks downward on the contingent and particular world of men and events. She is, in other words, the panoramic and synoptic version of Ireneo Funes. The philosopher, on the other hand, detaches his gaze from the human world of life and contingency and instead looks upward in order to contemplate the immobile otherworld of ideas. The truth and reality of his visions do not regard the human world of stories, but rather an otherwordly realm that opposes itself to the happening of stories, just as being opposes itself to appearing, the universal to the particular, the ideas to the plurality of things in the world. For example, the Muse sees the singular heroes who perform courageous actions; the philosopher, however, contemplates the idea of courage that offers itself, immobile and disembodied, to the eye of the soul. Philosophy is concerned with general essences; epic is concerned with the embodied uniqueness of singular existents and celebrates their actions by telling stories.[9] Unlike Plato and philosophy in general, the Muse does not know the idea of Man but rather, one by one, all the women and men who act and speak in her presence—distinguishing them from all others "in the unique form of the body and sound of the voice."[10]

With regard to this perception of detail—which the philosophical eye disdainfully refuses—we might momentarily recall the antiplatonic spirit of the tale by Borges to which I referred earlier. The similarities between the Muse and Ireneo Funes, to which I am alluding, might seem strange—but there is a foundation for this comparison. As I said earlier, the strange case of the Uruguayan antimetaphysician in fact regards not only an extraordinary capacity of perception, but also a prodigious memory. Just like the Muse, he preserves in his memory everything that he sees, in its smallest detail. Thus, these memories are anything but simple: "Two or three times he had reconstructed a whole day; he never hesitated, but each reconstruction had required a whole day."[11] Funes' memories thus have the same temporal extension as the things that are remembered. In order to remember and to recount a day, it takes a day. In Funes' memory—which saves every particular from oblivion, conserving it just as it appears to his infallible gaze—the time of the memory lasts as long as the time of the vision. It is a perfect copy of this vision. It is the absolute replication of reality.

The narrator of the strange case of Funes—an Argentinean whose memory is much frailer—understands very well what is at stake. He recounts his dialogue with Funes, which took place fifty years earlier. And he makes clear that he "shall not try to reproduce the words, which are now irrecoverable. I prefer to summarize with veracity the many things Ireneo told me."[12] Unlike the Muse and Funes, the narrator works within the limits of human vision and memory. He neither sees nor remembers all the details of Funes' face, even if he provides a good description of it. In the same way, he does not remember all the words of the dialogue, but he summarizes them in a faithful tale. As it is written out, this tale occupies four pages that correspond, more or less, to the time of one long night. Funes, on the other hand, would have taken an entire night to tell the same tale— and no syllable of the dialogue nor any detail of the scene would have escaped him. The infallibility of his perception and his memory, in a certain sense, would have produced what we can call an absolute tale of what happened that night.

The occasion of the dialogue between the Argentinean and Funes comes about because of some Latin texts that the former had lent the latter a few days earlier. Now the young Argentinean wants them back. When he arrives at Funes' house, the Uruguayan is reciting—in the dark—a passage from Pliny's *Natural History*. Its last words are *ut nihil non iisdem verbis redderetur auditum*, "until everything of what is heard is rendered in the very same words." Pliny's motto is quite apt for Funes. For nothing escapes him. The exactness of his perception extends to both sight and hearing. The discourses that he hears or reads can be repeated word for word. Almost as if the semantic aspect were of no importance, the difficulties of languages that he does not yet know pose no problem for him; all he needs is a guide to the grammar.

Predictably, Funes is quite interested in the cases of prodigious memory that Pliny records. Among these we find "Cyrus, King of the Persians, who could call every soldier in his armies by name."[13] Funes is, predictably, surprised that such a case deserves to be recorded by Pliny for posterity. We, on the other hand, are more like Pliny and can appreciate the wonder of such a case. Cyrus indeed seems to be divine, in much the same way as the Muse described by Homer. If Funes had been lent the *Iliad* instead, he would have seen the resemblance. And he would have recited to perfection the Greek verses, word for word.

In the *Ion*, Socrates is the one who recites Homer's verses. He disrespectfully steals the job of the "champion" of rhapsodic art with whom he is dialoguing. Thus, Socrates too risks involving himself in the poetic *mania*. Another platonic dialogue speaks of this *mania*—namely the *Phaedrus*, which discusses it as a particular type of possession and madness that comes from the Muse "taking over a pure and gentle soul, awakening it to a Bacchic frenzy through songs and poetry that celebrates the achievements of the past and teaches them to future generations."[14] The allusion to Homer here is clear. As the first and great educator of Greece, no one more than Homer corresponds to the poet who sings the glories of the past and educates the present generations. Just as happened in the pages on poetic magnetism in the *Ion*, so too in the *Phaedrus* there is still no particularly bitter tone in the words that Plato puts in Socrates' mouth. Possessed by the Muse, he says, delirious poets are the best poets.

This claim is in total keeping with the famous myth in the *Phaedrus* that binds the Muses even to the philosophers; namely, the myth of the cicadas, on which the entire theoretical axis of the dialogue turns.[15] We are told how the cicadas come from a certain type of men that lived before the birth of the Muses. When, with the birth of the Muses, song appeared, these men "were so overwhelmed with the pleasure of singing that they forgot to eat or drink; so they died without even realizing it."[16] Filled with compassion, the Muses thus transformed these men into cicadas, giving to them the privilege of being able to sing, without need of food or drink, all their lives until they die. "And, after they die, they go to the Muses and tell each one of them which mortals have honored her."[17] From that day on, through the mediation of the cicadas, each Muse comes to know and hold dear those who venerate her art—for example, the dancers of Terpsichore or the lovers of Erato. Indeed, even the philosophers get the protection of two Muses, Calliope and Urania, "who preside over the heavens and all discourses [*logoi*], divine and human, and sing with the sweetest voice [*kallisten phonen*]."[18]

According to Socrates' tale, therefore, the relationship between the philosophers and the Muses is mediated by the cicadas, just as happens with the poets and all those who honor the musical arts. Even if the delirium is no longer presented as a flux that descends directly from the Muse and possesses the soul, inducing it to song, this flux still pervades the entire myth. The cicadas are the ambiguous and metamorphic figures of a delirious song, and of a delirium that produces song. Compared by Socrates to other famous singers—namely, the Sirens—the cicadas are originally men who were taken to death by the pleasure of song and who then become creatures that live in the stupor of this pleasure, without eating or drinking. On the other hand, the cicadas are messengers of the Muse, men who dedicate themselves to song. Thus, at the center of the myth lies a possessing and enchanting stupor, similar to poetic delirium, which weakens the life instincts. In other words, it is a song that attracts and kills—just like that of the Sirens.

In the *Phaedrus*, Plato thus continues to analyze the effect of the enchantment and enchaining that comes from the Muse. The problem is always the same. The epic worries Plato above all for its musical and vocal performance, linked to corporeal pleasure. The harmonious voices of the Muses and Sirens, and the monotonous and penetrating song of the cicadas, continue to disturb the platonic imaginary whenever the philosopher seeks to critique the poets. The principal function of these figures—who are emblematically feminine—seems to be to emphasize the sonorous, libidinal, and presemantic materiality of logos. What is certain is that in this contagious pleasure, the acoustic register reigns sovereign and stands in opposition to the solitary style of *theoria*. This pleasure alludes to harmonious links that are different from those of the philosopher's logos; it alludes to a closer relation, at times too close, with the female body. What guides the platonic critique of Homer is thus "an implicit, although nebulous, association between the figure of the mother and the *oral work* of the poet."[19]

2.2

The Fate of the Sirens

"But if you take away my voice"—said the little mermaid—"what will I have left?"
—Hans Christian Anderson, "The Little Mermaid"

Born in Greece, the Muse passes into the western tradition as the inspirational source of a poetic activity that, while it assigns an essential role to the *phone*, nevertheless, because it renounces the sung performance of epic, takes away the power of its sonorous effects. No longer practiced, live or vocally, the poet's song becomes—in a culture of writing—a sort of metaphor that emphasizes the musicality of verse. The Sirens, however, have a different destiny.

The Sirens are monstrous figures who duplicate, in many ways, the function of the Muses; in the *Odyssey* they narrate by singing. Just as with the Muse, their song is a tale that says many beautiful things about the events of the Trojan War and the world of heroes. And as with the Muses, so too in the musical narration of the Sirens, vocality does not annul speech. For reasons that will not be difficult to uncover, however, the history of the western imaginary decides not to take this speech into account. In the tradition that runs from the Romans to the present day, the Sirens in fact tend to embody the lethality of a pure, harmonious, powerful, and irresistible voice that is almost like an animal cry. Half woman, half beast, they represent a vocal expression that is "different" from the humanized sphere of the *phone semantike*. One does not find this figuration in the Greek description of the Sirens from the *Odyssey*, even if there is already in Homer some elements that push them toward the song without words that will be their eventual destiny.

In Homer's tale, Circe speaks to Odysseus about the Sirens. Listen to my words, says the seductress to the hero. And she goes on to describe the tremendous peril: "you will come to the Sirens who seduce all men with their sweet song [*thelgousin aoide*]."[1] This seduction is, of course, deadly. The shore surrounding the Sirens' island is littered with skeletons and decaying corpses. And we soon find out that death came to the poor sailors who, pulled by the song, crashed on the rocks. To hear Circe tell it, this pull could be simply the effect of the Sirens' harmonious voice—a pure vocal sonority, a phonetic modulation without words. Odysseus is in fact put on guard against an irresistible voice [*phthogge*] that gives pleasure to whoever hears it. Circe does not warn against the verbal content of the Sirens' song. The entire pathos is concentrated on the deadly, seductive circuit between voice and hearing, sound and ear. As monstrous singers, or deadly women with powerful voices, the Sirens produce an acoustic pleasure that kills men. Circe thus advises the hero to melt some wax of honey, and use it to plug the ears of Odysseus' companions. His companions should then tie Odysseus himself to the ship's mast. Thus rendered deaf, the sailors can pass safely by the island of the singers. If Odysseus wants to listen to the voice of the Sirens—suggests Circe, somewhat maliciously—he must tie himself very tightly to the ship's mast and keep his ears open to enjoy the song. In this way, someone gets to enjoy the Sirens' song without dying. Of course, more than one of the men might have been tied to the mast with his ears open. After all, the sea is calm; there is neither wind nor wave. It would have only taken a few sailors to manage the ship. Still, only one gets to enjoy the song—namely, the astute man, the Greek of acute intelligence, the champion of persuasive discourses, the hero of reason.

Describing the adventure, Homer defines the Sirens' voice as a divine song [*thespesiaon*].[2] (The monstrous and the divine often go together.) When the cursed island gets closer, a god holds back the waves. In the flat calm of the water, a surreal silence surrounds the ship. Under the burning sun, the wax melts easily, the bonds are tied, and everything is ready. The sailors, deaf and perspiring, man the boat while Odysseus, all ears, is bound tightly to the mast. As he waits anxiously, the Sirens' song suddenly arrives. When the boat is "as far from the land as a voice shouting carries," the Sirens sing to him.[3] In other words, distance is measured by the sound of the voice and not by the purview of the eye (even if, as we shall see, the Sirens have acute vision). Something else is surprising, however. The monstrous singers do not simply emit from their mouths [*stoma*] a voice that, like that of the Muse, has a "sound of honey" (which is identified with the very voice of Homer).[4] They sing words, they vocalize stories, they narrate by singing. And they know what they are talking about. Their knowledge is, in fact, total: "we know all [*idmen*]," they sing.[5] Just as happened with the Muses, the Homeric language again makes seeing and knowing coincide. Indeed, just like the Muses, the divine singers narrate musically the things that they saw happen on the Trojan plain and all over the earth. They know all, completely and in detail, because they see all. What distinguishes them from the Muses, besides their monstrous body, is thus above all a voice that is audible to human ears. Simple sailors can hear from the Sirens what the Muse instead reserves only for the poet.

Seduced by the narrating song, Odysseus obviously goes mad [*smania*]. His heart [*ker*] wants to hear. Or rather—because he is listening with open ears—he wants to hear more, to hear longer, to hear forever the beautiful voice and the tale that it sings. Signaling to his companions with his eyes—for, because he is bound up and their ears are plugged, he is constrained to gestures—he invites them to untie him. He wants to go all the way—to enjoy and die. But they, as was planned, tie him even tighter. Only when they are far enough away do the sailors remove the wax and free their prisoner.

Could the deaf sailors have been commanded by the eye? Could a strong gesture from Odysseus have been enough to convince them to untie him? Would they have trusted a commanding gesture from their captain? The text does not say, and the Homeric tale naturally goes on to another adventure. But this episode remains the most memorable. As it gets sedimented in the collective imaginary for centuries to come, the episode of the Sirens makes feminine song into something quite disturbing.

Clearly, it is feminine song that is at stake. This is precisely why it is so disturbing. It disturbs, however, in a rather curious way with respect to the generic stereotypes that one finds in the western tradition. Homer in fact wants the monstrous singers to be omniscient, just like the Muses. In other words, he wants them to be a counterfigure for himself, as he narrates the stories of Troy. There is no doubt about the sexual origins of Homeric poetics: the feminine song, as the source of epic, is what guarantees the truth of the story and lends it its seductive power, both narratively and vocally. What is important, for Homer, is that epic produce an irresistible pleasure, that it seduce the listeners, even if this pleasure is not necessarily a lethal pleasure. This is why the Muse is a more apt figure than the Sirens to represent the source of epic. Her song does not kill—even if, seeing as how only the poet can hear it, there must be something dangerous about it that is filtered and translated into something humanly audible. The difference between the Muse and the Siren, both of whom see omnisciently, both of whom know and narrate all the events of the Trojan War, is thus above all the lethal effect of the latter's song. The Sirens' song can be heard by all mortals who venture on their island. The Muse's song is only heard by the poet who is privileged among mortals and who does not die from having heard it. In a certain sense, the poet experiences what Odysseus experienced—he enjoys the divine song without dying from it. Unlike Odysseus, however, the poet transmits vocally to humans this enjoyment. The fact remains that the first source of this pleasure is feminine. As happens for every human who came into the world, the first voice is a woman's voice.

This is, among other reasons, why Homer wants the voice of the song to be feminine. However, he wants it to be narrating, articulated in words, fully semantic. After all, at play here is not a voice as voice, but rather a particular voice, the sonorous voice of epic. Thus, the two different receptions of these Homeric figures in the western tradition is all the more significant. Again, in the western imaginary, the destinies of the Muse and the Siren diverge. The first continues to inspire verses to poets who, strictly speaking, no longer sing. The second tends instead to lose speech and to become pure voice, inarticulate song, acoustic vibration, cry. Thus, through the betrayal reserved for the Sirens alone, a minor history unfolds—one that is entrusted to legends and fables, where the pure voice prevails over speech. Importantly, this minor history is the converse of the major history in which the pure semantic opposes itself to the sonorous power of speech.

In the iconography of the minor story, most Sirens sing, but they no longer narrate. Nor do they know all like their ancient mothers. They become sinuous, fishlike creatures—something that the Homeric monsters never were—who seduce men not only through their song, but also by their beauty. The charm of the voice, rendered even more disturbing by the absence of speech, still calls men to a pleasurable (and often explicitly erotic) death. The historical metamorphosis of the Homeric Sirens thus seems to coincide, finally, with the way in which Circe described them. There is a feminine voice that seduces and kills, and that has no words.

As Greek vase paintings teach us, the Greeks imagined the Sirens as women who had the body of a bird. They had a round torso and claws.

Beautiful they were not. They lay in the rushes along the shore, near the sea, but they had no common ancestry with fish. Moreover, because they had such vocal power, it is obvious that they call to mind birds instead of fish. Whoever is mute like a fish certainly cannot produce a monstrous song. Many species of birds, on the other hand—as our modern languages say—sing; some are even famous for their incomparable musicality. Plato, for example, tells in the myth of Er how the singer Thamyris chose to be reincarnated as a nightingale in order to fully express his art. In short, the song—which is made of air—belongs to creatures of the air, not creatures of the deep.

And yet the reception of the myth in the western tradition consigns this song to the depths. This change of abode is highly significant. The descent of the Sirens into the water, their metamorphosis into fishlike creatures, is in fact accompanied by their transformation into very beautiful women. This process corresponds, in a rather significant way, to the one of the most stereotypical models of the female sex—namely, the stereotype according to which, in her erotic function as seductress, as an object of masculine desire, the woman appears first of all as a body and as an inarticulate voice. She must be beautiful, but she must not speak. What she can do, however, is emit pleasing sounds, asemantic vocalizations, moans of pleasure. Given that the voice comes from the internal body and comes out of the mouth to penetrate the ear of the listener, this figuration obviously works because the voice and body reinforce one another. The fact that the voice is a pure vocality that says nothing further assures an extraneousness to the semantic dimension of logos that only increases the feminine nature of the voice itself. In other words, in the (notoriously dichotomous) symbolic patriarchal order, man is conceived as mind and woman as body. The division of logos into a purely feminine *phone* and a purely masculine *semantikon*, finally, accomplishes and confirms the system.

This goes, in general, for the stereotypical representation of human women, but it is even truer, or more symbolically perfect, in the long, iconic reelaboration of the myth of the Sirens. As omniscient narrators, Homer's Sirens in fact work to upset the androcentric system; they usurp the masculine specialty of logos. In the case of the Sirens, obviously, this is a highly particular logos—a poetic, narrative, sung, and musical logos that stands in opposition to the silent logos of philosophy. And yet it is still a logos in which the vocal dimension of song accompanies the semantic dimension in putting a knowledge into words. These dimensions, as Homer continually underscores, are divine and extraordinary—they go beyond human capacities. After the decline of oral culture, however, a decisive symbolic gesture takes speech away from the Sirens, leaving only the voice. The ancient figure of the Siren thus undergoes a radical change: the Sirens survive as an image, but no longer as Homer's image. And this survival is linked to an embodiedness, a pure voice, which only strengthens the female stereotype.

To be sure, elements of this corporeality were already present in Homer's description of the Sirens. After all, unlike the Muse, the Sirens are horrible and murderous monsters. They are hybrid creatures—half woman, half animal—who are surrounded by the dead corpses of male sailors. And their repellent character has a precise role in Homer's poetry—namely, to guarantee that their charm comes only from song, or from the epic performance. Their seductiveness has, in other words, nothing to do with the beauty of the divine singers, a fact that Homer goes out of his way to emphasize by highlighting their monstrosity. This does not mean, of course, that the Sirens hide themselves from view. As its Latin root indicates, the *monstruum* is such because it offers itself to be seen [*si mostra*]; it is there to show off. The monster's anomalous body irresistibly attracts the gaze. As a result, the western imaginary has been able to play on this visible fascination of the monstrous Sirens by making the feminine part of the monster beautiful, turning it into the sinuous body of a sea creature. With their legs closed off in a smooth, silver tail fin, the Sirens entered the water.

Obviously, the water around the island was already there. The "sailor's story" that happened to Odysseus adapted itself quite well to future stories of fishermen, narrated by countless legends. Moreover, it is likely that the bond between women and amniotic fluid also determined the trajectory of the androcentric imaginary.[6] After the first voice, there is the first water: indeed, the figure of the mother seems to lead the myth of the Sirens in a certain direction. At times this is quite explicit. There are numerous popular versions of the legend in which the siren or mermaid embraces the fisherman and, in the passion of their last kiss, drags him with her to the bottom. Born from the water of a woman, he thus returns to the water with her to die. It is the common, ancient patriarchal fable of Eros and Thanatos, with the maternal body functioning as both cradle and tomb, as both origin and end of the living body.

Did not Odysseus himself wish to die of pleasure on hearing the Siren's voice? Did not the benevolent bonds of epic seduction perhaps save him, by tying him tightly to its mast?

There is a famous painting by René Magritte that depicts a siren stretched out on the seashore.[7] From the waist up it is a fish; from the waist down it is a woman. It looks like a fish onto which the body of a woman was grafted. The effect is startling. By effacing the human aspect, the inversion produces a figure in which the animal component prevails. No painter has known better than Magritte how to take measure of the fate of the siren. For it is her fate to be abandoned on this final shore, washed up by the sea of an imaginary that took her further and further away from Homer in order, finally, to kill her.

Indeed, Magritte's siren does not sing. Her fish mouth is mute. In fact, she no longer even breathes—she is a fish out of water, in agony. Her pubis and her naked legs, her hips and the roundness of her thighs, are, however, still able to solicit a kind of necrophilial sexual pleasure. The history of the imaginary that made her seductively beautiful, while not daring to admit it, wanted precisely this—namely, a woman's body to possess, a feminine body for the man's pleasure, something that no part of the body represents better than the dark triangle between her legs. And of course, the typical erotic fantasies involving sirens or mermaids inevitably encountered a certain difficulty when it came to the "technical" details of intercourse. This is why, for example, the beautiful Melusina had an interchangeable bottom half—sometimes she was fishlike, but when the need arose, she became a whole woman. Magritte's siren therefore makes clear for us the convenience, so to speak, of a final, drastic decision. If the monster is, classically, a hybrid creature, and if, in order to enjoy her, it is necessary to get rid of one part, then it is best to get rid of the face. Without a mouth to kiss or breasts to caress, the siren now has the face of a fish. Or, perhaps, like the dolphin [*delphis*] that she now resembles, she alludes to the centrality of her vulva [*delphus*]. Which might also mean—as misogynists maintain—that what identifies the female sex, what is proper to the female, is the part of the body that lies below the belt. Her head, the seat of intelligence, is of course hardly a necessary characteristic.

The siren is now speechless, incapable even of an animal cry. Having lost even the ancient memory of song, the modern siren thus dies.

Just as in the painting by Magritte—but for different reasons—the Sirens imagined by Franz Kafka are mute as well. They are properly Homeric in appearance, with the face of a woman and the body of a bird; and they await the sailors, ready to kill them with their deadly song. But they did not expect that such an arrogant man as Odysseus, with "a look of bliss on his face," would be waiting to hear their song. The surprise renders them silent.[8]

"It was known to all the world," writes Kafka, that no wax could block out the penetrating voice of the Sirens; nor could any bond resist the force of the longing that their song produced. And yet, Odysseus "trusted absolutely his handful of wax and his fathom of chain, and in innocent elation over his little stratagem he sailed out to meet the Sirens."[9] And by concentrating all his attention on the ridiculous solution of the wax and chain, he overcame the challenge. In fact, the hero showed such an arrogant, human happiness on his face that the Sirens for a moment forgot their singing. Amazed by his appearance, they were silent. Or, perhaps, they believed "that this enemy could be vanquished only by their silence." But Odysseus, "if one may so express it, did not hear their silence; he thought they were singing and that he alone did not hear them." For a "fleeting moment," writes Kafka, "he saw their throats rising and falling, their breasts lifting, their eyes filled with tears and their lips half-parted," and he believed that "these were the accompaniments to the songs which died unheard around him." This idea of a privileged deafness, a kind of antidote to the lethality of the song, only increases his pride. Then, without any regret, his satisfied eyes fix themselves on the distance; "the Sirens literally vanished before his resolution, and at the very moment when they were nearest to him he knew of them no longer."[10]

For Kafka, Odysseus is therefore a man of the gaze. Therein lies his power. This interpretation is supported by many ancient vase paintings in which Odysseus—bound to the mast of the ship and depicted in profile—looks decisively ahead of him, so that he can see the Sirens only briefly, in passing. In Kafka's ingenious parable, this interpretation also suggests that the hero belongs to the order of vision, just as the Sirens belong to the order of the voice. Odysseus' vision is hungry for new adventures, always looking ahead—but it is a vision that, like thought, does not perceive the surrounding circumstances and instead looks elsewhere. Everything turns, in any case, on the gaze of Odysseus. The most immediate sense of this gaze consists in the expression of joy—which comes from his thinking about the effectiveness of his "stratagems." This expression on his face is precisely what catches the Sirens' attention. As Kafka makes clear, they are above all captivated by "the radiance that fell from his great eyes." The mute logic of the gaze thus consumes even the singing monsters in their own realm; the seductresses are seduced. As they look on he who looks elsewhere, they remain silent because "they no longer had any desire to allure." The order of vision defeats the order of the voice and reduces it to silence.

Having won the challenge, Odysseus is able to reconfigure not only the Sirens' song but also an unforeseen—and even more terrible—weapon that men had never fully confronted—namely, their silence. A mere mortal, who came just to listen to them—full of stratagems to keep himself from succumbing to this pleasure—would not have been able to stand their silence. He would certainly have died from this silence—not so much from disappointment as from the feeling of having conquered them with his only strength; namely, a tremendous act of pride "that bears down everything before it and which no earthly power can resist."[11] And yet Odysseus does come out on top. Capable of turning every situation to his advantage, he neutralizes the weapon of silence, just as he was ready to neutralize their song. The extreme risk he took is thus transformed into satisfaction for a well-deserved privilege. Nothing can take from him his self-esteem, and he carries onward toward the next adventure, his confidence in his tricks further emboldened.

With a subtle irony, however, Kafka adds that the whole episode might have been a comedy or a pretense. After all, Odysseus is at bottom a master of the art of trickery. Perhaps he had noticed that the Sirens were silent and yet sly as a fox, he pretended that he did not notice. Thus, the terrible weapon of silence did not have the desired effect. On the contrary, he probably thought that it was a mere trick of the sorceresses, to which he quickly responded with a trick of his own. The most curious result of all this is that, in this way, Odysseus even mocked the gods and the whole of Homeric poetry—which, of course, keeps on narrating his encounter with the Sirens and the pleasure that he enjoyed. As a consequence of Odysseus' talent for *commedia*, we in fact do not know whether the Sirens really sang or if they remained silent. His companions at the oars, rendered deaf by the wax, certainly cannot bear witness. The intrepid captain—winking, raising his eyebrows, making faces—tricked them as well. Of course, we can count on Homer. But is not this episode perhaps part of Odysseus' autobiographical tale, which Homer is limited to simply reporting? Who, if not the Sirens, could narrate in a true fashion the story of their improbable silence?

Moving the date of the origin of the enlightenment back to the Homeric *epos*, Theodor Adorno and Max Horkheimer discover in the

Odyssey "a description of the retreat of the individual from the mythic power."[12] This is the rational and logocentric subject that the two Frankfurt School philosophers see—in an anachronism that is, to say the least, audacious—in the figure of Odysseus. As the figuration of a subject that is "still unreconciled to himself, still unsure," and who is "attaining self-realization only in self-consciousness," the hero embodies "the way taken through the myths by the self."[13] The archaic powers of nature that are evoked by the myth are therefore that to which the rational subject is opposed; but they are also, at the same time, his internal prehistory. Challenging nature in order to dominate her, the Self dominates even the nature that he himself was—and that still persists in him, violent and seductive, under the now vigilant control of reason. "Man's domination over himself, which grounds his selfhood," still has a ring of nostalgia.[14] In a certain sense, therefore, the Sirens sing only for Odysseus. Rather than simply being the lifeless bodies of naive sailors, the cadavers that surround the sorceresses' island evoke the mortal risk of the subject, the nature from which it emerges and against which it builds itself up.

However, this mortal risk is inevitable for the subject. Precisely because it is sedimented in the labor of its self-construction—like a sort of prehistoric stage of its nascent rational substance—the Self cannot avoid it. Odysseus does not try to find another way around the island of the Sirens. And as Adorno and Horkheimer diligently point out, he does not even attempt to survive the encounter with the Sirens by trusting his reason alone to overcome the primordial forces of nature. Still too fragile for a direct encounter with powers that, after all, pulse in his own breast, the Self takes recourse in a minor type of rationality—namely, cleverness. It finds the right stratagems to distance himself from nature, but it "remains subject to it if it heeds its voice."[15] Indeed, in the crucial moment, the subject tries to free itself from bonds that it had prepared, in order to give itself over to the call of the Sirens, to return to its own prehistory. What overcomes the seduction of this return is not reason in the fullest sense, but rather the techniques or stratagems of self-preservation that reason provides. Through such techniques the Self shivers from the feeling of its own self-dissolution; but having emerged from the challenge in one piece, the Self confirms and reinforces itself. To borrow the language of Michel Foucault, one could say that listening to the Sirens' song is a functional proof of the technologies of the Self.

One can easily complain that the thoroughly modern lens through which the authors of *Dialectic of Enlightenment* read Homer—suggestive as this lens is—ends up being an anachronistic deformation of the ancient text. They apply improbable and misplaced terms like "subject," "Self," "enlightenment"—not to mention "society," "bourgeoisie," "capitalism"—to the *Odyssey*. Obviously, every interpretation—especially interpretations of ancient texts—can withstand a free appropriation of the original text on the part of the interpreter. The pants of the bourgeois subject, however, are pretty tight for the hero from Ithaca. Still, precisely because it is a modern reading, Adorno's interpretation of the Sirens provides an interesting take on the problem of the *phone*—namely, on the usual error of seeing the Homeric temptresses as voice alone. For Horkheimer and Adorno, the Sirens in fact represent "pure" voice; they sing, but they say nothing, recount nothing. They do not belong to the world of Homeric orality. Rather, in them Odysseus "recognizes the archaic superior power of the song."[16] As with the later tradition of interpretation, Horkheimer and Adorno see in the Sirens a pure, melodious, asemantic vocality. The song thus concentrates in itself the whole of the challenge posed to Odysseus. As a result, the challenge is actualized between the sonorous physicality of the song and mute reason, between pure voice and pure semantic. The opposing sides are at the polar extremes of a logos that tends to split into a presemantic vocality and a devocalized rationality.

In the interpretation of Horkheimer and Adorno, this means that the Self recognizes the pleasure of the pure *phone* in its prehistory and, fortifying itself with bonds of reason, decides to run the risk of regressing to the joy of a presemantic stage for which it still feels nostalgia. It is as if the vocalizations of the *in-fante* called out behind the adult, returning the Self to the pleasure of the ear and phonetic emission. Given the inevitably ambiguous name of "Self," Odysseus not only represents the parable of the subject, but in fact represents the parable of a man who was an infant—that is, the parable of every human being as a speaking animal. As Adorno and Horkheimer suggest, the *Odyssey* lends itself to exemplifying many types of journeys—that of the subject and the Self, which they privilege in their interpretation, but also that of the human species as it leaves the caveman behind, or the infant who becomes an adult. There are many examples of this. Polyphemos, who still lives in a cave, has the kind of gigantic status that infants see in adults. The lotus-eaters, who are incapable of agriculture, recall an experience that is still "known to European children only in terms of cooking with rosewater and candied violets," and that is the "promise of a state in which the reproduction of life is independent of conscious self-preservation, and the bliss of the fully contented is detached from the advantages of rationally planned nutrition."[17] The infancy of the individual and the species converge in the evocation of a pleasurable state that both the adult and civilization in general must renounce. So too does the subject, or the Self as a completed form of self-consciousness, with respect to which mythical demons must be "forced back into the forms of rock and cavern whence they once emerged in the dread remoteness of antiquity."[18] What is certain is that the pleasure that comes from the Sirens' song is one of the crucial aspects of this logic of renunciation. After all, especially for Adorno and for his well-known reflections on music, the regression to listening is a phenomenon worthy of the greatest consideration. Adorno himself is, on the other hand, "a creature of the Hegelian tradition who postulates a historical cogent teleology which is capable of incorporating everything into its unstoppable progress."[19] In this sense, the Sirens must embody a musical vocality that is deprived of speech. Odysseus, for his part, must overcome it.

For Homer, who knows nothing of the modern rational subject, the Sirens do not at all represent a presemantic vocality. Rather, they sing and narrate; or they sing narrating. The irresistible charm of the song is inextricably linked to the charm of the tale. The pleasure that results is therefore not in some "prehistory," however one understands this; rather, it is the same pleasure that Homer himself is capable of producing in his audience. He is proud to trace the source of epic narration back to an omniscient female figure; the poet inherits from their song his own power to enchant. Moreover, the privileged relation that binds him to the Muse consists precisely in his function as a filter between the goddess and the listeners. He is the only one who can hear their divine song and translate it into a human song. He is the only one who can translate the vocality and the omniscience of the Muse into a narrating song that transmits to the listeners a humanly bearable pleasure. If they had access to the power of the original song, mere mortals would in fact die of pleasure. Odysseus tried this himself, and only his clever stratagems saved him from death. This does not take away the fact that—as far as his capacity for hearing and transmitting the divine song goes—Homer places himself slightly higher than Odysseus on the scale of mortals. In the Homeric economy, the poet is in fact superior to the hero—just as the art of epic is superior to the clever techniques or stratagems of the hero, just as the narrating song is superior to rational discourse, just as the power to produce acoustic pleasure is superior to the audacity of challenging its lethal effects. At bottom, the

Sirens are copies of the Muse, which Homer conceded to Odysseus' ears in order to prove the superiority of epic as a material that produces pleasure.

In Horkheimer and Adorno's interpretation, on the other hand, the question of a pleasure linked to the coincidence of voice and tale in epic performance disappears from view. The narrative aspect of the song gets overlooked. The Sirens sing, but unlike Homer, they do not sing tales. The Sirens' song as pure voice must in fact now work as a repressed pleasure, or as a primeval state that is the object of nostalgia. Detaching itself from speech, the *phone* thus comes to represent a primitive "physical force," not unlike Polyphemos' muscles. In contrast to what happens to the Sirens as they are "reinvented" by Horkheimer and Adorno, the giant Cyclops still speaks. According to the two Frankfurt School philosophers, however, he maintains an archaic relation to speech that is very different from that of the civilized Odysseus. Odysseus' play on his own name in fact serves to emphasize this difference. By playing on the etymological vicinity of *oudeis* (no one) and *Odysseos*, the hero tells Polyphemos that he is called No One. In this way, using his customary techniques and stratagems, Odysseus shows that he can calculate and plan, in great detail, his own escape from the Cyclops. After he is blinded, the giant Cyclops in fact will ask the other Cyclopses for help, declaring that "no one" is hurting him, and obviously, the other Cylopses do not come running to his aid. The main point, however, is something else. According to Horkheimer and Adorno, the point is Odysseus' ability to take the name away from the mythic sphere—in which the name and the thing magically coincide—by inserting "the intention in the name."[20] Poor Polyphemos truly cannot understand this meaning. For his archaic notion of logos, the relationship (or distinction) between acoustic signifier and mental signified is in fact inconceivable.

As a champion of semantic tricks and sophistic discourse, Odysseus—according to Horkheimer and Adorno—is also the prototypical narrator. There is no doubt that the central cantos of the *Odyssey* come directly from his mouth. The very episode of the Sirens is notoriously mise-en-scène by Homer as an autobiographical tale of Odysseus. Indeed, the Homeric poem here displays a textual complexity that deserves to be emphasized. The poet recounts for the public how Odysseus recounts for the Phoechians his encounter with the Sirens, who were themselves recounting to Odysseus his own story; and, because they (the Sirens) see all, they are obviously capable of recounting in turn how he (Odysseus) is now recounting his encounter with them. This is not a paradoxical confusion, but

rather a narrative model constructed through a circular plot of tales that—
by recalling the one to the other—stages its own movement.

It is thus surprising that Horkheimer and Adorno, by opposing the
narrator Odysseus to the mythic song of the Sirens, end up drastically over-
simplifying the complexity of the plot's self-conscious staging. By concentrating their attention on the hero, they short-circuit the complex narrative
tensions of the text. By trying to make Odysseus fit the clothes of the subject, they make Odysseus into the privileged narrator at the cost of all the
other narrators in the *Odyssey*. In keeping with his rational nature,
Odysseus thus puts into action the "cold distancing of narration" that
transforms the facts into something that "happened a long time ago."[21]
Through the use of memory, he places the stories at a distance, consigning
them to a temporal dimension that separates past events from the present
of the narrator. In short, this is, for Horkheimer and Adorno, just another
one of Odysseus' rational techniques or stratagems, one that gives the
Frankfurt School philosophers a further reason to see a kind of mastery in
Odysseus' logos. Whatever remains of the bodily pleasure thus gets reduced to mere relief at having passed the danger of the Sirens—if not to a
tale that "represents horror as if it were a conversational topic," without
even taking the musicality of the narrating voice into consideration.[22] It is
in any case symptomatic that, among the atrocities that abound in the
Homeric text, Adorno and Horkheimer decide to cite the brief episode of
the hanging of the maids, which "coldly compares the women's appearance
as they hang to that of birds caught in a net."[23] In fact, in this case
Odysseus himself is the executioner, not the narrator. Homer is the one
who tells the story of the maids.

And yet even Adorno and Horkheimer cannot help confusing
Homer with Odysseus, or the labor of epic with the character that (according to them) embodies the parable of the subject. In any event, the
fact remains that, according to the authors of *Dialectic of Enlightenment*,
the Sirens have nothing to do with the art of narration. They are limited to
raising their melodious voices in a nonsemantic seduction.

2.3

Melodramatic Voices

> The emission of song is, in and of itself, the acoustic exhibition of embodiment. It is not a sound that comes from a mechanical instrument; rather, it is produced by the very body of the singer, the corporeal flux that emerges from the most hidden cavities, and which determines its particular "grain" . . . ; not a generic timbre, codified in advance by technical instruments, but rather a peculiar, elusive, highly individualized, acoustic image of a specific embodiment.
> —Marco Beghelli, *Erotismo canoro*

The silence of Kafka's Sirens has, as we have seen, an unforeseen, extraordinary, and surprising meaning in the context of the short parable. However, the opposite happens to women, mere mortals, who remain silent. "Women should be seen and not heard," goes the famous adage of patriarchal wisdom.[1] Another proverb tells us that "silence is golden"—which here would mean that "whoever remains silent gives his consent" or obeys, as wives and daughters rightly should. Taking this to its logical conclusion, the perfect woman would be mute—not just a woman who abstains from speaking, but a woman who has no voice. Or, more precisely, not just a deaf-mute woman (who risks not obeying the man's words because she does not hear them), but rather a woman who has lost her voice. In short, a woman who listens but cannot speak.

However, it can happen that—by reflecting on this "ideal" muteness of their sex and recalling the Sirens—different women end up interpreting the whole affair in very different ways. Some of them have even suggested that, for a woman, there exists an emblematic way to lose one's voice.

In a story by Isak Dinesen called "The Dreamers," a young opera

singer by the name of Pellegrina Leoni loses her voice in a rather emblematic fashion.[2] The cause is a traumatic episode. During a performance of
Don Giovanni, a fire breaks out in the Scala Theater in Milan where Pellegrina is singing the aria of Donna Anna; the accident that follows causes
her to lose her voice—not her womanly voice or speech, but rather her
singing voice. As a soprano, Pellegrina dies; at least, this is what a world ignorant of the fact that she physically survived the fire comes to believe.
And given the total coincidence of Pellegrina with her operatic voice, she
in effect does die. Her existence under this name no longer comes together
with her voice. So the young woman decides to travel the world, changing
her name over and over, living many lives. No longer prisoner of a voice
that made her the greatest soprano of her day, she begins to play with other
possible existences. Her story is an intense and adventurous one. But in the
delirium of her actual, final death throes, her original identity as a soprano
returns. Once again as Pellegrina Leoni, the dying woman sings for the last
time the aria of Donna Anna, rediscovering if not her old voice, then at
least the emotion of the song.

Pellegrina's fate turns on a crucial aspect of the female voice. Silence—which according to the patriarchal order is "golden," especially for
women—concerns speech, not song. As the myth of the Sirens teaches us,
song is heard as naturally feminine, just as speech is naturally masculine.
Destined to substantiate themselves in the semantic, men's voices tend to
disappear in the mute labor of the mind, or thought. By modulating themselves in song, on the other hand, women's voices come to show their authentic substance—namely, the passionate rhythms of the body from
which the voice flows. In this sense, the woman who sings is always a Siren,
or a creature of pleasure, extraneous to the domestic order of daughter and
wife. The female singing voice cannot be domesticated; it disturbs the system of reason by leading elsewhere. Potentially lethal, it pushes pleasure to
the limits of what is bearable.

This is precisely the power of Pellegrina Leoni. She reincarnates the
sonorous seduction of the Sirens and reproduces their effects. As Dinesen
has Pellegrina's devoted admirer/companion narrate, when she sang, "your
heart would melt at the sound of her voice, until you thought: This is too
much; the sweetness is killing me, and I cannot stand it."[3] Pellegrina's song
is wonderful. It saves the listeners even as it drags them into the abyss, and
it opens for them the meaning "of heaven and earth, of the stars, life and
death, and eternity."[4] The notes that come out of the soprano's throat bear

witness to the fact that the world has not been abandoned by the angels. Whoever listens to her voice weeps from joy, forgets the weight of existence, and remembers lost paradise. In short, just as happens with the Sirens, Pellegrina's voice flows with an irresistible pleasure from which one could even die. The loss of her singing voice is thus more tragic than any other muteness, more tragic than any silence imposed on wives or daughters. In fact, with this voice, the formidable power of female song dies. No woman is as symbolically mute as the soprano who no longer sings—or, rather, no muteness is more tragic than the Sirens' silence.

The contemporary feminine imaginary still counts among its numbers some other sopranos who lost their voices—and also the power of speech—because of a fire that happened during a performance. This is what happened to Ada, the protagonist of the film *The Piano* (1992), directed by Jane Campion. Actually, the story did not go exactly like this, but Ada's daughter, indulging her childish imagination, justifies her mother's muteness by telling this story. A lightening bolt set fire to the outdoor stage where her parents were performing, killing the father and rendering the mother mute forever. The little girl thus becomes the mother's interpreter, while the mother communicates through sign language. As the point of transmission between her mother and the world, the little girl is her mother's voice, the sound of her speech. In this case, the mother's muteness is total; she cannot use her voice—which, in the child's imagination, gets emphasized by her prior career as a lyric singer. Again, no woman is more mute than the one who loses her singing voice. At the same time, however, the film takes as its focus the piano, the musical instrument through whose sounds the protagonist expresses herself.

The complicity between mother, daughter, and piano is presented as an exclusive threesome. In a certain sense, they are three emissaries of European civilization in the hostile world of New Zealand, where Ada arrives through an arranged marriage. The piano is the interpreter of her song, just as the daughter is the interpreter of her speech. Strangers in the society that surrounds them, Ada communicates with her hands and body. The work of her fingers is transformed into musical sound on the piano, just as her sign language is transformed into her daughter's voice. (Symptomatically, Ada "speaks" to strangers through writing, at least to those who know how to read.) The tragic twist of the story in fact concerns the hand as the means of sonorous transmission. Her cuckolded husband, in a fit of rage, exacts his punishment—not by killing her, but rather by cutting off one of

her fingers. Beyond simply being a horrendous act, this mutilation is crucial precisely because it puts her voice at risk—both her musical voice and
her discursive voice.

Indeed, it is telling that the "happy ending" of the story is not able to
erase the impression left by this terrible scene of mutilation. For the spectators, this attack on a hand that is the fundamental instrument for the
sonorous communication of a mute woman is the climax of the tragedy. As
for the narration—which has a kind of double ending—the silence of the
ocean depths into which the protagonist throws herself, along with her piano, is a far more convincing ending than the artificial finger that is ap-
pended to her hand after she is rescued from the sea. In the last scene of
the film, we even see Ada as a happy housewife, learning to speak. But the
true Ada remains the other one—the one who belongs to musical passion,
where the seduction of sound is also an erotic experience. She is a peculiarly feminine type: lethal, and enigmatically bound to the sea.

Although she loses her voice like Pellegrina—worse, in fact, because
she is totally mute—Ada finds, through the piano, a way to still sing like a
Siren. Although it is only the childish dream of her daughter, her past career as a soprano also helps to explain the sonorous seduction that she turns
out to be capable of. Pellegrina, too, was a soprano—and she becomes one
again at the moment of her death. Full of references to ancient feminine
powers, irresistible pleasures, and erotic transgressions, there lies behind
both of these women's stories the strange world of opera.

At first sight, actually, this world seems more ridiculous than strange.

"*Sento l'orma dei passi spietati,*" sings the baritone. Justifiably famous
for the boldness of the metaphor, the phrase has earned for *Il ballo in
maschera* a seat of honor in the catalog of the ridiculous that characterizes
opera's texts. From this point of view, those who do not speak Italian are
saved, and naturally, the same happens to all those who listen to opera sung
in a language that they do not know: "who understands Wagner's texts in
Italy, or Verdi's texts outside Italy?"[5] The limit of linguistic fluency is itself
worthy of note and, together with the question of the ridiculous, constitutes one the many strange features of opera. Today, just as before, in the
theaters of the world, an adoring public sits through hours of a sung drama
that it, more often than not, cannot understand. Of course, today there is
the modern expedient of the electronic supertitles. Yet what is certain is
that, leaving aside the meaning of the sung phrases, the public evidently

enjoys the musical instruments and the song as voice. As for the plot of the story, a printed summary in the program—or a quick summary from a friend—is sufficient. When Madame Butterfly sings "*un bel dì vedremo,*" everyone knows that she is singing of love and useless hope. Her voice alone is capable of expressing what the words—which are a sort of secondary apparatus—simply punctuate.

Of course, one does not have to be a foreigner in order to be ignorant of the words of melodrama sung in another language. Only the real experts know the libretto, and thus only they follow the song word for word. Indeed, because the performers generally employ a technique that emphasizes vowels and elides syllabic distinctions, the words that are sung are often incomprehensible to the listener. To this is added an emphatic and obsolete language, whose archaisms certainly do not help the text to be more comprehensible. And as we know, certain megalomaniac performers are known to "improvise" the text. Modifications and involuntary misunderstandings are part of opera, and part of its popularity. The ridiculous is, in fact, taken for granted in opera; it is evident not only in the text, but also in the costumes and the whole mise-en-scène. As the novelist Carlo Emilio Gadda describes it, there is a chorus that screams "at the top of its lungs the most bombastic extravagances" while one of the dancers seems "to want to fling off, sometimes in the direction of the audience, a slipper that is bothering her."[6]

There is no doubt. From a certain point of view, opera is a triumph of the ridiculous and of kitsch. And the libretto is often the instrument of this tragicomic undertaking. From another point of view, however, opera is something entirely different. It takes advantage of the ridiculous in order to anchor the seriousness of its vocal message in the lightness of a smile. In fact, opera is essentially the sublime working of the human voice, which conquers the meaning of words as well as the visible realm of representation. In this sense, what matters is not the point of view with which one regards opera, but rather the "point of hearing" with which it is approached. In order to touch the heart of opera, in order to see past the ridiculous, it is necessary for the eye of the body and the eye of the intellect to be usurped by the sovereignty of the ear. This is, of course, somewhat paradoxical, given that the melodrama consists of a musical and vocal spectacularization of the plot. At first sight, in fact, opera seems rather simple. As in the theater, there is the staging of a story and there is an audience that looks and listens, except that instead of speaking, the protagonists of this story sing.

Recent decades have witnessed another interesting admission in the world of opera—namely, that gays love opera and, as Wayne Koestenbaum puts it, opera loves gays.[7] Koestenbaum defines himself as an *opera queen*, a term that names those homosexuals who go wild for opera and regularly attend performances. They are quite often distinguished, according to Koestenbaum, by outrageous outfits that would not clash with the costumes of the spectacle itself. Notoriously characterized by masking, transvestitism, eccentricity, and excess, opera turns out to be the occasion for a gay party where the bond between melodrama and homosexuality gets joyously exhibited. This bond not only consists in the obvious process of identification of the homosexual with the prima donna, the diva, the "divine," or the "queen." According to Koestenbaum, this bond depends instead on the primacy of song over speech—or, rather, the victory of a voice that, even when it is a man who sings, evokes the feminine, just as speech, understood as the power to signify, evokes the masculine. As Hélène Cixous notes, "musicians have never lost the sense of mystery that is the song of truth. What sings in a 'man' is not he, but she. Musicians have always known this."[8]

As Homer already knew, and as stereotypes ever since prove, the sexual difference between the vocal and the semantic, which is modeled on the difference between body and mind, continues to work in the contemporary imaginary of melodramatic opera. When there is song, melody, and a voice, then there is generally a feminine experience, whether or not the composer or performer is a man (and all the more if she is a woman; the prima donna is the fulcrum of nineteenth-century opera). When, on the other hand, the words and their meaning come to the fore, then it is a masculine experience in which the intellect reigns sovereign. Opera is in fact a good place to play out a confrontation between the masculine and the feminine in this regard, for in a certain sense, it unites and confuses them. And yet, as most divas know, in opera, the song is more important than the meaning, the voice matters more than the words, and the music matters more than the story. The libretto is not undone by the ridiculousness of the language but by the power of the song. Put simply, in the sung discourse, the feminine is confused with the masculine and conquers it. This is the work of opera [*l'opera dell'Opera*]—voices that frustrate the role of speech, an enjoyable triumph of the vocal over the semantic.

This happens on both small and large scales, according to the case. For example, thanks to a certain contrast between verses and melody, the modest Lorenzo Da Ponte works as a good librettist for Mozart's music. The catalog of Leporello is perhaps the most famous example of an enjoyable marriage of music and text. In the absurdly meticulous "*mille e tre*," what is more pleasurable, the words or the arching crescendos? Symptomatically, the opera queen tends to go to the melodramatic opera of the nineteenth century, rather than that of the eighteenth century—not only because the melodrama of the nineteenth is the genuine home of the prima donna, but above all because Mozart's theater—while sensitive to the vocal virtuosity that marks the disturbing femininity of the Queen of the Night, and while the genius from Salzburg is totally convinced that in opera "the poetry must be the obedient daughter of the music"—is perhaps too close to the birth of this new musical genre.[9] Thus it is too far from the crucial feminine fate of the genre itself, which only comes to full fruition in the nineteenth century.

Opera has a precise date of birth. It came into the world in Florence at the end of the sixteenth century with the help of a group of musicians who were interested in ancient Greece as the homeland of a tragic theater that used song. Bearing in its very name the intention of its inventors, melodrama [*melos-drama*] is thus born from a plan for a *drama with music*. Monteverdi's *Orfeo* (1607) is its first triumph. Born from the dubious hypothesis that ancient Greek tragedy was sung, and from a productive confusion of epic and tragedy, this new melodrama finds success. Crucially, from the very beginning, there emerges the feature that is destined to mark its fate—namely, the fact that the song prevails over the text. The theorists of this new genre in fact try repeatedly to bring about a reconciliation of the two elements—the music and the virtuosity of the singers should not obscure the meaning of the words. The *phone* should not devour the semantic. The principle is clear: to maintain an equilibrium between voice and speech. But this equilibrium is lost from the very start, and the listeners and performers are soon brought together in a common acoustic pleasure. The audience delights in this "drama with music" not because it understands the meaning of the words but because it is seduced by the singers' voices. As Koestenbaum says, the care of balancing the feminine/feminizing role of the voice with the masculine/masculizing role of meaning turns out to be in vain.[10] A good librettist is required by opera only in order to avoid totally drowning in acoustic pleasure. And yet no matter how good the author of the text is, the voice ends up winning. The power of the song takes control over the words. Opera is the realm of the bel canto, not the *bel testo*. If this were not the case, opera would have sunk under the weight of its own ridiculousness long ago.

In effect, opera does not make us laugh. Rather, it makes us cry; it moves us. It often moves even those who find it ridiculous or inexorably dated. As Augusto Illuminati rightly notes, opera is full of "unlikely plots, and ridiculous verses; and yet the heart beats, the tears flow and it is pure art."[11] A genre from another time, against all odds, opera has survived and still demonstrates its enchanting effects on audiences today, not only for a gay public, or sophisticated music lovers, or irrepressible megalomaniacs, or capricious intellectuals who are prone to follow the latest retro fad, and not even for the stereotypical bourgeoisie who has season box-seat tickets. The anthropology of the opera-going public is much wider. And it even has its predilections.

Perhaps the first, or best-known, predilection is the figure of the young woman who weeps on hearing the song. As the Hollywood film *Pretty Woman* (1990) demonstrates, no audience member is more emblematic than the (probably unrefined) young woman who, on being dragged to the opera, finds herself moved by what she hears. Of course, *Pretty Woman* plays on the numerous homages that cinema has paid to opera. These homages generally emphasize the emotional sensitivity of the female soul, her natural receptivity to the music—demonstrated by the fact that she probably has little or no musical culture, or is unrefined in general. In a simple sense, these are the stereotypes of a romantic sentimentalism that has long been transmitted and reinforced by cinema's self-referentiality. But there is something more. Among the banality and the misogyny of the scene lies the correct focus on the rather peculiar relation that women have with opera.

If the triumph of the feminine principle lies at the heart of opera, it is in fact obvious that opera concerns women even before gays. Yet the reasons, according to Catherine Clément's well-known study, are not the same—because not only the *melo* as voice but also the *dramma* as story concern the feminine.[12] The supremacy of music and song over speech in fact produces ambiguous consequences. On the one hand, it signals the victory of the feminine. On the other hand, however, it distracts the audience's attention from the plot of a story that is obsessively misogynist. Celebrating before the audience what amounts to a kind of patriarchal ritual, opera speaks of women who must die and who are on stage in order to sing their death. Through the enchantment of song, the ritual can thus pleasurably repeat itself and disseminate its message, all without any recourse to the critical work of consciousness.

The misogynist structure of the melodrama is actually quite simple. There is the drama that, like all drama in the western canon, seems to narrate many variants on the usual patriarchal story: having been enamored, betrayed, mocked, tricked, and having then gone mad, a woman dies. And there is the *melo*, which, as it captures the audience in an acoustic passion, lets the story reach its conclusion, even making it pleasurable along the way. According to Clément, however, things are more complicated. In general, the heroine of the drama embodies a female figure who is somewhat anomalous or out of place. Carmen is a gypsy, Butterfly and Turandot are exotic women, Tosca is a singer, Violetta is a ne'er-do-well. As women who live outside familiar roles, as transgressive figures who are often quite capable of independence, they do not just die—they must die so that everything can go back to normal. Does not Violetta die so that a young maiden who is "as pure as an angel" can be married, and so that the bourgeoisie can breathe a sigh of relief? The seductive power of opera, its melodic trick, consists precisely in making these undomesticated heroines die singing. "*Lasciatemi morir*," sings Monteverdi's Arianna—and the audience in fact lets her die, while deeply enjoying her sublime voice.

Because the audience is composed of both men and women, one presumes that the sense of this pleasure is different. From the perspective of the plot, the men enjoy, so to speak, in keeping with their patriarchal victory. The women, on the other hand, enjoy—in spite of themselves—their own undoing. It is thus above all the female audience that is pulled in and betrayed by the enchanting *melo*. It is precisely in this sense that the opera scene in *Pretty Woman* is emblematic. The film's protagonist, a happy and proud young prostitute, finds herself moved at *La Traviata* by the death of Violetta (her operatic double). Weeping for this beautiful death, which touches the melodic sensibility of her heart, she participates with delight in the representation of her own end.

According to Clément, therefore, the libretto, the words, count. They count precisely because their meaning is erased by a singing voice that makes even those who know it forget the text. Without the musical emotion, opera would be ridiculous—not only because of the literary style of the libretto, but also because of the stereotypical banality of the misogynist story that it stages. Sung by a voice that challenges human possibilities, this story becomes sublime. Through words that are unheard yet understood, the ritual repeats itself. The supremacy of the feminine principle that characterizes melodrama, as a victory of song over speech and of the vocal over the semantic, is thus somewhat less favorable to women than it would first appear. The director's eye knows this, and does not hesitate to make it clear. As in the case of *Pretty Woman*, the director focuses on the moved face of the protagonist while the volume of the prima donna's song sweetly inundates her ears, and the ears of all those present, with a kind of communion of irresistible pleasure. After all, it is not by chance that cinema cites opera so often. As "the acoustic mirror" where the feminine voice often functions as a pure sonority disarticulated from speech, cinema takes advantage of its power to duplicate the sacrificial ritual of melodrama and to multiply its seductive effects.[13]

The conclusions drawn by a feminist reading like that of Clément are, in a certain sense, obvious. The libretto in opera obeys the misogynistic laws of the western canon—it tells a story in which the women are the victims and men the victimizers. We would be surprised if it were otherwise. What is less obvious, however, is the role played by the voice in all of this—not so much because we discover that the voice evokes a feminine principle, but rather because the mixing of words and song of which opera consists works precisely as an anomalous site of challenge and confusion, of seduction and trickery. In the final analysis, the fundamental question is this: why does the voice win? Why does it conquer all—men and women, homosexuals and heterosexuals?

No matter what anthropology of the opera-going public one constructs, the problem remains that opera can be received by different subjects precisely because the power of song triumphs over the words. What keeps opera going throughout the centuries, down to our own, is precisely its musicality. With all due respect for the work of Lorenzo Da Ponte, opera does not survive thanks to his texts. If anything, it survives thanks to the myths that these texts celebrate (and this is certainly the case with *Don Giovanni*).[14]

Song and musical instruments are obviously not the same things. What distinguishes them is the human voice and, especially in the case of opera, a human voice that is inseparable from speech. As Edward Said puts it, "music does not denote, and does not share with language the register of discursivity."[15] Only in song is there this place for the confusion and the challenge of the human as human. Only in song does the *phone semantike* let itself dissolve into its two elements, letting the first win over the second.

The soprano who sings "like a nightingale" is, in this sense, a misplaced metaphor. As in a musical instrument, in the animal voice, the sound does not challenge speech because it does not carry speech in itself. In human song, however, the voice carries speech. Even when it renders speech incomprehensible or breaks down its syllabic texture, the voice still carries speech and recognizes in it its essential destination. The *phone* is, even when it negates the semantic in its sonorous ocean, nevertheless *semantike*. Speech, no matter how frustrated by song its semantic valence may be, nevertheless continues to be what song is destined toward.

Of course, there are "mute" songs, like the famous chorus of *Madame Butterfly*. And more recently, there is the possibility of synthesizing the human voice with digital techniques and transforming it into the sound of a musical instrument. The voice imitates, or makes itself into, a musical instrument. But then it becomes music, not song. All the more with opera, the distinction between music and song is in fact necessary, not only because without song, opera would not be a *melo*-drama, and thus would not be at all, but above all because this popular scene, where the femininity of the phonic takes the masculinity of the semantic head on, would disappear. In this sense, opera comes to show that the reality of speech does not coincide, immediately and exclusively, with its semantic substance, or with the urgency to signify that goes back to the videocentric sphere of the signified. Speech is rather the point of intersection, or tension, between two poles: the voice that makes up its sonorous texture, and the verbal signified that it is bound to express. Thus, what gets conquered in the victory of the feminine over the masculine is not really speech, but rather the videocentric pole of the signified, or the register of thought to which the metaphysical tradition subjugates speech.

Musical instruments and song, although distinct types of emission—mechanical and corporeal—share a crucial feature that opera, in fact, emphasizes. In both, the pleasure of the ear is at play, not the ears as the vehicles of a signified that goes straight to the mind, or as tubes of transmission from one intellect to another—but rather as acoustic chambers that enjoy the vibrations and resonances, just as the palate enjoys the sweet and the salty. It is hardly surprising that the problem concerning the triumph of the vocal over the semantic applies not only to opera, but traverses the whole history of western music, from its origins in Greece. Plato inaugurates this problem when he worries about how to reduce the *melos*—vocal and instrumental—to a numeric harmony, and how to subordinate it to logos. In the Christian era, Augustine continues down this same road, ready to confess that he "was enthralled by the pleasures of sound" [*voluptates aurium tenacius me implicaverant et subiugaverant*] before God liberated him.[16] The remedy for this enthrallment, in his *De musica*, is the disciplining of sounds into a music that he intends to be a science by numbers, and an experience of divine order inscribed in the world. Analogous to this is the theoretical background of music in the sixteenth century, where "the primary given is not the sonorous musical aspect, but rather a conceptually formulated content; listening presupposes that the score is followed section by section, and the motives are understood starting from the words."[17] Thus when melodrama raises the problem of the relation between the acoustic and the verbal spheres, it recalls a long tradition in which the former is commanded by the latter. Moreover, precisely in the sixteenth century there emerges a model that invites the listener to "follow the music on its morphological level as an autonomous construct, not as a bearer of a text and its meanings."[18] The tyranny of speech over sounds, which should obediently follow speech, thus begins to topple.

The ear is a delicate and vulnerable organ, which also has a precise spectrum of pleasure; when the sound is too loud, it suffers. As people who go to discos know all too well, when the sound is really loud, it is the internal body that gets whipped with pleasure by the sound waves. Both music and song, in short, already at the level of their mere reception, concern the body and its pleasures. In fact, closing one's eyes can intensify the sensation. Caught up in the enjoyment, the one listener lets herself get totally wrapped up in the sound, penetrated and inundated by it—"like a woman," as experts on feminine eros would say. But then, the soprano becomes an extraordinarily powerful figure, for she is a woman who not only carries and conquers the semantic in her voice, but also takes the active "masculine" part of the one who penetrates and inundates, or inseminates, the listener.[19] As if this were not enough, the accompanying instrumental music facilitates the whole operation. The androcentric tradition that celebrates the superiority of the semantic really does have something to worry about! In the west, the history of the devocalization of logos is also the history of this understandable preoccupation.

The contrast between the feminine principle of the vocal and the masculine principle of the semantic is, however, only one of the ways in which sexual difference interferes with the world of opera. There are, in fact, formalized norms that regard the vocal register of the two sexes. By fixing the four principal voices of song, these norms assign the role of the soprano and the contralto to the feminine voice, and the tenor and basso to the masculine voice. The natural phenomenon of the sexual difference [*sessuazione*] of the voice thus comes to organize the rules of opera. This complicates, in and of itself, the principle according to which song—especially when it manifests the victory of the voice over the semantic—always alludes to the feminine. When a basso sings, given that in him the deepness of the masculine voice is exhalted, the feminine valence of the vocal is directly challenged. At stake, in this case, is not the victory of the vocal over the semantic, but rather a victory of the vocal sphere as intrinsically feminine over a voice that not only comes from a man but moreover underscores the masculine timbre. In a certain sense, this might seem presumptuous. And at least from the perspective of an elementary phenomenology of the voice, it is. Among the characteristics of the voice as voice, there is in fact the revelation of the sex of the one who emits it. This only confirms that the voice is rooted in an embodied—and therefore sexed—uniqueness. Opera, however, has to do with song and with the exaltation of the vocal register over the semantic. Sexual difference, starting from the symbolic elaboration that our tradition gives it and from all its stereotypes, is what is at work here. To this we might add the fact that transvestitism is one of the typical features of melodrama. Opera has an irresistible tendency to stage drag: women who dress like men, and men who dress like women.

In Rossini's *Conte Ory*, for example, the tenor and the entire masculine chorus are cross-dressed as nuns. In Verdi's *Forza del destino*, Leonora puts on a young man's pants, and so forth.[20] Drag, more often than not, is as ridiculous as it is out of place.[21] By use of the categories of Judith Butler, one could in fact say that in addition to stabilizing the stereotypes of sexual identity through their apparent transgression, operatic drag confuses them and unleashes all the unsettling effects of parody.[22] Symptomatically, transvestitism is an essential element in the historical emergence of operatic melodrama—not only because men put on women's clothes within the plot of the story, but also because of a more austere "vocal transvestitism" in the strict sense. As is well known, in the early period of operatic melodrama, women were in fact prohibited from being on stage. The female characters were played by men who sang in falsetto, or, more especially, by castrati. The ability of these singers to bring the audience to the point of delirium is legendary; and in the baroque theater, of course, this becomes one of the most celebrated chapters in the history of melodrama.[23] However, significantly enough, the castrati ruled the stage even in the middle of the eighteenth century, by which time women were generally allowed on stage. The need to replace the female roles, or the technical need for vocal transvestitism, is therefore only present at the beginning; the voice of the castrati continues to exert a charm well beyond the historical moment that renders this voice technically indispensable. The transvestitism of the voice, its incongruence with respect to the sexual identity of the one who emits it, turns out to be an essential source of pleasure in opera. In the castrato, the intrinsic femininity of the vocal seems to celebrate its most direct triumph: the masculine body renounces its own sexual organs in order to make itself into a feminine voice. Indeed, the castrati do not fake it, as do those who sing in falsetto; rather, they conserve their "virgin," or feminine, voice of childhood through a surgical intervention that impedes the vocal change of puberty. They sacrifice—or, better, are sacrificed—for the feminine principle of song.

In fact, it appears that some female singers, who were jealous of the careers of the castrati divas of the day, tried to pass themselves off as castrated boys—and they were even able to pass the genital exams organized by the authorities in order to prevent such tricks. Curious as this might seem—or perhaps it is only further proof of misogynist discrimination— it shows how the world of opera goes well beyond conventional transvestitism. The supremacy of the feminine voice, quintessence of the femininity of the vocal, may determine the many versions of drag and help to proliferate its meanings—and yet, this supremacy as such is certain. No matter how parodied, falsified, or destabilized, sexual difference directs the acoustic sphere toward a precise source of pleasure. The prima donna—an expression that, after all, also indicates the mother—embodies this source.

2.4

The Maternal *Chora*; or,
The Voice of the Poetic Text

> As soon as I would read a writer, I would discern almost immediately under
> the words the air of a song, which is always different in each one; and, as I
> would read, without realizing it, I would sing. I would raise the notes or
> slow them down or interrupt them, as one does when one sings—keeping
> time, following the rhythm, before saying the end of a word.
> —Marcel Proust, *Contre Sainte-Beuve*

The young Nietzsche claims that his considerations of Wagner's *Tris-
tam and Isolde* can only be understood by those who speak "music as a
mother tongue" and have an "immediate kinship with music, and who
find in music their maternal bosom, so to speak."[1] This is not simply an innocent metaphor; nor is it a particularly original thesis. The pleasure of the
acoustic sphere, symbolized since antiquity by female creatures, sooner or
later evokes the figure of the mother. However, what is remarkable in
Nietzsche—also because of his influence on a broad section of twentieth-
century thought—is the link he establishes between the maternal character of musical pleasure and the way in which it liberates the listener from
the chains of individuality. The Nietzschean inheritance, which is sometimes mixed with that of psychoanalysis, in fact flows into a certain stream
of contemporary thought—namely, a predominately French matrix that
includes especially Julia Kristeva and Hélène Cixous. By insisting on the libidinal register of the vocal, these thinkers trace vocality back to the preoedipal phase. That is, they trace it back to the originary scene in which
the fusional relationship between mother and child also works to frustrate
the category of the individual. From this perspective—which is not at all

far from Barthes' notion of the "pleasure of the text"—the pleasure rooted in the acoustic sphere has above all a subversive function; that is, it destabilizes language as a system that produces the subject. Rather than stand in opposition to writing, as happens in the studies focused on orality, in this case, the voice stands in opposition to language—that is, to the disciplining codes of language, to grammar and syntax, to the "Law of the Father" that separates the child from the mother by consigning the child to the logic of individuality. In addition to constituting the two poles of a contrast between eye and ear, voice and writing here come together against a certain systematic and normative conception of language.

According to this broad, speculative horizon, in fact, insofar as the voice can be traced back to the orality of the maternal scene (which is, so to speak, a radically primal orality where the semantic order has not yet made its entrance), the voice penetrates and invades writing. Writing is here understood as a practice but, moreover, as a text—above all, the poetic text; that is, the rhythmic and musical texture of speech. The attention here does not fall on the characteristics of oral culture as distinct from literate culture; rather, the focus is on the relationship between vocality and textuality. The aim is to feel how the principle of sound organizes the text and, at the same time, disorganizes language's claim to control the entire process of signification. Speech [*la parola*], even when it is written, thus gets analyzed through its sonorous matrix. In other words, this is a theoretical perspective that traces both spoken and written language back to a vocal sphere that is the common matrix of both. And this perspective is therefore quite different from those insisting on the dyad orality/writing.

Very early on, babies pronounce "articulate sounds which easily outstrip the register of their mother tongue," says Julia Kristeva; these sounds "do not correspond to any signifier in the sense of being 'inherent to the sign.'"[2] Thus, before learning to speak, babies are capable of a broad, timbale spectrum of phonic expression that has nothing to do with the classic, linguistic "semiotic triangle"—referent/signifier/signified. The entrance into the semantic, or the acquisition of speech, cuts and reduces precisely this variegated infantile vocality. Every language has its phonematic code—in the work of signification, some sounds are admitted, others not. Language imposes a "phonematic austerity" that stands in contrast to "the untamed sounds" that babies make. In other words, language asks the sacrifice of their free vocalization, which is still rooted in the biological. Incapable of speech, nightingales on the other hand continue all their life to emit thousands of love songs in infinite variations, or, as Deleuze would say, "*la ritournelle.*"[3]

It is difficult to say whether or not human adults, at some point, come to regret not having been born nightingales. If we believe Plato's myth, the singer Thamyris actually succeeded in being reborn as one.[4] And even those human beings who do not excel at singing still seem to preserve a trace of their extraordinary infantile vocality. For Kristeva, this is the trace of what she calls the "semiotic *chora*": the preverbal and unconscious sphere, not yet inhabited by the law of the sign, where rhythmic and vocalic drives reign. This semiotic *chora* has a profound bodily root and is linked to the indistinct totality of mother and child. It precedes the symbolic system of language, or the sphere of the semantic where syntax and the concept rule—the paternal order of the separation between the self and the other, between mother and child, and between signifier and signified. Although they are different, according to Kristeva, the two spheres are not in simple opposition to one another, nor in a relation of pure chronological succession. The vocalic practice of the semiotic—in which the child is immersed, in the free play of the articulation and differentiation of sounds, tones, and rhythms—ends up being indispensable to the phonematic system of language. Language, in short, exploits, reduces, and regulates the marvelous exercises of the infantile voice. Stripped of its excesses and its imagination, the infant's emission is frozen into the syllables and tones that language permits. Indebted to the semiotic *chora* for the articulation of its phonemes, the symbolic system still has trouble finding a home beyond the cut that separates it from the *chora* and at the same time unites them. The semiotic drives of the phonic thus find some fissures through which to invade language and disturb it with the agitation of its rhythms. This is, put simply, the musicality that breaks down and reorganizes the sense of what Kristeva calls text. Poetry is an excellent example of this.

Revolutions in Poetic Language is a complex book. The Freudian and Lacanian psychoanalytic horizon in which Julia Kristeva moves—along with her use of an arduously technical lexicon taken from linguistics, and an anomalous use of Hegelian and Marxist categories—complicates her theory somewhat. Still, it is not difficult to isolate the original point of this book. It consists in an implicit rethinking of the Aristotelian *phone semantike* that—instead of neglecting the phonetic in favor of the semantic (as philosophers have done for millennia)—valorizes the fundamental role of the voice and simultaneously underscores its essential destination in speech. This is a voice that not only is the sonorous material of language, but also, above all, is the vocalized rhythm and corporeal drives that anchor the "speaker" to the embodiedness of his or her existence. If it is true, as Aristotle says, that man is a speaking animal, then it is also true that the subject and speech are constructed together through (to use Kristeva's terms) a signifying process that is rooted in the biological and in the economy of unconscious drives. In the vocal exercise, lungs, throat, mouth, tongue, and ears all take pleasure. This happens, especially, in the child, but also again in the adult. In phonic emission, there is a musical pleasure that the semantic order both exploits and limits, and yet still fails to control. More archaic than verbal communication, the drive substrata of the phonemes—like the rhythmic pleasure of sucking—works in the oral cavity, and it does not easily forget its pleasure. Unlike thought, which tends to reside in the immaterial otherworld of ideas, speech is always a question of bodies, filled with drives, desires, and blood. The voice vibrates, the tongue moves. Wet membranes and taste buds are mixed up with the flavor of the tones. As Mallarmé says, "the Word presents itself, in its vowels and its diphthongs, like flesh; and, in its consonants, like a skeleton to dissect."[5]

The term *chora* is explicitly stolen by Kristeva from Plato's *Timaeus*. In the cosmological context of the *Timaeus*, Plato speaks of a great maker or builder who shapes the world. For this work of molding, three elements are needed. The first is the divine model that the builder looks at, which is composed of eternal and immaterial forms or ideas that pertain to the sphere of thought and thus correspond to the videocentric order of signifieds. The second element is the physical world in which we live, and which is the material copy—visible to the eyes of the body—of the divine model. The third element, rather more problematic, is the *chora*: a sort of unformed material that gets used in the shaping of the world. Plato compares these elements, respectively, to the Father, the Son, and the Mother.[6] Even more interesting, from Kristeva's point of view, is the fact that the philosopher finds himself in some difficulty when it comes to naming and defining the *chora*. Because the whole sphere of noetic intelligibility is reserved for the ideas that appertain to the realm of the Father, and the whole sphere of material visibility is reserved for the realm of the Son, the *chora* in fact gets situated at once outside intelligibility and outside visibility. The *chora* is neither intelligible nor visible; it cannot be contemplated by the eyes of the soul, nor observed by the eyes of the body. Deprived of every material and conceptual form, it is the unformed maternal receptacle in which the Father generates the Son as his copy through the imprint of his forms. It is the amorphous receptacle, the space of materialization, the wet nurse. Plato speaks of the *chora* through a metaphor, but in all rigor, he admits that it has no name and that one can only give a bastardized discourse about it.[7]

The problem of not being able to define, conceptualize, or say the *chora* makes of it a dimension that exceeds the system of language that Kristeva identifies with the symbolic. What is extremely problematic for Plato on a logical plane becomes, for Kristeva, precisely because of this difficulty, a motive of great interest. The *chora* of the *Timaeus*, in fact, not only exceeds the symbolic but also ends up being necessary to the productive work of the symbolic itself. Or, to put it in platonic terms, the generative process of the paternal ideas must imprint their forms in the *chora* in order to produce the visible world. There are, of course, other reasons for Kristeva's interest in Plato's text—namely, the *chora*, in addition to being a site of the indistinct, is a place of continual movement, a constant motility that knows no quiet. The *chora* has its rhythms, which cannot be comprehended or cataloged by the symbolic system. In the *chora*, a vertiginous motility and movement prevent anything from being separable from anything else—just as the child is, for psychoanalysis, inseparable from the mother in the preoedipal phase. In fact, Plato calls the *chora* Mother. And Kristeva echoes this when she speaks of a semiotic that is "indifferent to language, enigmatic and feminine . . . rhythmic space, irreducible to an intelligible verbal translation; musical, anterior to judgment."[8]

As it is read by Kristeva, the videocentric logos of platonic metaphysics thus gets finally bent—or rebent—to exigency of the phonic. This is rendered possible by a vocal conception of the *chora* that the philosopher does not foresee. The *chora* of the *Timaeus*, at least from Plato's point of view, is in fact not *phone*—just as the forms or ideas are not words, but rather pure signifieds, noetic objects. However, the characteristics of the platonic *chora* are perfectly adapted to Kristeva's semiotic *chora*, insofar as it is a sphere of rhythmic drive and motility that precedes and sustains the symbolic system of language. For Plato too, the *chora*—if for no other reason than that it is unformed and thus unnameable—refers directly to language. Moreover, the *Timaeus* in fact presents yet again the double platonic conception of logos: that constitutive ambiguity that enables logos to indicate both the otherworldly realm of forms and the realm of speech. The result, as far as the *chora* is concerned, is a problem that Kristeva too must take into account. A simple formulation of this problem could be the following: how to say the extralinguistic? How to conceptualize the extraconceptual?

Curiously, this is a problem that is taken quite seriously by Plato himself, the most drastic of metaphysicians, as well as by his poststructuralist adversaries. In order to reserve intelligibility for the sphere of the Father, Plato must in fact resort to the rather dubious contrivance of a bastard logos when he speaks of the maternal unform. In order to emphasize the performative effect of language as an absolutely productive power, contemporary thinkers have had to consider all material things, and the "material" itself, as a product of language. At bottom, the two approaches are similar. They absolutize the conceptual or the linguistic—and declare that the extraconceptual, the extralinguistic, does not exist, or that it has no reality except for that produced by the conceptual and the linguistic. In other words, nothing is outside the symbolic system, if not what the system itself produces as its outside. Indeed, in spite of the fact that it declares the *chora* to be unsayable insofar as it is unformed, Plato says that it is unformed. Where is the *chora*, if not in Plato's system?

Kristeva's powerful materialist formation, which has little in common with classical metaphysics or its poststructuralist critiques, fortunately avoids this vicious circle of the symbolic's omnipotence. As is obvious, Kristeva knows that to speak of the preverbal means to reduce it to the verbal and to reconfigure the heterogeneous in the homogeneous. She knows that, when she speaks of the *chora* in *Revolutions in Poetic Language*, she is conceptualizing what exceeds the concept. But she neither doubts the existence of bodies nor postulates that the process of signification is an operation that is played out exclusively in the realm of the symbolic. Language has, precisely, a materiality that is rooted in the drives of the unconscious, a materiality of which language bears the traces. The eroticization of the vocal apparatus—although blocked in the phonematic code of language—makes its presence felt in the combinatorial play of tones, sounds, repetitions, and rhythms. This is evident in the poetic text, but it also operates in ordinary speech; the work of the *chora* always permeates the sphere of language. The age-old problem of the sayability of the preverbal thus finds a solution: one can speak of the semiotic *chora* because one can retrace its effects in language—including the language that says this *chora*—including the theoretical treatment that Kristeva provides. In short, not only does the pure semantic not exist (as Plato dreamed), but the semantic role of speech is intrinsic to a vocalic that anchors it to the bodily drives. It is at this point that vocalic pleasure passes from orality to the practice of writing. For there are texts that are pervaded by a musical rhythm, in which vocality explodes through the linguistic signifier, comes to the surface, and commands the meaning. Poetry, understood as "poetic text," is the most efficacious example of this.

Reading a text by Mallarmé, Kristeva underscores that the term *prose*—from the Latin *prorsus*—indicates a straight, linear process that "faces forward." The verse—from the Latin *versus*—instead denotes a backwards process, a turnaround. It would therefore seem that verse "reverses" the natural linearity of prose. In this sense, prose (characterized by a writing that goes from the top to the bottom of the line, and marches forward like reason itself) would be normal, whereas verse (which goes its own way, indulging syntactic flights of fancy) would be the overturning of the norm. Symptomatically, according to Kristeva, things are not so simple. In fact, with the term *prose*, "classical rhetoric designated a type of discourse that originally resulted from a rearrangement, we could say a 'reversal' of verse."[9] Moreover, at the beginning of the literary history of the west there lies epic, Homeric verse. The poetic voice, a song, lies at the Greek origins of the western tradition. An analogous thing could be said about the Bible, in which prose is given as the transcription of a more ancient versification. From a historical point of view, in short, verse comes before prose and prose *reverses* verse.

According to Mallarmé, as Kristeva emphasizes, one does not even need the historical point of view in order to understand the phenomenon. The drives that are manifested in verse are part of the general mechanism of language and its immemorial past. It precedes historical time and conquers it—"in the Verse, dispenser, arranger of the rhythm of the pages, master of the book"; dissimulated in the linearity of writing, it is also present in prose where "there remains some secret pursuit of music in the reserve of Discourse."[10] If the semiotic rhythm, which shakes up language and rumples its flat surface, is at work, then the ordinary distinction between prose and verse tends to be erased. Pervaded by a dimension that is immanent to the functioning of language, and that is "deeper than the deep structure that articulates linear signs," verse and prose flow together in the musicality of the poetic text.[11]

In Kristeva's words, this is a text that is poetic over and beyond the genres and classifications of literary canons. It does not matter if this text is written or oral; strictly speaking, the poetic text is every text in which the semiotic rhythm erupts into the symbolic system of language, breaking down its borders and inundating it with phonic pleasures. Broadly speaking, it is also the semiotic dimension that is deeply at work in the phonematic codes of all languages. Namely, the semiotic *chora* is rooted in the very functioning of language. In the signifying process, there is no symbolic without the semiotic. In logos, there is no *semantike* without the *phone.* As the material of an originary acoustic pleasure, the voice precedes and makes possible a language that always bears its traces. Both generating and destabilizing, the semiotic vocalic is therefore—at the same time—the precondition of the semantic function and its uncontrollable excess. When this difficult control openly surrenders to the reemergence of vocalic pleasure, we have the poetic text. Thus, the poet simply indulges an ancient pleasure and resurrects the rhythmic waves whose undulation makes language move.

Inscribed in the libidinal drives of the body, language for Kristeva comes precisely from the lungs, from the mouth, from an eroticized apparatus of phonation. In spite of her homage to the *Timaeus,* nothing could be further from the absolutizing of the semantic sphere that characterizes platonic metaphysics. After all, it is no coincidence that—when it is disembodied from the vocalic and sequestered by the metaphysical videocentrism—the semantic appears dead. Indeed, as Plato puts it, the philosopher "is living for death." If the life that drives language as voice is taken away, then language ends up being a system whose "rigor" depends on rigor mortis. The free vocalizations of the infant are replaced with a grave silence.

2.5

Truth Sings in Key

> We know that, from its remote origins and in all its variety, human language is one. But perhaps the secret laws of rhythm have a sex.
> —Sibilla Aleramo, *Apologia dello spirito femminile*

Working in a vein that has a lot in common with Kristeva's reflections, Hélène Cixous also emphasizes rather explicitly in her work that the logocentrism of the western tradition is also a phallocentrism. "Philosophy is constructed on the premise of woman's abasement . . . this being the condition of the machine's functioning"—namely, the typical binary economy on which the metaphysical system is built.[1] There are many series of oppositions that organize this system as a hierarchy, but for Cixous perhaps the most symptomatic of these is the opposition of writing to speech. Refuting this dichotomy, Cixous theorizes—and practices—an *écriture féminine* that is capable of reverberating the infinite, uncontrollable, rhythmic drives of the voice.

"The Voice sings from a time before law, before the Symbolic took one's breath away and reappropriated it into language under its authority of separation."[2] In the psychoanalytic lexicon employed by Cixous, this means that the symbolic, as the "law of the father," breaks the unity of mother and child, and by separating them produces the self-conscious and autonomous individual, the subject. To separate, to oppose, and to subordinate—the work of the phallogocentric tradition consists in nothing other than this. In this tradition, language is presented as a system of signification that uses and controls the vocalic, forgetting its origins. The source of the vocalic lies, for Cixous, in that maternal time of pleasure in which the voice is mixed with milk according to the sweet and generous

rhythms of sucking. Warm and bodily, like the mother's breast that nourishes the baby, the voice flows and inundates, like a song, inaugurating the
musicality of language. "Song, the first music of the voice of love, which
every woman keeps alive . . . because, within each woman the first, name-
less love is singing."[3] Because there is "always, more or less, something of
the 'mother' in every woman," women have a privileged relation with song
and with the musical materiality of language. These elements are never
completely distanced from the mother—"mother" being understood here
as a source of goodness, rather than a role in the social order. Every woman
always carries with her the first love—that "language-milk" [*languelait*]
that, in its spontaneous generosity, fills the entire register of oral pleasures
and infantile vocalizations.[4]

"I was raised on the milk of words," declares Cixous in her typically
autobiographical style.[5] She tells how, as a child, she made a pact: she swal-
lowed her food only if, at the same time, her ears were given something to
listen to. This infantile "thirst of the ear" gets satisfied above all by her
mother's tongue, a German Jew who brings the baby to identify German
as the language for singing. Anyway, it is not so important that it is German, instead of another of the many languages spoken and heard by the
young Cixous. What matters, rather, is the auditory sucking of a mother
tongue that is not only maternal because it comes from the mother's
mouth, but also because it is *langue* both in the sense of a vocal emission
and in the physiological sense of the term. "In the language that I speak,"
says Cixous, "the mother tongue resonates, tongue of my mother, less language than music, less syntax than song of words."[6] The vocalic not only
precedes the semantic, but permeates every language and exceeds the very
codes of language.

There is a language that I speak or that speaks (to) me in all tongues. A language
at once unique and universal that resounds in each national tongue when a poet
speaks it. In each tongue, there flows milk and honey. And this language I know,
I don't need to enter it; it flows, it is the milk of love, the honey of my unconscious. The language that women speak when there is no one there to correct
them.[7]

Because it belongs to an unconscious set of drives, the mother tongue that
Cixous speaks of is therefore not far from the semiotic *chora* that Kristeva
theorizes. This is borne out, moreover, from the privilege that both accord
to poetic language. What is original in Cixous, however, is the way in
which she links this maternal set of drives to writing. *L'écriture feminine* is

a fluid, overwhelmingly rhythmic writing, which breaks the rules of the symbolic, making syntax explode. It precedes and exceeds the codes that govern the phallocentric logos. Like the "writing from hearing to hearing" that the Spanish philosopher Maria Zambrano also evokes when she speaks of the "remote song" that comes from a maternal, vocalic source, *l'écriture féminine* maintains the vocal rhythm of the *languelait*.[8] With the taste of mother's milk still in her mouth, Cixous "writes with white ink"—that is, as she often repeats, she writes with flesh, with the body.[9] Her writing is a potentially infinite pleasure without borders. Akin to song, this writing "plays its own score on our own body" and turns the text into music.[10]

The opposition between voice and writing, which comes to the fore in studies on orality, is thus dissolved into a soundtrack, written in words, where vocal rhythms decide the movement of the text. The result is the proliferation of a sense that does not coincide with the phallogocentric dominion of the signified, but rather flows from the movement that combines words according to the laws of rhythm, echo, and resonance. The sound of one term calls another; the placement or displacement of a letter produces different names and generates neologisms. This is, de facto, the difficult and suggestive writing of Cixous: a text, at once legible and audible, which allows sense to flow from the cracks in syntax, or from the breaks that arise from its sonorous drives.

Although she is also an author of theoretical essays, Cixous is not a philosopher and does not want to be one. She does not follow—on the contrary, she fights—the principle of the univocal signified on which philosophical truth insists, and which is supposed to guarantee the coherence and the intelligibility of the text. The work of writing, for Cixous, consists rather in letting language flow in the musical rhythms of language, listening to words as they vibrate, so that they can begin to signify and resound in one another—for example, "one" [*l'una*] is also "moon" [*luna*]—according to a play of assonances that permit the ear to reverberate the breath of language without, however, abandoning the sphere of meaning. "What is musical and phonic in language, which could also appear as an accompaniment, is in effect inseparable from a *significance*," writes Cixous.[11] And this is true for a mysterious and marvelous reason: "the music and the meaning are absolutely indissociable."[12] Cixous thus says that she has the impression that "truth sings in key," in a way that is contrary to "the imperatives of language that obligate us to construct grammatically correct utterances, following the rules of gender."[13] In Cixous' writing, "music does not accompany or follow, but rather quite often opens, inaugurates, precedes, calls."[14] It is a sonorous writing in which the voice does not merely represent the side of an opposition, but rather plays all over the field.

As Cixous emphasizes, her intention is not to "create a feminine writing, but to allow to pass in writing what has until now always been prohibited, namely, the effects of femininity."[15] *L'écriture feminine*, in other words, is not a new style, a modern literary genre; rather, it is a practice that—by submitting to the phonic seduction that the androcentric tradition itself links to the feminine—subverts and overturns the metaphysical strategy that has produced the devocalization of logos. The "feminine" thus indicates song, rhythm, and, above all, an imaginary that is linked to the maternal body. The feminine evokes warmth and fluidity—or, rather, a whole metaphorical constellation referring to the mother's body, which has by now become a standard lexicon among feminists. All the features that characterize the rigidity of metaphysical logocentrism—from its oppositional economy, to its privileging of mental signifieds over sonorous signifiers—are thus dismantled through a return to the sphere of the vocalic. Symptomatically, this is a return that concerns both the relation with the mother and the vocalic matrix of poetry. Before it is broken by the law of the Father, the pleasure of the maternal bond corresponds to the pleasure of the poetic song—the very song that, since Plato, metaphysics has sought to oppress. From Cixous' perspective, as from Kristeva's, this pleasure coincides with the register of the unconscious. Therefore, there is no self-conscious "subject" here, no *ego* that could be linked to a *cogito*. The unity of the "I"—along with any other cultural or social system, including language—gets broken down precisely by the unconscious drive that blurs this "I's" boundaries. Just as in the texts of Clarice Lispector, to whom Cixous dedicates some of her best theoretical essays, the codes that organize the "I" and discourse are broken under the wave of a vocal flux in which someone laughs, cries, screams, and breathes, singing in writing the advent of his or her own disorganization.[16]

According to Lispector, this depersonalizing experience is like a passion.[17] Taking up one of the classic themes of epic, Cixous in turn claims that writing consists of both a process of possession and dispossession. The latter has two sides. Writing dispossesses us of ourselves, freeing us from the system of the "I"; but unfortunately, it dispossesses us of our originary phonic possession as well, which is fully enjoyed only in infancy.[18] The tragedy that writing tries, endlessly, to remedy is precisely this: to write with white ink means to contrast the dispossessing of possession, to fight the disciplining effects of the system in order to return to the sweetness of the mother's vocalic body. *L'écriture feminine*—both active and passive, because their opposition no longer matters here—lets the voice of the mother tongue flow with its rhythms, disordering the codes that organize the subject and language. "When I write," says Cixous, "I do not write, I curl up in a ball, I become an ear, I am a rhythm."[19] Just as for the king who listens in Calvino's story, Cixous' fundamental strategy consists of concentrating on acoustic perception. This perception, which might seem passive, is, however, already actively a rhythm that pulsates in her and pulls her body toward writing. The music of language, which even plays in the nonverbal languages of animals and things, reverberates in the sonorous cavities of the body, moving it to the pleasure of the text.

Brought back to life by its first love, the voice, the text therefore sings: it becomes musical, enchanting, just like epic song. It is made more for the ears than for the eyes. That is, it is made for an ear that, from infancy, "thirsts" for words in which sounds, and not concepts, vibrate. Again, the privileging of the vocalic facilitates the disorganization of the semantic.

Yet in its movement that flows from unconscious drives, this disorganization ends up washing away, along with the subject, the uniqueness that the voice (because it is always the voice of someone) announces. In other words, from the perspective of Cixous, Lispector, and Kristeva, the discovery of the subversive and antimetaphysical role of the acoustic sphere still does not explicitly thematize vocalic uniqueness. The dismantling of the "I," or the depersonalizing effect of possession, does not reveal the unique existent that vibrates in each voice; instead, these processes allow a multiple "I" with many voices to emerge, in the register of the unconscious. The register of the unconscious thus captures, in a zone of indistinction, the very reason for which we can rightly say that "truth sings in key."

Much contemporary theory—especially feminist theory, and in particular Anglo-American feminist theory—reads Cixous' position from a poststructuralist perspective. Rather than focusing on the transgressive sense of a rhythmic drive that breaks down both language and the subject, most feminist readers emphasize a practice of writing where meaning proliferates in multiple, uncontrollable ways, preventing the text from being a closed unity. The voice—which Cixous often spells with a capital "V"—is assumed as a plural dimension, but it is assumed as an indistinct polyphony, rather than a plurality of unique voices.[20] Besides, what feminist theorists have most often appropriated from Cixous is the subversive effect that *l'écriture feminine* has on the communicative or expressive aim of language. Obviously, the influence of a Lacanian lexicon on contemporary feminist theory plays a role in this reading of Cixous.

And yet, precisely in Cixous' own writing, there is another aspect worthy of critical attention, which brings the theme of uniqueness to the fore. For this writing is, in fact, autobiographical. And it is autobiographical especially in those texts that are closest to the genre of the "theoretical essay." This is not the traditional genre of autobiography, but rather a sort of self-portrait painted blindly—which, in Cixous' case, corresponds to a strong myopia that requires her to "use my ears in order to see better."[21] Trusting the memory of her ears, Cixous begins with herself [*parte da sè*] and tells her story, especially her infancy and her relationship with her mother. We could therefore say that her coming to writing concerns the unique and unrepeatable course of a singular existence that, while it may find correspondences in other existences, does not get confused with them. Even the happy discovery of Clarice Lispector's books gets narrated by Cixous with autobiographical accents. Although Cixous' writing is sustained by rhythms that come from the unconscious, and although it avoids the pretentious style of a writer who always keeps his or her life story almost under control, it thus ends up continually manifesting, singing, and intoning the presence of a uniqueness that makes itself text. The continuity between the body of the text and the body that writes comes from a singular life that overflows into writing. Thus, in an oblique way that is more practiced than theorized, there emerges from Cixous' work a substantial ambiguity that turns on the problem of a singular experience that is, nevertheless, deindividualized. The "Voice" is in fact the name of a pleasure that overflows language—but it is at the same time that which opens, encourages, and sustains every speaker/writer in the singular course of a pleasure that implicates possession and dispossession.

What can be useful for feminism, however, is Cixous' insistence on a vocalic sphere that is relational—not only because this relation is centered on the maternal figure and does not exhaust its potential in the scene of infancy, but rather because this relation, by operating in the register of speech and writing, makes itself heard as rhythm, reverberation, echo. This echo, this play of assonances and acoustic repetitions, is an originary opening to the other. "The source is given to me," says Cixous. "It is not me. One cannot be one's own source."[22] This source, in the context of Cixous' repeated allusions to her Jewish roots, is above all a reference of the voice of God. And yet it is also an evocation of the mother as the first source of song, the sweet and inexhaustible source of infinite, musical pleasure, language-milk. The other thus seems to give him- or herself in a vocalic relation that determines the echoing movement of rhythm rather than the linearity of monotony. *L'écriture feminine* flows freely according to laws of resonance that constitute its meaning, and yet precisely because of this, it depends on a musical song that is its source. The other, the mother, is the source of language and its rhythm. The libidinal economy, which makes language into music, has an ear cocked to the rhythmic enchantment of the first voice. The first song announces, in the song itself, the sonorous relation that inimitably forms its soundtrack.

2.6

The Hurricane Does Not Roar
in Pentameter

> I can read verse much better than most English poets alive. That is a fact.
> And I read it [at the ICA, London] exactly as I would have done in the
> West Indies. After all, it was my poem. I had made it. It was my own trum-
> pet; and I knew the keys. If I were afraid to blow it, whom could I expect to
> do it for me? So I made a heaven of a noise which is characteristic of my
> voice and an ingredient of West Indian behaviour. The result was an im-
> pression of authority.
> —George Lamming, *The Pleasures of Exile*

Hélène Cixous, born in Algeria to a Jewish family, writes in French.
"I learned to speak French in a garden from which I was on the verge of expulsion for being a Jew."[1] In this sense, Cixous brings to mind the experience of the young Jacques Derrida, who was also born in the Algerian Jewish community, and to whom the French language presented itself as "a
mother tongue, whose origins, norms, rules and laws lay elsewhere."[2] At issue here is not only the common experience of the Jewish people who, as
Rosenzweig would say, speak "everywhere they speak the language of their
external destinies, for example, the people in whose dwelling place they reside as guests."[3] In Algeria, of course, French is not the language of the
country but rather the language of the colonizers. As a daughter of the di-
aspora, Cixous knows how to write in a language that, beyond being the
language of her father, is the language of a colonizing nation. Moreover,
having in her ear the music of her mother's German, she tries to synthesize,
out of the different sounds that she hears, a "unique and universal" language "which resounds in every national language when poets speak it."

Other acoustic modulations come to her from "Africa sung by the sea day and night."[4] Cixous' French, entrusted to the sonorous fluidity of a Voice that breaks down its syntax, is not only the national language of the French people; rather, it is also the language in which the sounds of the city of Oran reverberate with the echoes of the voices of her Jewish ancestors, figures of a family album that bind the dead to the missing and to the survivors. Derrida, too, notes that "this great-French-Sephardic-Jewish-woman-writer-from-Algeria, who is reinventing, among others, the language of her father, *her* French language, an unheard-of French language, is also a German-Ashkenazic-Jewish-woman through her 'mother tongue.'"[5]

Cixous' many languages, which are neither combined nor mixed, flow together in the sonority of a Voice that makes them breathe. The typically Jewish theme of a divine, originary language toward which all languages would tend is taken up by Cixous in the (perhaps more ancient Hebrew theme) of the reverberation of the *qol* and *ruah* in these languages, as the originary meaning that generates and exceeds the system of speech. The Jewishness of Cixous, however, is oriented toward the political rather than the theological. *L'écriture féminine*, which is more a political than an aesthetic gesture, consists above all in a subversive practice that penetrates the language of the dominators. This penetration disorganizes the dominant syntax through the musicality of a vocalic that is, at the same time, pleasure drive, maternal vicissitude, surrounding environment and historical memory.

For the contemporary Caribbean poet Edward Kamau Brathwaite, the language in which he composes his verses is English. His English, however, is not the Queen's English, but rather a language that is more akin to creole English, to that which takes the name "nation language"—that is, the English spoken by the Africans who were taken to the Caribbean. Over the course of the generations, the structure and the sound of their original languages—of which there are many, but which can be traced to a common base—have acted like a hidden language, capable of modifying English and of undermining the cultural imperative of European languages. This phenomenon, as Brathwaite notes, is not simply a matter of the dynamic contamination of difference languages. Rather, it is a question of their belonging to the different sonorous universes of the natural environment in which these languages are born and in which they develop.

Languages have a sensibility all their own with respect to the acoustic experience of the environment. As Brathwaite notes, English lets the snow fall on roofs with a soft and delicate sound, but in English "we haven't got the syllables, the syllabic intelligence, to describe the hurricane, which is our own experience."[6] There is no universal sonority that is equal for all languages, for all mouths or all ears. The voice is not only sound; it is always the voice of someone as it vibrates in symphony with the natural and artificial sounds of the world in which she or he lives. Language imitates the sonority of the environment; it is attuned to its music. This particular musicality is, moreover, what allows us to recognize a language of which we do not understand a word. The great travelers of the past knew this well, as they distinguished the different languages that they encountered by the sound or musicality before syntax or grammar. Today, of course, one need hardly travel to have this experience. Any Venetian is able to recognize by sound the Japanese language, as it is spoken by tourists around town, even when these tourists are behind her back and she does not catch a glimpse of their faces, their physiognomy. A blind New Yorker in Chinatown hears full well where he is, even if he does not understand a word of Chinese. Contemporary metropolises are practically concert halls for the babelic variety of linguistic orchestrations. In the spoken word, the phonic communicates the language well before, and totally aside from, any semantic communication.

Brathwaite's central thesis is that, through its syllabic intelligence, the vocalic is the essential nucleus around which even the semantic structure of language is organized. Thus, the onomatopoeic sound of speech plays a central role. Rather than imitating things, as the theory of language-as-imitation would have it, this is a vocality that imitates above all the surrounding environment. The ear of the speaker is immersed in an acoustic universe that transmits to him its tones, its cadences and rhythms. The vocalic's base is thus essentially musical in the sense that it conforms to the contextual sonority of the world, to its noises; and it participates in it as well. Of course, most poets, by entrusting the sound of the words to the musicality of the meter, work under this very presupposition. For the poetry of the English tradition, for example, pentameter is the most apt meter. But "the hurricane does not roar in pentameter," laments Brathwaite.[7] In addition to making the English language bend to the sonorous universe of the Caribbean, the Caribbean poet must also force it to vibrate in a meter that it—for environmental, cultural, and historical reasons—does not foresee. The language, no matter how modified or hybridized, remains English—but its music becomes something else.

The term *music* should be understood in the strict sense of the word. Instrumental music, nonverbal and nondiscursive by definition, not only reflects the experience of the sonorous environment that surrounds it with immediate fidelity, but also belongs to a sphere of expression that is independent of speech. In a postcolonial world, this means above all that music can enjoy a broader autonomy with respect to the language of the colonizers. The rhythm of Caribbean music and, more generally, musical genres that are linked in some way to Africa not only explain the phonic inflections of the national language, but also stand in direct and explicit contrast to the sonorous universe that is transported by the English language.[8] The legend of Bob Marley, and the revolutionary potential attributed to his songs, are a peculiar symptom of this. The current era of the market and of globalization obviously makes it hard to give a simple account of the phenomenon. Jazz, R&B, and rock and roll are famous examples of a rather complex hybridization between African and European sounds that, however, the society of spectacle and capital has been able to absorb and normalize. The cultural—and thus political—battle that is fought through the sound of music is not at all an easy undertaking in the era of globalization. And yet even the ear of a distracted listener is today capable of distinguishing European from African sounds, although these sounds are sometimes closer to a sort of "pure" original, and other times a hybrid, reciprocal mix. Still others are full of citations and riffs whose history is, by now, forgotten or difficult to trace. According to Brathwaite, this history is also a history of the voice, which renews its memory in the sonority of poetry.

By upsetting the order of the British-English flutes with the percussion of tambourines, shattering pentameter with the dactyl of Calypso, Caribbean poetry—and, more generally all poetry in which an African voice vibrates—bends the dominant language to a vocalic that is at once direct experience of the environment and memory of the lost world. A "decorative noise" of high energetic potential accompanies it, says Brathwaite.[9] In this noise, the vibrato of the voice is mixed with the humming of the banjo, hissing sounds with crashing sounds, the noise of scraping with a pounding beat, while the tambourines roll louder and louder until they sound like thunder. Were it detached from this powerful acoustic accompaniment and transported into a soundless environment, poetry would not only be incomplete, it would be false. It would not sing with its own voice.

As any audience that has been lucky enough to hear him can testify, Brathwaite is an extraordinary reader of poetry. He provides not only the kind of experience that can be enjoyed when the poet "makes his poetic activity into pronunciation," exhibiting himself in a "live reading" that restores the voice to the text.[10] Rather, Braithwaite maintains that poetry cannot exist in the written text, because it belongs exclusively to the world of speech, or orality. "It is based as much on sound as it is on song"; hence, its acoustics are part of its meaning.[11] Once the voice is eliminated, the meaning is lost. This meaning, although essential to poetry, does not belong to it in an exclusive way. It concerns rather the so-called total expression that is typical of languages that are rooted in an oral culture. An oral tradition requires that, in addition to the griot who speaks, prophesizes, or sings, there are listeners who complete the community. "The noise and sounds that the maker makes are responded to by the audience and are returned to him."[12] The meaning resides precisely in this vocalic continuum of the community. In the case of African peoples who were uprooted from their land and their language, the "total expression" is in fact linked to the historical experience of people who have been able to count on breath rather than on a memory archived in books and museums. Transmitted through breath and sound, the voice therefore represents the vital element of the community. Experience and meaning coincide in the vocalic work that the poet exchanges with his audience.

Orally composed and often improvised, Brathwaite's poems—which are especially enjoyed aloud—can also be read as a printed text. This text is not a simple transcription, however. Precisely because the fundamental site of meaning is the voice rather than speech, a transcription would be an erasure. If entrusted to the written sign, the vocalic—and therefore the meaning—disappears. As the author wanted it, the books that print Brathwaite's poems are thus presented as an extraordinary graphic composition in which the character, the body, and the disposition of the letters are called on to translate a universal sound. Uppercase and lowercase letters of varying dimensions, the use of boldface and italic type, the horizontal and vertical spacing, all strive to represent the voice through the disruptive frame of the optical effect.[13] As in oral performance, the voice supersedes the semantic so that the design comes to take precedence over the significance of the written word in the graphic transposition. The text addresses above all the bodily eye and seeks to claim its attention before addressing the work of the mind. This principle comes from a long tradition that, starting with the transfiguration of the letters of the alphabet into images that is typical in medieval codices, goes all the way to "painted poetry" and the "figured word." By exalting the visual register to which it pertains, the text makes itself into a design and obeys the economy of figures. In this tradition, however, an ornamental idea of writing prevails, one that tries to superimpose itself on the semantic order of language. In Brathwaite's case, however, the texts are intentionally "noisy"; the acoustic reality transmits its energetic potential to the black marks on the page and makes them graphically dance. Brathwaite's writing does not therefore flow generously and infinitely, like Cixous' *languelait*. Rather, it dances like the rhythmic sound of the Caribbean voice.

2.7

The Harmony of the Spheres;
or, The Political Control of *Mousike*

> Professor Schwarzbrod who, once he overcame his shyness, did not lack for
> insolence, assured us that even the musical notes were under surveillance.
> They were not all equal: *do, re, mi* and *sol* were considered monarchic. The
> case of *fa* was ambiguous, and therefore was the subject of many studies.
> *Sharps* and *flats*, on the other hand, were decidedly revolutionary and proba-
> bly Jacobean, for obvious reasons. The elderly naturalist declared with rous-
> ing bellows that series of *sol-fa* were distributed to the policemen, and that a
> spectator at the Opera, caught enraptured by a *flat* and a *sharp*, risked prison.
> —Gilles Lapouge, *Le bataille de Wagram*

For Plato, bitter enemy of the rhapsodic voice, music is essentially a
political problem. He does not think, like Brathwaite, that music reflects
the sonorous universe of the environment, but rather that it reflects the
mute world of numbers. He agrees with Pythagoras; he places his trust in
the well-regulated sequence of numbers in order to render the acoustic
sphere of *mousike* politically inoffensive—useful, even.

In Greek, one of the many meanings of the term *logos* is in fact
"number." Distinguishing arithmetic from the science of calculation [*logis-
tike*], Plato says that the latter is "a science of the odd and the even, not
only with respect to their own qualities, but also with respect to their reciprocal relation."[1] Precisely here lies the secret of the mathematical valence
of the term *logos*, and the reason Plato favors it. For the science of numbers
has to do with *legein* in the sense of "linking," "binding," "gathering together." Moreover, it does not bind at random, but rather presents numerical progressions whose order is defined by a certain type of relation between numbers of a series. From Pythagoras onward, the entire speculative

framework of the number suggests the existence of a necessary structure, which is independent of human arbitrariness, and which is organized around an internal ratio between its elements that binds them together in a system. The succession of even and odd numbers, which comes about through the adding or subtracting of a single digit, is the simplest example of this. The number is logos—link, bond, ratio. There are different types of ratios, of course. Analogy is one of the most important types, because it shows equality or proportion between two ratios.

According to Plato, there are many explicit features that mathematics shares with philosophy. The register of pure signifieds or ideas that occupies philosophy and the register of numerical entities that occupies mathematics share the vision of a system of ratios in which each element is linked to the other according to the order of the whole. This is why Plato maintains that, because it too deals with the visual sphere, the study of mathematics prepares one for the study of philosophy. Calculation and arithmetic require one to take the eye of the body away from material things, and to turn the eye of the soul toward numbers as intelligible entities. By this, Plato does not mean that one should practice mathematics the way that a merchant or shop owner does when he counts his money; rather, he means that mathematics accomplishes the conversion of the soul from the perishable world of things to the eternal world of truth and being.[2] In other words, the objects of mathematics, insofar as they are contemplated by the mind, already have the status of the idea. Even when scholars of geometry trace figures and seem to be working on an image, in truth they are working on the idea of which the traced figure is only a sensible and imperfect copy. Mathematics thus has an affinity with all the sciences—including geometry and astronomy—that deal with intelligible entities and train the eye of the soul to look in the right direction. Plato's appreciation of numbers thus regards their belonging to a system of binding, and their belonging to an intelligible vision that characterizes that system. After all the *legein* that concerns numbers—a "binding" that is not to be confused with speaking—does not even have to make an effort to free itself from the *phone*. Inhabited by pure, intelligible, proportionate, regular ratios, the world of mathematical entities seems to have all the qualities that make it perfectly suited to the sphere of the eye. This is borne out by the fact that astronomy, for example, departs from the observation of the stars in order to contemplate the numerical laws of their regular motion. The affinity between this activity and the philosophical contemplation of ideas is quite explicit—for example, in the myth of the cave. Having come

out of the darkness of the cave, the philosopher lifts his gaze to the luminosity of the stars, the moon, and the celestial bodies.[3] In the metaphorical construction of the myth, these bodies represent the ideas, just as the
sun represents the supreme idea, namely the "good."

And yet as Plato knows well, Greek speculation on astronomy still allows the acoustic realm to play a central role, and to interfere with the
realm of the eye. This is because of the Pythagorean origins of the science
of numbers. Pythagoras' followers are the first to interpret the regularity of
the stars' movements in terms of a sophisticated musical theory. In Anaxi-
mander's work, preceded by Babylonian and Egyptian mathematical models of astronomy, we already find a spherical conception of the universe
that implies a geometric space defined by ratios of symmetrical and re-
versible positions.[4] Here the cosmos is already constructed on the law of
the number, although it does not yet play music. But because it can—indeed, it must—play, it happens that the number reveals itself to be the generating and regulating power behind the acoustic sphere. The Pythagoreans are the ones who discover this. With them, astronomy—the science of
the observation of the heavens—becomes, through the law of the number,
a music of the spheres. This is why, still today, "three quarters of the musical vocabulary—from 'design' to 'form,' from 'interval' to 'ornament'—are
borrowed from the world of sight."[5]

Hippasus notes, for example, that bronze disks of equal diameter but
different thickness, once struck, produce sounds whose tone is directly
proportional to the thickness of the disk.[6] The harmony is not only measurable, but it depends on, and is produced by, the size of the proportion.
Archytas of Tarentum, a great scholar of this phenomenon, also states that
things that crash and collide, including the breath when it is pushed into
the holes of a flute, produce an acute sound if the collision is fast and forceful, and a grave sound if the collision is slow and weak. According to
Archytas, this law of proportions between movements, which produce
sounds of different tones, also works for sounds that are inaudible to human ears. Some sounds, in fact, go unheard because they occur too far
away, or because the crash is too weak.[7] The music of the celestial spheres
belongs to these "unheard" sounds. Because they move at a different speed,
the heavenly spheres produce a marvelous, but inaudible, harmony. Of
course, it does not matter if human ears can enjoy the cosmic chords, or
provide the acoustic proof of the sublime concert. For Archytas, it is
enough to have gathered sufficient evidence to formulate his thesis, according to which the law that is manifested in the vibrating chord of a mu-

sical instrument is the very same law that moves the stars. Worthy of being called "origin," *arche*, this law of the number generates and rules over everything.

Thus, the Pythagoreans claim that even the soul is structured like a harmony of its parts. Of course, in this case it is not a soul that produces music, but rather a soul that is constructed like a unity of elements whose coordinating principle is proportion. In the Pythagorean universe, the harmonic law of number is at work in all things, and at all levels, including the heavens, the *polis*, and the soul. Obviously, not all these levels produce sonorous harmonies, and yet sonorous harmony has the privilege of being the audible form of the numeric structure of each one of these levels. This ends up attributing an important position to the acoustic sphere. On the one hand, human ears, through sensations of pleasure or annoyance, act as the sensory organs that are best capable of naturally recognizing an accord, or a discord, which has numerical foundations. On the other hand, these same ears transmit to the harmonic structure of the soul a music with which the soul feels in tune. As the venerable Julius Stenzel puts it, "that in the 'irrational' and sensorial position taken by the soul there is manifested a state of extreme rational pregnancy" reinforces the belief that the numerical law of the harmony regulates all things, including the passion of acoustic pleasure.[8]

According to Stenzel, the question concerns precisely the relation between the "rationality" that is at work in the numerical structure of the soul and the "irrationality" that the sensory organs traditionally evoke. Among these, the organ of hearing deserves special attention. As epic certainly knew, and as Plato never tires of denouncing, the effect of the *phone*—voice and sound—provokes pleasure and solicits the passions. What is new here is the fact that, with the Pythagorean doctrine, this pleasure throws off its irrational character and finds a justification in the numeric roots of the universe whose sonorous harmony has a perceptible expression. In its meaning as a "connection" among sonorous elements, the term *harmonia* is less explicit than another term that often accompanies it: *symphonia*, or in Latin, *concordia*. In this case, in fact, to the prefixes *sun* or *con* (which indicate "connection"), the *phone* or *cordia* gets added. This explains, moreover, why *harmonia* has an original semantic proximity with the term *rhythm*—which precedes the stabilization of both in musical language.[9] *Ruthmos* or *rusmos*, as Heidegger also notes, in fact signifies "the stillness that joins the movement of dance and song."[10] According to the Plato of the *Laws*, the term designates more precisely the order of movement in dance; or, rather, it consists in the forms or dispositions that connect the movements of the body, transforming them into figures of dance.[11] In the same passage, Plato adds that the order of the voice in which the acute and the grave are linked together [the verb is *sun-kerannumi*] is called *harmonia*. Again, harmony connects, links, or articulates. It is worth repeating here that the term derives from the Greek verb *harmottein*, which indicates the world of the carpenter who connects two pieces of wood.[12] In the process that brings these terms to rest in the lexicon of music, *ruthmos* and *harmonia* refer to different realms—movement for the first, and the acoustic sphere for the second. But both evoke a power of connection that relates to an order structured by measure and proportion. Put simply, the problem is not only connecting something to something else, but rather how to connect many things in a unity that ends up being stable thanks to an equilibrium produced by the "right joining" among the parts. The things that are joined by rhythm and harmony are in relation with each other according to a reciprocal tension that defines the position of every element, as well as the whole.

Significantly, the lexicon that refers to the problem of connection or joining comes to rest in the lexicon of music, above all through the mediation of the Pythagorean doctrine. The ability to read the ratio between sounds in numerical terms eventually allows for the precise classification of different types of harmony, and for their standardization in a unified theoretical framework. Music becomes a realm that lends itself to be regulated by forms and norms. Deprived of its secret power of enchantment, the acoustic realm of *mousike* falls under the regime of logos of which it is the perceptible expression.

Plato is highly enthusiastic about the Pythagorean doctrine of the number. In addition to the reasons listed above, another reason for his enthusiasm is the idea of a single principle connecting all things in a whole. As Socrates emphasizes in the *Gorgias*, something common [*koinonia*] keeps together heaven, earth, and men, and this is why the whole [*holon*] gets called "cosmos." This connective force—which can also be given the name of friendship, justice, and temperance—consists above all in geometric equivalence, a principle "of great power between men and gods."[13] Plato's homage to the Pythagorean doctrine here is, among other things, because of the philosopher's great interest in a category that plays a decisive role in the science of the number. This category is not logos, but rather a term that resembles it: *analogia*. Translated in scientific vocabulary as "proportion," or the equivalence of two ratios, *analogia* is, to the letter, "the same logos giving itself again." And this can mean (1) that the same discourse [*logos*] is applicable in two or more cases, or (2) that the same relationship [*logos*] is found in two or more cases. In the analogical construction of platonic metaphysics, the difference between these two alternatives is nonexistent.

This construction, which is given a magisterial description in the *Republic*, is in fact analogical not only because the order of the cosmos, the *polis*, and the soul correspond to one another, but also because this order is founded on a logos (understood as the right joining) that is the same in each of the three levels, and that allows Plato to repeat the same discourse for each one. Making the same discourse [*logos*] on the soul, on the *polis*, and on the cosmos means, therefore, to rediscover in all three cases the very same structure—that is, precisely the structure of the joining that has its foundation in the order of the ideas. The devocalized logos, or the order of pure signifieds with which it coincides, in fact functions as a model of the right joining on which not only the meaning of the words, but the entire ontological status of the universe, depends (soul, *polis*, heaven and earth included). In other words, the order of the ideas not only joins the ideas but it is mirrored, and it returns, in various levels of the whole universe. This explains, moreover, why Plato—inheriting a saying of Parmenides, and foretelling a opinion that extends to Descartes and Hegel—claims that there is an identity between thinking and being. The register of the ideas cannot but entrap in its own realm those *realities* that it has generated and organized. Put simply, platonic metaphysics does not claim that everything that is real is thinkable; rather, it proclaims that everything that is thinkable is real.

The best *polis*, thought and constructed by the philosopher, is thus maximally real. It would be an error to conclude that because it is only thought and does not in fact exist, it is an unreal *polis*, or as is often said, a utopia. For Plato, this *polis* is real precisely because it is thought. The philosopher models it on the order of his soul, which in turn is modeled on the contemplation of the order of ideas. In the *Republic*, in fact, the ideas function as criteria for constructing the best *polis*—namely, the famous *polis*, understood as a harmonious whole constituted by the three parts of craftsmen, soldiers, and philosopher-rulers. "The absolute priority of 'seeing' over 'doing,' and of contemplation over speaking and acting," is at work in the application of theoretical principles to politics.[14] Philosophers, says Plato, are "painters of constitutions" who look at the divine model of the ideas and copy its order.[15] The visual sphere generates and decides the norms of politics. It is thus hardly surprising that this videocentric *polis* banishes epic song and places music under strict regulation.

Here, too, one can trace these features to Pythagorean precedents. Damon, the famous teacher of Pericles, says that music pushes men to be courageous, wise, and just.[16] This is *mousike* in the Greek sense. This *mousike*, which can include dance, as far as the acoustic sphere is concerned, consists in a song of words with instrumental accompaniment. However, Damon's position is remarkable because he reforms the musical tradition by showing how certain harmonies can form a good citizen, while other harmonies have the opposite effect. In Greece, music is a fundamental part of the *paideia*, or the education that forms the virtuous man and the good citizen. Music thus pertains to the political arena and not to entertainment. Before the advent of the modern era—as Adorno would say, before the late Beethoven—music does not belong to aesthetics, but rather to politics.[17] For Plato, who throws the *mousike* of Homer out of his *polis*, the fundamental problem is how to replace this *mousike* with a music that can play a role in the formation of the philosophical soul. Imagining a political education entirely without music is, for the Greeks, impossible.

The platonic critique of Homeric culture, and of the musical innovations of the time, thus leads to the distinction between a type of music that is apt to form a good citizen and the type of music that instead has negative effects. As Damon says too, in this framework good music appears as ordered and ordering, whereas bad music appears disordered and disordering. It is a delicate matter, because music is poured "into the soul through the ear, as if by a funnel."[18] According to Plato, the listener is passive; all he can do is receive a joining of sounds that is objectively good or bad. We have to wait for Descartes before listening becomes a mental activity of a subject who is capable of linking perceived sounds into a coherent unity through his imagination.[19] For Plato, and for treatises on music until Descartes, the joining of sounds does not depend on the subject, but rather on an intrinsic quality of the sonorous object. So too the joining of which logos consists is intrinsic to the order of ideas. The problem is thus to distinguish the right joinings from the wrong ones. Plato therefore excludes the sweet, maudlin harmonies of the flute, the warbling of song, and every kind of acoustic pleasure that is likely to solicit the passions that disorder the soul. He reserves "his preferences for less musical and less modulating modes; for the austere and cold Doric monody."[20] In addition to the wind instruments, polychord instruments are eliminated as well. The rhythm that is useful for the *polis* must be simple and uniform. The souls must be disciplined by the sounds, not inebriated or distracted by them.

However, the crucial point regards the words. For Plato, "purely instrumental music is a heresy."[21] Unlike the Pythagoreans, Plato has very little faith in the capacity of pure sounds to "pour" into the soul the numerical harmony that they must express. The *phone* understood as an instrumental sound, disciplined by austere harmonies, must accompany the *phone* understood as a voice that vocalizes words. Words constitute the hegemonic element in musical performance. Music is organized around logos. Accompanied by the cithara, the song [*ode*] in fact consists in a melodic voice that says words. The melody, the *melos*, is also always logos. Indeed, it is first and foremost logos. By examining music from the point of view of rhythm and harmony, Plato in fact establishes a primary, foundational principle: harmony and rhythm must follow logos, and not the other way around.[22] In the *Republic*, this means that the words of the song—that is, the contents of the poetic narration—must conform to that which, according to the philosopher, it is right to say.

Logos therefore commands melodic performance in various senses—senses that are inscribed in the polysemy of the term *logos* itself, and that coherently relate to one another. According to the most general sense logos, understood as speech, admits a certain musicalization but does not admit that there is music without speech. The ears and their indiscriminate thirst for acoustic pleasure must be governed by speech. The flute, which keeps the mouth busy, gets excluded all together. According to a more specific sense, *melos*, vocal or instrumental, must adapt itself to the words and not the other way around. Socrates suggests that one first establish the verbal text, and then adapt the music to it. Plato therefore proposes judging the words themselves, detaching them from their musical context. However, according to an even more fundamental sense, the philosopher is the one who is able to look at the order of ideas, silently dialoguing with the vocalized logos of his own soul; he is the one who decides which topics the words of the song ought to express. And, finally, according to the sense from which all the previous senses derive, there is the order of ideas (which is truly the logos as right joining) that the philosopher looks at in order to construct the *polis* and regulate the laws of the *paideia* and the *mousike*. The result is a music that is well tempered politically, a music in which the acoustic register is subordinated to a verbal register that is already, in turn, disciplined by the mute and videocentric order of ideas on which everything is based.

Many interpreters have noted that today such an art would be called "state art." However, this is only the most scandalous aspect of the problem from a modern point of view, because in the paidectic sphere of *mousike*, already what is at stake is necessarily political. Precisely in these scandalous pages, Plato is taking on the cultural transition from the ear to the eye. As Hannah Arendt has pointed out, Plato is founding the videocentric criteria of politics, along with the disciplinary status of political philosophy, through the application of a fixed order of ideas to the contingent, plural world of action.[23] One of his most serious problems therefore consists in the effort of adapting the power of the sonorous arts to a model of the city whose criteria are founded on the vision of the ideas. Given the privileged relation between the ideas and logos, it is therefore obvious that the first censureship is addressed to the poetic logos—that is, to the words of the song, in order to confirm logos as the dominant element in *mousike*. *Mousike* must be the bearer of topics that are preselected by philosophy. Rhythm and harmony, happily reduced to the law of the number, are little more than an accompaniment that must be adapted to the logocentric structure. As often happens with this structure, the platonic *mousike* thus shows that its regulation is essentially decided by that which it must exclude. And with respect to this normative music, anything in the entire sonorous universe that oversteps the canons becomes a dangerous excess. Thus, the great power of the voice, of which—according to Plato himself—Homer is the undeniable champion, gets reconfirmed. As a matter of fact, the philosopher of ideas fears the acoustic sphere and tries to submit it as much as possible to the disciplining of logos.

By inaugurating itself as a logocentric metaphysics that is prudently founded on a devocalized logos, platonic philosophy illustrates why the western tradition—while it ends up transferring music into the realm of aesthetics or entertainment—still tries to maintain control over it. For there is a subversive potential in the voice, which is redoubled when the voice itself vibrates with the universe of sounds instead of merely clothing the concept in acoustic vesting. Of course, Plato could not even imagine the impact of jazz, R&B, rock and roll, and similar rhythms on the western ear. He could not imagine how, in modern times, the unsettling effects of the melodramatic theater could be passed on to an audience at a rock concert, where the ritual of a "loss of self-control, collective delirium, tears, fainting, fanaticisms of all sorts" is once again renewed.[24] Still, Plato left precise instructions that the cause of these phenomena be banished from the *polis*.

Plato's *Republic* ends with the famous myth of Er, which narrates the destiny of the souls and the cycles of their reincarnation. Along the way, the movement that produces the music of the spheres gets described in some detail. This is, of course, the ingenious astronomical model—obviously taken from Pythagoras—that Plato presents in order to describe the rotation of the seven heavens of the planets around the axis of the eighth and most luminous heaven. However, Plato does come up with one original feature with respect to the Pythagorean doctrine. On each one of the eight celestial spheres, he says, there lies a Siren "who emits a single voice [*phonen*], a single note. But from all these eight voices resounds the concord [*symphonein*] of a single harmony."[25] More or less stolen from the Homeric imagination, Plato's Sirens are therefore already synonymous with a wordless song. The pure voice of each one is only a single, monotonous note—which, attuned to all the others and proceeding linearly one after another according to the Greek principle of the monody, contributes to a common harmony. Symptomatically, this harmony is also a music that functions as an instrumental accompaniment for the songs of Lachesis, Clotho, and Atropos—the three Fates who, as true substitutes of the ancient Sirens in both knowledge and omniscience, sing the past, present, and future. In addition to singing, they regulate the rotation of the spheres. Touching at regular intervals the various rings of the spheres so that they continue to spin, the Fates control the sonorous emission of the heavens.

Thus, this cosmic harmony appears as a curious mixture of technical elements and mythical figures. At the same time, the acoustic phenomenon seems to have two sources: the throat of the Sirens and the rotation of the spheres. Symptomatically, Plato's addition of the Sirens to the Pythagorean model represents the capture of the voice in the cosmic mechanism of sonorous emission. Of course, this voice is no longer a human voice, or even a divine voice, like the song of the Fates carrying words. Rather, every Siren emits but a single note. A single harmony binds them—perfect, repetitive, regular. And this harmony traps forever, in the discipline of its numerical rules, the most dangerous vocal creatures that the west has ever imagined.

PART III

A POLITICS OF VOICES

3.1

Echo; or, On Resonance

Auribus in vestris habito penetrabilis Echo.
—Ausonio, *In Echo pictam*

Myth is full of female vocal creatures. Among them is the nymph Echo who, instead of singing, repeats the words of others. The repetition begins, however, with a certain temporal overlap, while the other is still speaking. The echo thus makes itself into a resonance according to a musical rhythm. As a pure voice that refracts another voice, Echo makes the musicality of language sing. The poet Ovid wisely places her alongside Narcissus. The eye and the voice, which so tormented Plato, thus encounter one another in the Latin fable. And as with Plato, in Ovid's text there is no shortage of mirroring effects or produced copies—Narcissus' reflected image, and Echo's reverberating voice. The story tells of their impossible reconciliation.

At the beginning of the story, according to Ovid's original version, Echo is a loquacious nymph; in fact, she is positively verbose, capable of entertaining people with long-winded discourses [*sermones*].[1] She is not just any conversationalist, therefore, but a young girl who has total command of the language, possessed of a typically feminine rhetorical talent. She is able to distract Juno with her chattering while the other nymphs bed Jupiter. Realizing that she has been tricked, the goddess takes her revenge. Echo is condemned to repeat the words of others, duplicating their sounds. Rendered incapable of taking the initiative in order to proffer discourses of her own, she becomes a vocal nymph who only echoes sounds. *Vocalis nympha, resonabilis Echo*, like a voice that functions as an acoustic mirror, the young girl is transformed into an effect of resonance. She cannot speak first; but she cannot remain silent. She speaks *after*, she depends on others' discourses and becomes merely their echo. Moreover, only the last words that are uttered by her voice—which are superimposed on the words that the speaker is pronouncing—are heard. Thus separated from their context, they take on a different meaning. They are a forced and unintentional repetition, but they can appear like a response.

Narcissus, who enters the scene at this point, encounters Echo. Narcissus is young and beautiful, and the nymph falls in love with him. The occasion of their first—and last—encounter is in a wooded glade where Echo, hidden in the bushes, can only repeat his words. Believing that he is holding a conversation with a girl who does not want to show herself, the young boy invites her to join him. "Come here and let us meet [*huc coeamus*]," he says. And the voice of the nymph repeat, "Let us meet [*coeamus*]." Her response is naughty. For without the *huc, coeamus* alludes to coitus. The nymph goes on to make the situation worse by jumping out of the woods and throwing her arms around Narcissus. Scandalized by her ardor, the boy then declares that he would rather die than couple with her; and Echo, automatically, invites him to couple, or rather copulate, with her. The result is an unequivocal and definite refusal on the part of Narcissus. He would of course have refused her in any case, because he is capable of loving only himself. But Echo's story requires this cruel turn. For right after this unhappy episode, she in fact begins to physically wither away from her unrequited love. "She became wrinkled and wasted; all the freshness of her beauty withered into the air." As if by a progressive dissolution, her body vanishes until "only her voice and her bones remain." Soon after, her bones become stone. Disembodied, Echo finally becomes echo, the sound that the mountains send bouncing back, a pure voice of resonance without a body. Without a mouth, or throat, or saliva, without any human semblance or visible figure, the beautiful nymph is sublimated into a mineralization of the voice.

The myth is rich with symbolic references. Following the classical tradition, it confirms that the voice is feminine. Unlike the Muses or the Homeric Sirens, however, Echo's is not a singing or narrating voice, but rather a voice that results, like a mere residual material, from its subtraction from the semantic register of logos. Rather than repeating the words, Echo repeats their sounds. If these sounds, separated from the context of the sentence, come together to form words that still signify something (or something else), then this is a matter for the listener, not the nymph. After Juno's curse—following the usual rule of feminine envy—Echo is no longer a *zoon logon echon*; she no longer possesses a *phone semantike*. She is instead pure *phone*, activated by an involuntary mechanism of resonance. Only because of Narcissus do Echo's responses form a dialogue. In this sense, in the economy of the patriarchal symbolic order, Echo is but the younger sister of the mute woman. Neither of them speaks; but the prohibition that denies them speech is different in each case. Women in general, it could be said, adapt themselves to a silence that conforms to a "natural" feminine inadequacy when it comes to logos. For Echo, on the other hand, it is a matter of revocalizing logos through a voice that is totally drained of its semantic component. The revocalization is thus a desemanticization. It falls to Narcissus to resemanticize the sounds that the nymph proffers. In the end, in his exemplary narcissism, Narcissus "dialogues" coherently only with himself, not with Echo. He dialogues with himself, he interprets himself, and he misunderstands himself. The whole, somewhat obscene game that Ovid plays is developed on the semantic level.

Echo is the designated victim of this game. Pure voice, restricted to repeating the words of others, she provides a sonorous substance to a semantic that is not organized according to her intentions. She vocalizes a meaning that not only depends on Narcissus' words, but on the language game that appears in Ovid's text. And this meaning is what allows her to suddenly throw her arms around Narcissus—the only act that is properly hers, spontaneous, out of the norm of repetition. By embracing Narcissus, the enamored Echo shows that she is still a singular body that expresses itself. It is precisely this initiative that provokes Narcissus' refusal, which brings her to wither away from love and lose her body. This process of withering has certain anatomical details; first, her flesh dries up, then her humors vanish, and then her bones turn to stone—not the stone of a statue, but rather stone in general: rocks, boulders, mountains. The nullifying of her body is thus the definitive dissolution of a uniqueness that, as echo, Echo's voice does not possess. Echo's voice is, in fact, not *her* voice; it does not possess an unmistakable timbre, and it does not signal a unique person. It simply obeys the physical phenomenon of the echo, repeating even the timbre of the other's voice. It is a mere acoustic resonance, a voice that returns, foreign, to the one who emitted it. The juxtaposition of Echo and Narcissus is therefore perfect. The absolute ego of Narcissus, for whom the other is nothing but "another himself," corresponds to the reduction of the vocalic nymph to a mere sonorous reverberation of the other. The mechanism of repetition in the voice produces the annulment of uniqueness. The same mechanism of the eye produces in Narcissus an absolute duplication of himself. Lovesick for his own image, the beautiful boy dies, leaving the flower that bears his name. Echo instead lives on without a body and still functions as an acoustic mirror for the play of the voice that, from afar, returns through its own rhythmical extension.

As Ovid knows, there is something infantile in this game which is played on mountain paths the world over. As a master of language and a devotee of the musicality of verse, Ovid constructs a text which the sounds reverberated by Echo not only substantiate the meter, but reorganize the semantic register through the dialogue's equivocations. Beyond the entertaining construction of the dialogue, however, Echo remains pure voice, vocal resonance, not speech. As in the case of the infant who repeats the mother's words, stripping them of their meaning, Echo is acoustic repetition, not intentioned toward meaning. Just as the myth recounts, her story alludes to a sort of regression to the mimetic vocalization of infancy, to the so-called la-la language. Before Juno's intervention, the nymph not only spoke, but was capable of discourses that could entertain even the gods. As is typical of women, she was skilled in the semantic art of rhetoric—which makes her transformation into a pure vocal mechanism of resonance, in and of itself indifferent to the semantic, all the more significant. Through the fate of Echo, logos is stripped of language as a system of signification and is reduced to a pure vocalic. And yet this is not just any vocalic, but rather a vocalic that erases the semantic through repetition. Repetition—the very repetition that is the famous mechanism of the "performative," through which meaning is stabilized and destabilized—here turns out to be a mechanism that produces the reverse effect. Echo's repetition is a babble that dissolves the semantic register entirely, leading the voice back to an infantile state that is not yet speech.

Literary modernism—especially those texts that employ experimental techniques in order to liberate language from the urgency of signification—intuits the power of this regression. Some texts by Samuel Beckett, for example, produce a linguistic flux that—through repetition and syntactic breaks, phonematic substitutions, and ambiguous resignifications—results in a babble where the semantic system, and the subject that should sustain this system, are dissolved.[2] Hélène Cixous' work is similar, and yet different, in this regard. Her work against the codes of the language of the Father is explicitly aimed at freeing the maternal, rhythmic voice of the mother, which precedes and exceeds the system of logos. Cixous, like Kristeva, recuperates for the voice an originary scene of infancy as a link with the mother. The element of repetition in their texts is more than babble; it becomes resonance, music, and acoustic relation. If we transport Echo onto this scene—which is renewed wherever the semantic succumbs to the vocalic—then the Ovidian nymph ends up recuperating a different sense for her vocalic repetition, one that is no longer punitive or forced. For as Ovid himself no doubt knew, Echo is not so much a tragic figure of interdicted speech as she is a figure of a certain pleasure. This pleasure in vocal repetition is not even perceived as compulsive; rather, by evading the semantic, it rediscovers a time in which such pleasure was free from the very problem of this evasion. In other words, the echo that mobilizes the musical rhythm of language does not simply coincide with an infantile regression; it rediscovers, or remembers, the power of a voice that still resounds in logos. By devocalizing logos, metaphysics wants to immunize itself from this power. The privileging of *theoria* over speech, as Plato knew well, is first of all the erasure of the voice.

In the etymology of the Latin *vox*, the first meaning of *vocare* is "to call," or "invoke." Before making itself speech, the voice is an invocation that is addressed to the other and that entrusts itself to an ear that receives it. Its inaugural scene coincides with birth, where the infant, with her first breath, invokes a voice in response, appeals to an ear to receive her cry, convokes another voice. The intrauterine bond—which is already rhythmical, musical—is broken. The first cry thus invokes a new sonorous bond, as vitally important as the breath that sustains it. Existence hangs on a push of the lungs, which is at the same time an invocation of the other. The voice is always *for* the ear, it is always relational; but it is never as relational as it is in the first cry of the infant—an invoking life that unknowingly entrusts itself to a voice that responds. For at the beginning, in the cold and blindness of the first light, in the expulsion from the warmth of the uterine water—at the newborn's emergence "in order to have what it did not have inside; air and breath, indispensable for phonation"—there is nothing but the sonorous bond of voice to voice.[3] This bond establishes the first communication of all communicability, and thus constitutes its prerequisite. There is nothing yet to be communicated, if not communication itself in its pure vocality. The voice first of all signifies itself, nothing other than the relationality of the vocalic, which is already implicit in the first invoking cry of the infant.

During the first crucial months of life, this vocalic relationality takes its time and its pleasure before handing itself over to the system of language. The maternal tongue is not only the language that we speak because we learned it from our mothers. It is also, before this, the wordless language of vocalizations that the mother exchanges with the infant. Whether she utters words with meaning, or indulges in nonsensical baby talk herself, the mother tongue touches the infant's ear with unmistakable tones and teaches the infant the mimetic cadences of the sonorous relation. This is an acoustic-vocal relation in which, importantly, what gets said is, as yet, nothing. There is not yet any signified in this voice—no reference through the linguistic sign to the noetic *presence* of an absent object. Materialized by the physicality of the vocal exchange, the only presence is the act of the relation. This relation often involves a "face to face," a contiguity of the face, of touch, of odor. The indexes of uniqueness quickly add up and are soon recognizable to the infant. But only in the vocalic sphere does the relation take on the status of an active, spontaneous communication that the facial expressions sustain and reinforce. Symptomatically, even from a developmental point of view, the exchange of voices precedes the exchange of smiles. Invoked from the very first cry, the vocalic dialogue begins straight away.

Obviously, in this case, "dialogue" is not the right word. For there is no logos here, just as there is not yet any system of language. There is, however, a cadence of demand and response—or, better, a reciprocal invocation in which the voices convoke one another in turn. This cadence has its temporal rhythms, its communicative soundtrack, its la-la melody—it has a certain measure, if not yet a law. In the play of voices that invoke each other, the sequence of emissions configure a reciprocal dependence—not just the obvious dependence of the infant on the one who nourishes and cares for her, or the originary dependence of each existent on the woman who brought her into the world, but rather the dependence that is inscribed in the very relationality of invocation. It is configured as a resonance where the emission, although free, spontaneously follows the relational rhythm of repetition. This rhythm confirms that each voice, as it is *for* the ear, demands at the same time an ear that is *for* the voice. In the phenomenology of the maternal scene, the cadence of the vocal exchange shows in an evident way that this "for" alludes to the ear and the voice of the other. The invocation, *incipit* of a vocalic dialogue, implies at the same time the ear and the voice of the other—someone else who is here, in earshot. The invocation depends on this. The "sharing of voices" [*la partage dex voix*], to use Nancy's phrase, is first of all a sharing that complies with the relationality of the voice. It is hardly surprising, in the maternal language of vocalizations and gurgles, that this sharing has a musical quality. Because it is modulated on the elementary structure of the echo, its form is a duet—a sonorous texture for two voices, which are structurally *for* the other.

This is the very music that Kristeva and Cixous speak of when they name the maternal figure as the sonorous, presemantic source of language. Because they rely on a psychoanalytic framework, however, their attention goes to the pleasure drive that is inscribed in this musicality, linked to the mouth as the center of oral pleasure. The *languelait* of the mother, voice and milk, is given to the ear and the mouth. The shadow of psychoanalysis thus ends up obscuring the relationality of the scene, sacrificing it to the originary bond [*fusione originaria*] between mother and child. As a result, the phenomenon of vocalic uniqueness is once again effaced. Unlike the bond [*fusione*] of mother and child, a relation carries with it the act of distinguishing oneself, constituting the uniqueness of each one through this distinction. In the case of the vocalizations and gurgles that the mother and the infant exchange, this uniqueness makes itself heard incontrovertibly as voice. The infant recognizes the mother's voice and sings a duet with her. Resonance, daughter of invocation, links the two voices in the form of a rhythmic bond. What makes the uniqueness of the two voices stand out, in fact, is this repetition, echo, and miming, because they duplicate the *same* sounds. The voice is always unique, but all the more so in the vocalic exercise of repetition. In fact, by challenging the economy of the same, uniqueness is here entrusted to nothing other than the singular voice. This does not mean that in this vocalic language mother and child are constituted as subjects. The phantasm of the *subject* is a fictitious entity generated by philosophy; it belongs to language as a system of signification; it comes from the devocalizing strategy of *theoria*. And yet this does not mean that there is no distinction between mother and infant. On the contrary, there is a process of self-distinction in the repetitive rhythm of the duet, in the reciprocal giving of uniqueness and relation, just like a song for two voices—communication, already regulated, of language whose rules are not semantic but acoustic. It is indeed a song, no longer intentioned toward speech, with which each invokes the other and communicates him- or herself in the interdependent form of the resonance. The uniqueness of the vocalic is inaugurated on a scene where, unlike what happens on the scene of the "subject," there are no dreams of autonomy or hierarchical principles. Free from the pretenses of Narcissus and from Ovid's textual games, Echo comes to appear as the divinity who teaches an acoustic relationality, still linked to infantile pleasure, in which uniqueness makes itself heard as voice.

3.2

A Vocal Ontology of Uniqueness

> Since sound indicates an activity that takes place "here and in this mo-
> ment," speech as sound establishes a personal presence "here and in this
> moment."
> —Walter Ong, *The Presence of the Word*

In the uniqueness that makes itself heard as voice, there is an embodied existent, or rather, a "being-there" [*esserci*] in its radical finitude,
here and now. The sphere of the vocal implies the ontological plane and
anchors it to the existence of singular beings who invoke one another contextually. From the maternal scene onward, the voice manifests the *unique
being* of each human being, and his or her spontaneous self-communication according to the rhythms of a sonorous relation. In this sense, the ontological horizon that is disclosed by the voice—or what we want to call a
vocal ontology of uniqueness—stands in contrast to the various ontologies of
fictitious entities that the philosophical tradition, over the course of its historical development, designates with names like "man," "subject," "individual." For what these universal categories share is the neglect of the
"uniqueness" of those human beings (or, to use the metaphysical lexicon,
their "particularity" and their "finitude"). It is therefore not surprising that
the "subject," in its classic Cartesian clothes, has no voice and speaks only
to itself through the mute voice of consciousness. This metaphorical voice
of the soul or consciousness, so dear to philosophy, is a crucial rhetorical
figure through which the voice—through its identification with the silent
work of thought—gets transformed into a negation of the voice. Thought
has no voice; it neither invokes nor speaks—it cogitates [*cogita*]. Thinking
is structurally immune to the musical and relational interference of the

acoustic sphere of speech. A vocal ontology of uniqueness must therefore first overturn the old metaphysical strategy that subordinates speech to thought. The first step toward freeing the voice from *nous*, the first gesture against the devocalizing canons of philosophy, also passes through a privileged thematizing of speaking. At least potentially, Levinas' *le Dire* could be of interest in this regard. But it is another Jewish philosopher of the early twentieth century who comprehends the heart of the question: Franz Rosenzweig.

Rosenzweig is aware of the novelty of his perspective, and calls it—with a rather infelicitous expression—"new thought." Also defined as "experient philosophy," this "new thought" tries to distinguish itself from "old" thought, or from the Greek philosophical tradition. More than a "new" thought, in any event, at stake is a horizon whose novelty consists in opposing the centrality of *speaking* to a philosophical tradition that instead has focused on *thinking*. "In the place of the method of thinking, as it has been constituted by all preceding philosophies, there comes the method of speaking."[1] Thinking and speaking are rather different activities. Thinking wants to be timeless; it poses a thousand different connections in a single stroke and assembles its objects in an eternal present. Furthermore, it is always solitary, even when it takes place between several people "who are philosophizing in common, even then the other only poses an objection that I would have been able to pose all alone."[2] According to Rosenzweig, this accounts for the artificial effect of Plato's dialogues. As Maria Zambrano notes, too, "*logos* proceeds without any other opposition than what it, in order to better show itself, poses to itself."[3] The thinker, including the platonic Socrates, knows his own thoughts beforehand. The time required for the questioning and answering thus ends up being an obstacle or a delay with respect to the speed of thought. Speaking, on the contrary, is always bound to time. It does not know in advance where it is going, and it entrusts itself to the unpredictable nature of what the interlocutors say. In short, thought is as solitary as speech is relational. Speaking "lives above all through the lives of others, whether they are the listener of a narration, the interlocutor of a dialogue or the member of a chorus."[4] There is a dependence on others that passes through a plural connection of mouths and ears. Unlike what Plato believes—when he inaugurates the metaphorical voice of the soul—speaking is not at all a thinking that expresses itself out loud, nor is it merely vocalized thought, nor is it an acoustic substitute for thinking. The phenomenology of speaking possesses an autonomous status in which the relationality of mouths and ears comes to the fore.

Speaking in fact means to speak to someone, "and this someone is always quite precise, and not only has ears, like the collectivity, but has a mouth as well."[5] In other words, speaking is an interlocution with others and requires a reciprocity of speech and listening. Unlike thinking, speaking does not allow its protagonist to be an abstract subject; instead, it implies that the speakers are human beings in flesh and bone, with mouths and ears. Rosenzweig effectively defines each one of these speakers as "very common individual, dust and ashes." In other words, this is an existent in flesh and bone, unique and unrepeatable, which philosophy declares unreal because he or she does not belong among the universal and atemporal objects of thought that, alone, are true and real. It is thus hardly surprising that the "I name and surname" ends up being unsayable (or, as Arendt would say, "superfluous") within the canon of philosophy. But this is not the only consequence. Rosenzweig in fact notes that "philosophy has declared that I, name and surname, must remain silent." Thus, not only does philosophy claim the epistemological ineffability of the single, particular human being, but it also orders human beings not to make their voices heard. The famous *individuum ineffabile* is, in the end, a unique being whose voice was taken away.

Indeed, this voice was taken away even more than Rosenzweig imagines. Although insisting on the physicality of mouths and ears, he in fact stops at the phenomenology of "speaking." Although he is open to a relational and antimetaphysical ontology, he does not root this ontology in the voice. As a result, rather than being denied, the uniqueness of the voice remains, in his texts, an implicit given that merely confirms the embodied singularity of the "I name and surname." One of the consequences of this is that Rosenzweig thus overlooks the possibility of emphasizing the vocal uniqueness of that *I* that philosophy, along with modern linguistics, ends up negating. For both linguistics and philosophy, the "I" functions as an empty, mobile indicator. Because everyone says "I," this "I" would stand for everyone and no one; or, better, for the speaker who appropriates the pronoun in the act of designating himself as "I." Even paying the slightest attention to the voice of this speaker is, however, enough to complicate this linguistic analysis and to push it in another direction. Consider the rather banal, everyday occurrence of the telephone or intercom, where one asks me "who is it?"—and I respond without hesitation "it's me," or "it is 'I.'" The depersonalized function of the pronouns "I" or "me"—highlighted here by the fact that the speaker does not show her face—gets immediately annulled by the unmistakable uniqueness of the voice. The sound conquers the generality of the pronoun. This everyday scene, a kind of banalization of the story of Isaac and Jacob, shows that every human being has, in the uniqueness of his or her voice, a sonorous self-revelation that overcomes the linguistic register of signification.

As a fact of everyday experience, the voice appears as the elementary principle of an ontology of uniqueness that radically contests the metaphysical tradition that silences the "I" in flesh and bone. Not that my face, as Levinas would say, does not appear as unique to the one who is next to me, looking at me. Yet this looking runs the risk of continuing to pay homage to the philosophical centrality of *theoria*. This ontology entrusted to the eye has been the lifeblood of western metaphysics since Plato. Narcissus is only its tragic and suggestive variant.

Unlike the detached, objective gaze that characterizes platonic metaphysics, Narcissus in fact represents the gaze of the subject on himself, the autocircuit of the eye. The act of looking at himself forces the reciprocity of the gaze and produces a sort of autistic face to face of the self with the self. Narcissus' narcissism, in addition to the many ways in which narcissism has been considered by psychoanalysis and contemporary thought, also has the following basic function.[6] It opens the sphere of the eye to a horizon of reciprocity, ignored by metaphysical *theoria*, and at the same time closes this very same horizon on a self-reflection of the self. It alludes to the possibility of "looking at one another" and then nullifies this possibility by looking at itself. In this sense, Narcissus announces the narcissistic self-referentiality of the modern subject—or, better, the modern figure of self-consciousness—but he also supports the general philosophical tendency born in Greece to ignore the reciprocity of looking and (therefore) the uniqueness of the other's face.

Metaphysics not only constructs itself on the primacy of sight, but also decides to ignore the reciprocity that is inscribed, as a decisive relational factor, in the economy of the gaze. The metaphysical eye, starting with Plato, fixes as its model a gaze that allows for the isolation, distance, and noninvolvement of the observer. This in turn legitimates the reduction of whatever is seen to an object. Thus, Levinas is not wrong when he proposes the face to face of the reciprocal gaze as a fundamental alternative to the objectifying effect of metaphysical *theoria*. Symptomatically, this alternative allows him to understand differently the category of *presence*. Rather than functioning as an eternalizing quality of *being*, the presence of those who look at one another face to face is guaranteed by the empirical contingency of the context. In the reciprocal gaze, the presence of the other is always the presence of an other who is *here*, who looks at me *now*, in the unrepeatable time of a present that is inscribed in the actuality of the context. It thus cannot be transformed into a hypostasis of a determinate duration. Rather than the atemporal dimension of a lasting permanence, the face to face evokes a discontinuous becoming, characterized by the ever-new "present" of the "nows" in which the gazes intersect. This is, moreover, why the Levinasian ontology of the face to face has an immediate ethical tonality. The face of the other is presented, *in the moment*, as a demand of responsibility that cannot be deferred. The ones who look at each other are not called on to respond—in general—for "man" or other fictitious entities. Rather, they are called on to respond, now, for the uniqueness of the other. The face, which is always the unrepeatable face of someone, punctually represents every time the same demand. It is enough to look at one another, to expose oneself reciprocally to the gaze. To make the eye a medium of communication. To distract it from the usual metaphysical (or scientific) orientation toward the object.

This work of distraction is, symptomatically, a quite natural effect of the voice. The voice never comes from an object, nor is it addressed to an object. Rather, the voice—as in Aesop's fable—subjectivizes the one who emits it, even when it is an animal. The voice belongs to the living; it communicates the presence of an existent in flesh and bone; it signals a throat, a particular body. For this reason, there is a certain wisdom in those modern languages that—breaking with ancient Greek, for example—distinguish "voice" and "sound" with two different words. Every human voice is obviously a sound, an acoustic vibration among others, which is measurable like all other sounds; but it is only as human that the voice comes to be perceived as unique. This means that uniqueness resounds in the human voice; or, in the human voice, uniqueness makes itself sound. The ear, its natural destination, perceives this unique sound without any effort, no matter what words are spoken. No matter what you say, I know that the voice is yours. Jacob's voice is not only different from Esau's, but it is different from every other voice. The voice is always unique, and the ear recognizes it as such. Indeed, the ear perceives the voice's uniqueness even when, never having heard it before, it cannot "recognize" this voice.

Unlike the gaze, the voice is always, irremediably relational. It does not allow a detached focus on the object because, properly speaking, it has no object. The voice vibrates in the air, striking the ear of the other, even when it does not mean to do so. Listening, as Koestenbaum puts it, is a reciprocal exercise, "grateful for what the ear receives, the truth responds by opening."[7] The elementary phenomenology of the acoustic sphere always implies a relation between mouth and ear. Because it belongs to the world of humans, the voice is *for* the ear. The thesis that the ear is there—as Derrida puts it—to "hear oneself speak" is curiously narcissistic (and metaphysically suspect). The emitted voice always comes out into the world, and every ear within earshot—with or without intention—is struck by it. The ear is an open canal; it can be surprised from anywhere at any moment. It is always cocked to a sonorous universe that it does not control. It can try to decipher the sounds, as Calvino's king tried to do, but it cannot decide on, or control, their emission. The ear receives without being able to select beforehand. The ear distinguishes the sound of the voice and knows it to be human not only because it vibrates in the specifically human element of speech, but also because the ear perceives its uniqueness. And this happens, obviously, even to the ears of philosophers. This is why they must mute their soul with the silent vision of *theoria*: in order not to run the risk of hearing the uniqueness of the voice that sounds in every spoken word.

After all, the strange poverty of the Greek philosophical language—which indicates both "sound" and "voice" with the single term *phone*—is due precisely to this muting effect of *theoria*. For the hearing of the metaphysicians—and for the linguists who inherit their acoustic pathology—the human voice is simply a sound among other sounds. The mouth, the living body are aligned with other sources of sonorous emission. It is true that Plato and Aristotle are interested in the phonic organs as instruments that articulate the vocal flux in discrete sounds, but this interest is already oriented toward the centrality of a speech that is characterized by the urgency to signify. The uniqueness of the voice as voice, as a sort of superfluous given, does not get thematized. Founded in the visual realm of the signified, speech blinds the natural sensibility of the ear. The most important consequence of this, from the perspective of the history of metaphysics, is a devocalization of logos that sweeps the voice from the realm of truth and allows philosophy to construct a system that neglects uniqueness and relationality.

An antimetaphysical strategy, like mine, aiming to valorize an ontology of uniqueness finds in the voice a decisive—indeed, obligatory—resource. The point is not simply to revocalize logos. Rather, the aim is to free logos from its visual substance, and to finally mean it as sonorous speech—in order to listen, in speech itself, for the plurality of singular voices that convoke one other in a relation that is not simply sound, but above all resonance. The fact that this resonance leads back to the scene of infancy does not mean that the sense of the vocalic exhausts itself in this dynamic of regression. In fact, the problem does not consist in recuperating a voice that is still pure voice because it precedes the advent of speech, but in recuperating the voice in the realm of speech toward which the voice is itself essentially destined. On the scene of infancy, it is precisely the mother who links the sphere of the voice to that of speech. She does not just respond to the infant's invocation by singing a duet; rather, as the source of language and the storyteller for the infant, she musically gives the register of speech to the child. However, the insistence on the mother as the source of this vocalic pleasure—no matter how good or theoretically grounded the intention may be—does not therefore justify her stereotypical opposition to a father who would be instead the one from whom speech ultimately comes. This opposition in fact goes on corroborating the old metaphysical dichotomy between "pure" phonic and "pure" semantic, which identifies the semantic itself with thinking rather than with speaking. In other words, the Law of the Father—if we want to call it that—concerns the semantic, universal, disciplining, rational side of language, not the communicative and relational side of speech. The Law of the Father deals with the Said, not with Saying. *Saying* [*le Dire*] pertains philogenetically to the figure of the mother—who in fact takes care that speech begins by singing, and who nourishes the infantile ear with the sweetness of music rather than the rigor of concepts.

It is often emphasized that "mother and baby are united by an umbilical cord of sounds."[8] Already in utero, an internal musicality wraps the unborn in the rhythms of the maternal body; it envelops the baby in its sonorous texture. In this sense, the vocalizations between mother and baby, modulated on the play of echo and resonance, would be nothing but a continuation of the intrauterine sonority. Precisely because the mother gives language to the infant, there is no rupture between this music and speech. The lullaby, or the song of words that rocks the baby to sleep with rhythmical movements, is perhaps the clearest example of the absence of such a rupture. In his book *The Songlines*, Bruce Chatwin notes how Aborigine women walk with their children, giving names to things while combining these names into the rhythm of a song that follows the pattern of their footsteps.⁹ In this case, therefore, the singing voice, the heartbeat, the footstep, and nomination are all one. As Maria Zambrano puts it, "the footsteps of man on the earth seem to be the imprint of the sound of his heart, which orders him to walk."¹⁰ An analogous phenomenon can be found in the Muslim and Jewish practice of reading the sacred text aloud while undulating the body back and forth—as if, to paraphrase Carmelo Bene, the movement of the reading restored the original rhythm of the "writing in Voice; Voice as the reanimation of the oral dead [*rigor mortis*] which is writing."¹¹ Speech, in its acoustic essence, has at its heart a rhythmic soul. This means that there is an intrinsic and substantial link between voice and speech, between the rhythmic embodiment of the voice and the expressivity of saying. The maternal figure is precisely the conduit that, in all of our lives, embodies this link—to which, as it were, metaphysics reacts in the name of the father. She is voice *and* speech; or, better, she is the originary sense of the voice insofar as the voice is destined to give speech its essential sense.

Instead of transmitting speech to the infant as something that can be taught and learned—a system, a language—the maternal voice transmits to speech the primary sense of the vocalic, the sonorous self-expression of uniqueness and relation, the self-invocation of embodied singularities through a spontaneous resonance. This resonance, begun by the duet between mother and infant, is not simply music—it is *the* music of speech, the specific mode for which speech sings musically. It is, in other words, the musical way in which the speaker cannot help but communicate him- or herself by invoking and convoking the other. The fact that there does not exist a language without music, without accents or rhythms, depends on this law of resonance that lies at the origin of all communication. Speaking does not have in the voice a mere instrument; rather, it has in the voice the *sense* that was maternally destined to it. Rather than being the irresistible pole of a regression, the scene of infancy is therefore instead the site of an imaginary that gives us an opportunity to rethink the maternal link between speech and voice. The point is not to separate the "pure" voice from speech, but rather to reorient speech toward its vocalic nucleus, stripping away at the same time the armor of the semantic that metaphysics put on it. In the end, it is a question of the imaginary that Echo leaves us— namely, a speech that is stripped of the semantic, a speech that represents itself as a pure voice, and that alludes to the resonance of an infantile voice that is not yet speech, but whose meaning is already destined to resound in the musical sense of saying.

Unlike Echo, however, speakers do not return to the experience of infantile vocalizations that are not intentioned toward speech. What is usually said about language goes for speakers as well: the time of the *origin* is already lost and unrecoverable. In the case of the speaker, this origin is, however, not a muteness or a silence that precedes speech. It is voice, cry, invocation that calls for the duet, a rhythm of reciprocity. It is communication that not only exceeds the register of verbal signifieds, but that is also not reducible to the general system of signs. Neither semantic nor semiotic (in the Aristotelian sense of these terms), vocal communication consists entirely in the uniqueness that is communicated. Paraphrasing Hannah Arendt, we could say that before communicating "merely something—thirst or hunger, affection or hostility or fear," the human voice communicates itself, its uniqueness.[12] Without this communication, the scene of infancy and the relation of the infant with the mother is reduced to a mere semiosis of needs.

As vital as it is for the survival of the infant, communicating something is only a secondary function of a gamut of the communicable that is engendered by this primary self-communication to the other. Symptomatically, this goes for those pragmatic forms of communication in which gesture supplants and accompanies speech, but it goes for verbal communication in the strict sense as well.[13] The relationality of saying, in the proximity of mouths and ears, is a necessary prerequisite for the communication of the Said. As Levinas emphasizes, only platonic metaphysics can postulate as self-sufficient and originary the reality of a Said that does not depend on any act of Saying. However, this Saying, precisely because it is a *saying*—in spite of what Levinas himself claims—implies the voice rather than the gaze. On the plane of speech, the communication of oneself—although not excluding the face to face—is necessarily vocalic. In speech, even in that speech that Aristotle calls logos and defines as *phone semantike*, it is the *phone* that is in play. Logocentrism and the ontology of fictitious entities find in the voice a theme that was always, inevitably destined to confront it.

There are many reasons for rooting an ontology of uniqueness in the phenomenology of the voice, rather than in that of the gaze. It is worth repeating that the main reason is the necessity of adopting a perspective that challenges, in a direct fashion, the logocentric tradition. In other words, what makes the voice a necessary point of intervention now is the strategy of devocalization that accompanies the history of logos from the very beginning. This logos strives to prevent the voice from entering the realm of meaning. In the economy of logos, vocality belong to the horizon of nonsense. Given that the semantic claims to cover the entire territory of meaning, a *phone* that evades its *semantic* function becomes meaningless, irrational—indeed, when reduced to its semiotic function, at best it becomes animal. From the perspective of logos, the vocal ends up being funneled into a nostalgic regression toward nonsense, where the infant and the animal coincide. According to metaphysics, once the voice is taken away from language as a system of signification, it becomes meaningless. This view is obviously a certain interpretation of "signification" that demands, in the name of logos, the entire sphere of meaning. "Signification" implies here the work of a code and the structure of the sign. By the same token, the voice gets trapped in the realm of the semantic or the semiotic as the sonorous articulation of the signified or as a symptom of affection. The result is a voice that remains unthought because it lies outside of the logocentric domain of meaning.

Instead, in my view, the voice pertains to the very generation of meaning—the very meaning that renders logos itself as a system of signification possible. Beyond the visionary dreams of metaphysics, the "linking" [*legare*] in *legein* is at the same time a "speaking," which announces the relation between mouths and ears that logos carries inside of itself from the beginning. By misunderstanding this, the metaphysical tradition has instead focused on a relation among the various elements of a logos that is, above all, a system or a structure. It has focused on a relationality that, in platonic terms, consists in a connection modeled on the order of ideas, a "right joning." However, what is really at issue in speech, in my view, is a vocalic relation that convokes mouths and ears, making the uniqueness of the voices vibrate in their resonance. This resonance, the first matrix of every poetic song, does not exhaust its meaning only in determining the musicality of language. Rather, the meaning of the resonance lies first of all in the vocal relation to which the singular voices are called. In other words, the resonance is musicality in relation; it is the uniqueness of the voice that gives itself in the acoustic link between one voice and another. It is a vocal exchange where the repetition of sound, and all its tonal rhythmic variants, expose uniqueness as an understanding [*un'intesa*] and a reciprocal dependence.

3.3

Logos and Politics

> This concept of speaking, which also lies at the base of the discovery of the
> autonomous force of logos by Greek philosophy, becomes secondary already
> in the experience of the *polis*, and then totally disappears from the tradition
> of political thought.
> —Hannah Arendt, *Was ist Politik?*

Logos is *phone semantike*, says Aristotle who, unlike Plato, insists on
understanding logos above all as speech. The definition, which compares
the human voice with the animal voice, is in the *Poetics*, but it is implicitly
recalled—together with the ever-present comparison with the animal—in
a crucial page of the *Politics*,[1] namely, the passage where having logos—nature's gift given only to humans—confirms the final design of nature herself in making man a *zoon politikon*. That is, rather than a "political animal"
(the usual translation), man is an "animal of the *polis*," just as the bee is an
animal of the apiary. The initial pages of the *Politics* are dedicated to illustrating how the *polis* is a kind of community [*koinonia*] that is proper to
man. By adopting a method that parses the *koinonia politike*—here assumed
to be the final synthesis of the various elements that constitute the community's own articulation—Aristotle begins by analyzing the genesis of the *polis*. Within this genetic analysis, logos does not yet play a crucial role.

According to the Aristotelian doctrine, the *koinonia politike* is the result and at the same time the final goal of a natural process of association.
Man, by nature, "cannot be without others."[2] What makes man a political
animal depends first of all on this ontologically rooted aggregating drive.
Unlike the modern individual, Aristotle's man is neither self-sufficient nor
autonomous. The ontology that concerns him is instead rooted in a state

of dependence. This dependence places man in the first natural form of the *koinonia*—namely, the union of man and woman that forms the family as a locus of generation. Likewise, the community in the larger sense is just as natural as the family, and this community in fact foresees the union of more families in the village. Only the union of more villages into the *polis*, however, constitutes the perfect, self-sufficient *koinonia*—which the whole aggregating process foresees from the start. Man is a *zoon politikon*, Aristotle concludes, because the being-with-others of an animal "that cannot be without others" has its best, most complete form in the *koinonia politike*. This *koinonia politike* does not summarize the individuals one by one, nor does it simply keep them together in some ordered way; rather, it brings the aggregating nature of man as species to full realization and thus allows man to live a happy life. As the organic synthesis of the subordinate forms of unions that constitute it, the *polis* is the final community of natural bonds. The *zoon politikon*, at this point in Aristotle's analysis, is such, even without taking the capacity for speech into consideration.

However, at this point, logos is called on to resolve an embarrassing question. There are certain animals, like bees, whose aggregating drive carries with it organized and complex forms of living together. From a methodological point of view, the problem lies, so to speak, in distinguishing the apiary from the *koinonia politike*. It is here that the human specificity of logos comes into play, as a sort of supplement to the argument that had been conducted up until this point. Animals perceive pleasure and pain and, through the voice, indicate this to one another. "Nature does nothing without a purpose," says Aristotle, and nature has given man speech so that he can express the useful and the harmful, the just and the unjust, the good and the evil.[3] In other words, man can express things that relate directly to the sphere of the *koinonia politike*. And his capacity to signify these things depends in turn on the fact that he has a perception [*aisthesis echein*] of them.[4] Man, therefore, does not make these things common because he communicates them by signifying them. Rather, these things appertain objectively to the community. The just, for example, as Aristotle makes clear, depends on justice as the intrinsic order of the political community.[5] The just belongs to the political community; it is part of its genesis and makes up its natural organization. Man, as a political animal, perceives the just and, through logos, signifies it. But this signifying does not regard things "that are always the same way," as happens with the theoretical sciences that take incontrovertible truth as their object. Rather, this signifying regards things that "are mostly the same way." Politics, like ethics, is a practical science—that is, a science linked to the contingent sphere of action. Acting in the right way implies a knowledge of the just that has a nonnecessary character—a character that is instead probable or opinible. When many people are called on to deliberate on what is just for the *polis*, a space of confrontation and discussion is opened for speech.

Symptomatically, however, in the passage that links the *zoon politikon* and the *zoon logon echon*, the accent does not fall on the communicative function of speech as a privileged medium of public discussion, or an element that is characteristic of democracy. First, according to Aristotle, man is not political because he speaks and thus mobilizes the intrinsic communicativity of language. Rather, man is political because he perceives and speaks of things that belong, per se, to the political community. Generated by a natural process of aggregation, this political community can take many forms—among them democracy. Indeed, through discussion and deliberation, the citizen of the democratic *polis* shows himself to be a *zoon logon echon*—one who knows full well the political role of speech. However, speech is inscribed in the natural state of the *zoon politikon* whether or not it takes place in a democracy.

From the perspective of modern democracies, Aristotle's position appears interesting for many reasons. The most notable of these is the contrast between the communitary substance of the Aristotelian man who, by nature, "cannot be without others" and the absence of natural bonds that characterizes the modern individual as self-sufficient, and thus free or autonomous. The political anthropology of the ancients and the moderns describes, as is well known, two very different theoretical frameworks. The *polis* and the state imply radically different types of ontology. This is demonstrated by the artificial genesis of the state, illustrated by the modern doctrine of natural law—namely, the social contract through which atomized individuals are linked together—which produces at the same time the juridical and procedural form of their union. This union—of which the individualistic ontology is both the presupposition and the result—can only be called *community* if the term is understood in a strictly non-Aristotelian sense. As Roberto Esposito notes, the state manifests the effect of immunity that the *communitas*—as *immunitas*—assumes as its intrinsic possibility. The "immunization project" of modern politics basically consists in thinking individuals as free and autonomous in order to save them from the "contagion of relation."[6] In contrast to what happens in the Aristotelian *koinonia,* modernity erases the natural bond and thinks of individuals as autonomous, isolated, and competitive. No one means anything to anyone else; each is already complete in the self-sufficiency that encloses them in themselves, like a world apart. And thus they are prevented from "recognizing" the other because what is lacking here is precisely the context of community in which each can exist and be recognized.[7] Because they replicate the same, each one is worth *one.* And the community that keeps them together—namely, the state—therefore cannot have its generating principle in the formal and quantitative mechanism of the majority. Modern democracy, as a procedural form that organizes the representative body, is founded on this very principle—that is, a principle totally in keeping with liberal individualism, according to which "the State was supposed to rule over mere individuals, over an atomized society whose very atomization it was called upon to protect."[8] The so-called pathologies of democracy that were the object of much debate in twentieth-century political thought depend on this very logic, which is called on to construct the political bond on the constitutive unbinding that guarantees the autonomy of the individual.

This explains why Aristotle is invoked by those who want—like the "communitarians,"[9] or all the champions of a "communitary ethics, hierarchically modeled on the priority of the collective over and against that of individual rights"[10]—to contest the logic that postulates the originary absence of any bond. And this also explains why a certain Aristotelian influence, amended by Kantian parameters, is also at work in those thinkers who, like Habermas, do not give up on the universality that is inscribed in the modern notion of the individual, but by considering that this individual is suited for the social bond, nevertheless persist in focusing on the political role of speech.

Actually, however, Aristotle's work does not really lend itself well to such an appropriation precisely because it is extraneous to the individualistic ontology that characterizes modernity. Aristotle's work authorizes the recuperation of the community neither through the rubric of identity nor through a linguistic or discursive rubric. And anyway, what is interesting here is not the philological plausibility of a modern use of Aristotle. What matters instead is the relationship—which is already remarkable, but which is symptomatically not really essential—between logos and politics that Aristotle proposes in his work.

According to Aristotle himself, politics as *koinonia politike*—the final and self-sufficient union in which the subaltern unions that compose it are articulated—consists in the full realization of a community bond that is natural. But logos is not what binds them. Logos as speech instead has the function of expressing signifieds that are inherent to the order of this community bond—a bond that is constructed in another way, through the natural process of association. In the exercise of this expression, the communicative dimension of speech is as obvious as it is inessential to the genesis and structure, or the constitution, of the community. In other words, when Aristotle reflects on the general (and generating) principles of politics, although he appreciates the deliberative scene of democracy, he does not think of the community of speakers, nor does he ground politics in the relationality of speaking. Rather, according to Aristotle, political community and speech are in a relation that is guaranteed by the teleological order of nature. Nature, "which does nothing without a purpose," assures the correspondence between the register of logos as the sphere of verbal signification and the register of the aggregating drives that make man a *zoon politikon*. Having been given a signifying voice, man signifies the things that are proper to the political community for which nature destines him. In Aristotle's view, the political nature of logos is thinkable only as an attribute of an animal that is by nature communal. Logos is common, but it does not make the political community. Logos signifies the political community, and is therefore functional to it.

Such signification—while it has specific objects within the sphere of politics, like the just and unjust, good and bad—belongs to language as a general system of signification. According to Aristotle, having logos makes man first of all an animal that signifies everything of which he has perception. And when this perception regards the things of the political community, then logos is revealed to be a fundamental gift of the *zoon politikon*. A certain portion of the semantic, a series of signifieds that concern the community, thus confers to logos a political valence. This obviously does not exclude—on the contrary, it implies—that logos mobilizes its persuasive, argumentative, and communicative power in the political sphere. And yet it does not show that it is precisely this power that renders the *zoon logon echon* an animal that is, as such, political. Unlike the moderns, Aristotle does not have to insist on the coincidence between politics and the communicativity of language—because the community has other foundations. For him, language constitutes a rational sphere wherein men come to understand one another, by perhaps discussing or arguing their opinions; but the political community is not generated by this understanding. The *zoon politikon* rather understands through words because nature assures the objective correspondence between the order of the community and the order of language that expresses its signifieds.

Symptomatically, the logos that reaffirms the communal essence of the political animal in fact subordinates the exercise of Saying to the order of the Said. Men are not political because they speak to one another but rather because they speak of political things. The relationality of speaking becomes a function—expected, but secondary—of signifying. What is important for the *phone semantike* is, precisely, the semantic, or the register of verbal signification as a rationally organized structure. Logos, as Aristotle points out in his "logical" works, is characterized by an objective rationality, by procedures and rules—among which the principle of noncontradiction stands out because it assures the validity of the signifying process. And this goes for both the objects of theoretical knowledge and the objects of practical knowledge, over and beyond the speakers themselves. For Aristotle, as for Plato, the question of the bond between the speakers depends most of all on the firm belief that language binds the speakers to its rules. And it is precisely this feature of Aristotle's thought that turns out to be crucial for the democratic rehabilitation of logos on the part of some modern authors. Even if it does not found the political community on the binding power of these rules, Aristotle's work in fact ends up providing modernity with a linguistic figure of the bond that functions as a remedy for the immunizing pathologies of individualism. The free and equal individuals, who have nothing in common with one another, finally find their community in the communicative rationality of a language that binds them because it binds them to its procedural norms. Language becomes the bond of the unbound. It becomes a universal bond that makes the linguistic community the most suited for constituting a democracy of individuals.

"Wherever the relevance of speech is at stake," writes Arendt, "matters become political by definition, for speech is what makes man a political being."[11] This sentence appears in the introduction to *The Human Condition*—a work that, according to Jürgen Habermas, not only reveals Arendt's sympathy for Aristotle but moreover supports Habermas himself in the notion that democracy finds its most genuine principle in language as an intersubjective medium of communication, an act that regulates public discussion and produces understanding.[12] Insofar as language is characterized by a rationality that is normative (or universal) for all those who are bound to it, language constitutes the bond between individuals as members of the "ideal linguistic community."[13] However, if one reads Arendt's text, one discovers that it develops a line of thinking that is quite far from the Aristotelian conception of the *zoon logon echon*, as well as from the Habermasian notion of communicative rationality. For Arendt, what makes speech political is not signification, expression, or the communication of something, even if that "something" is the just, the useful, the good, or the bad. Rather, the political essence of speech consists in revealing to others the uniqueness of each speaker. It should be pointed out that this is not a vocalic uniqueness—not because the voice does not reveal uniqueness in Arendt's view, but because it is, according to her, speech that qualifies this self-revelation as political. What Arendt calls "political" is in fact a space that is materially shared, whereupon those present show to one another, in words and deeds, their uniqueness and their capacity to begin new things. Although it already appears "in the unique shape of the body and sound of the voice," uniqueness assumes a political status only through the words and deeds of those who, in this way, actively show their uniqueness to one another.[14] The political sphere is generated precisely by this sharing of words and deeds that Arendt puts under the name of action.

This sharing is the political form of a bond that is inscribed in the ontological condition that makes human beings a "paradoxical plurality of unique beings."[15] The essential difference between men and animals— about which Aristotle cared so much—for Arendt, before having to do with language, has to do with this plural, and therefore relational, ontology of uniqueness. Every human being is unique, different, distinct from every other: "But only man can express this distinction and distinguish himself, and only he can communicate himself and not merely something—thirst or hunger, affection or hostility or fear."[16] Political action essentially coincides with this expression and communication of oneself, through words and deeds, which allow each one, already physically distinct, to distinguish him- or herself actively, and therefore politically, from every other. By founding politics on the ontology of plurality, Arendt understands politics as "the practice through which each human being gives meaning to his or her existence, and redeems the naturalness of human-kind by affirming his or her singularity."[17] With respect to Aristotle, therefore, the conceptual framework changes radically. The celebrated confrontation in Aristotle between the animal voice, which is a sign of an affective state, and the human voice, which instead expresses a mental signified, is not at all determinant of the political sphere for Arendt. According to her, speech—even when it is understood as *phone semantike*—does not become political by way of the things of the community that speech is able to designate. Rather, speech becomes political on account of the self-revelation of speakers who express and communicate their uniqueness through speaking—no matter the specific content of what is said. The political valence of signifying is thus shifted from speech—and from language as a system of signification—to the speaker. The speakers are not political because of what they say, but because they say it to others who share an interactive space of reciprocal exposure. To speak to one another is to communicate to one another the unrepeatable uniqueness of each speaker.

According to Arendt, speech falls under the political name of action. It is an act. As with Levinas, Arendt is interested in Saying and not the Said—and in a Saying that is a "speaking to someone," whose sense lies in communicating the speakers to one another.[18] What is at stake, therefore, is that Saying of everyone and no one that we call language. Put differently, Arendt is interested in the relationality of the act of speaking, not in speech as a system of signification characterized by objective rules that bring the speakers to an understanding. As Ireneo Funes understood, this system functions because of its generalizing power, which captures the contingency of the particular in the universal web of the semantic. Under the regime of the name as a universalistic system of the Said, the plurality of unique human beings becomes "man." But as Arendt notes with wise ingenuity, on this earth and in the world live men, not man.[19] "Man"—a name in language—is an abstraction that creates a disembodied and fictitious entity; it makes of plurality a faceless one, without biography. And this, obviously, does not change—indeed, it gets worse—when in modernity the term *man* gets replaced by the name "individual" or "subject."

As a fictitious entity of the ancient philosophical vocabulary, man inaugurates a tradition in which the plurality of unique beings appears from the beginning as an insignificant and superfluous given. This is even true for Aristotle's "man," "who cannot be without others." For at stake is "man" as a species, a universal substance modeled on the paradigm of the free, male adult—whose community is generated, tellingly, by a union between man and woman that gets configured as a hierarchy. In the first phase of the associative process—that is, in the family—the others, without whom the Aristotelian man "cannot be," are "by nature" subordinated to him. The *zoon politikon*, as Arendt would say, is founded on a clamorous falsification of the plural and antihierarchical matrix of politics. In *Was ist Politik?*—an incomplete text that testifies to her complex relation to Aristotle—Arendt in fact emphasizes that "Man is apolitical. Politics is born *among* men, and is therefore decidedly *outside* Man."[20] Because "Man" assumes and neutralizes the plurality of all men (and, what's more, excludes and subordinates women), it cannot be political because, in this horizon, there is no plurality and thus no relation. In the economy of the One—mirror image of the economy of the Same—there is no *in between*, no common space to share.[21] What the western tradition calls politics is in truth a model of depoliticization that, starting with Aristotle, excludes the plural and relational foundation of politics. According to Arendt, even the modern form of democracy falls under the rubric of this depoliticization, for this continues within the economy of the One, through a notion of the "individual" that is "more or less equivalent to the Same."[22] The basic lexicon of equality, while allowing for a pluralism of opinions and political parties that represent them, denies plurality—and therefore politics.

The Arendtian horizon of plurality, in fact, should not be confused with the pluralism invoked by contemporary thinkers who defend freedom of expression, or with respect for difference in multicultural and multiethnic societies. The recognition of the pluralistic instance—through which the abstract universality of democracy is opened to the concrete reality of differences—does not get rid of the ontology of the individual. Rather, it tries to reconcile the individual with the various group identities or affiliations into which the individual finds itself historically dropped. The Habermasian notion of logos as communicative rationality—characterized by objective and universally valid norms that assure understanding among the individuals of a pluralistic society—is part of this same logic. This logic is, in short, completely extraneous to the Arendtian notion of plurality. For Arendt, plurality has nothing to do with the theme of pluralism, which arises from the question of communitarian identities. Arendt's plurality is, first of all, a character of the human condition, the incontrovertible fact of an elementary ontology, or, perhaps, a radical phenomenology. Every human being appears to others and thus is different from "anyone else who ever lived, lives or will live."[23] From birth, which announces the human being as a new beginning, everyone shows him- or herself to be unique. This is what men have in common: uniqueness in plurality, or the uniqueness that makes them plural and the plurality that makes them unique. As the greatest sphere of activity in which men communicate and distinguish themselves, politics is called on to respond to this plural status. Therefore, it is not the pluralism of opinions—nor, much less, is it the pluralism of cultural identities—that qualify this interactive sphere as politics. If anything, for Arendt, the pluralism of opinions functions as an indirect proof of a plurality of unique beings that is translated into a multiperspective disposition of their worldview. In other words, for Arendt the political lies entirely in the relational space between human beings who are unique and therefore plural. The faculty of speech is political because by speaking to one another in a relational space and communciating themselves, men at the same time communicate the political nature of this space. What they communicate—contents, signifieds, values—might be congruent with this space, but however it is secondary with respect to the political act of speaking. It is in fact the relational plurality of the unique beings that constitutes the criterion on which the congruence of "what gets communicated" can be judged. The dominance of a single thought, typical of totalitarian regimes for example, is in keeping with a mass society where the negation of plurality, or the reduction of all men to a single Man, is borne out by the existence of a single perspective.[24] The very same criterion allows the pluralism of opinions to be considered as a positive sign—but it is only a sign, not a foundation of the political. The political, the exclusively human sphere of the world, consists in the "in-between," in what relates and separates men at the same time, revealing their plural condition.[25]

In claiming that it is "language that makes man a political being," Arendt, on the one hand, radically changes the meaning of Aristotle's sentence, and on the other hand, focuses her analysis on a political notion of communication that has very few points in common with the communicative rationality of a Habermasian sort. Far from emphasizing language's normative valence, its rationality, its universality, its orientation toward understanding, Arendt in fact insists on a "concept of speaking" in which the relational and contextual act of self-communication comes to the fore. The bond is precisely this self-communication that, by actively linking the unique beings who are already ontologically bound, shows them as who they are to each other. In other words, the bond consists in a reciprocal exhibition that finds its active (and thus political) medium in speech. The Said becomes secondary—whether as specific content (what gets said), or as a structure (the system of signification that regulates what gets said).

And Saying becomes the privileged realm of a reciprocal self-communication, which simultaneously expresses uniqueness and relation. Significantly, those who communicate themselves in this way are not individuals. They are unique beings in flesh and bone who, unlike the abstract and universal "individual," have a face, a name, and a life story. Unrepeatable and different from every other, they communicate the uniqueness of their own personal identity; they communicate reciprocally who they are. Because it is abstract and fictitious, on the other hand, the modern individual is incommunicable. In the horizon of communicative rationality, it is in fact language itself that communicates itself, by binding the speakers to its rules. In other words, discursive democracy risks focusing too much on a language—guaranteed by understanding and rational norms—of which the speakers are nothing but a function. In this sense, democracy becomes a product of language, and the linguistic bond between individuals becomes the communitary essence of democracy.

It is worth noting that although Arendt is the first to denounce the traditional subjection of politics to the principle of *theoria*, she is not alone in conceiving politics in terms of an ontology that insists on a plurality of unique existents in relation to one another.[26] One finds a similar position today in the speculative thought of Jean-Luc Nancy. In his lexicon, which derives the name and concept of plurality from Arendt, uniqueness becomes "singularity" and relation becomes "knot." To "democracy's empty truth and subjectivity's excessive sense," he opposes a "politics of incessant tying-up of singularities with each other, over each other, and through each other, without any *end* other than the enchainment of (k)nots."[27] Such a politics consists, "first of all, in testifying that there is singularity only where singularity ties itself up with other singularities."[28] This is, therefore, a politics that coincides immediately with the ontological constitution of the being-in-common of singular existents: because "the singular is primarily *each* one and, therefore, also *with* and *among* all the others. The singular is a plural."[29] The singular implies the plural because it is constituted in relation: "being-in-common means that singular beings are, are presented, appear only insofar as they appear together (*cum*), are exposed, presented and offered to one another."[30] The political, for Nancy, corresponds precisely to the *in* of this being in common. Favoring, particularly in less recent works, the term *community*, he in fact grounds politics in the *with*, the *among*, the *in*—which corresponds in Arendt's lexicon to the in-between—that is, in any particle that alludes to the original, onto-logical relation inscribed in the plurality of singular beings. Politics is the bond—a bond inscribed in the ontological status of singularity, insofar as this implies plurality and relation. These three categories of uniqueness, plurality, and relation—which generate each other—determine the coin-cidence of ontology and politics.

For Nancy, this coincidence is absolute. Unlike what happens in Arendt, there is no difference between ontology and politics. Politics con-sists immediately in the given relation of the ontological condition. In other words, politics is already, right away, everywhere the existence of sin-gular beings who are tied to one another. And it is not just politics, in Nancy's texts, that gets flattened into ontology. Each disciplinary sphere—including the ethical, the political, and the aesthetic—is in fact reduced to a variation that articulates in different ways the ontological theme of the knot. The question that draws in the various disciplinary horizons is pre-cisely the *among* and the *with* of a singularity that is a plurality, or, to put it in Arendtian terms, it is the in-betweeness that "relates and separates men at the same time."[31] Existence, writes Nancy, "*is*, only if it is shared." What binds us together, the political or the community, is the same thing that shares us. It shares us, and at the same time, it shares itself. Sympto-matically, this is also true of logos.

As Heraclitus understood, logos is common. Glossing a famous verse of Holderlin's—"since we are a dialogue"—Nancy explains that we are our dialogue: "we are this between-us, that is language, and reciprocally, lan-guage is the between-us."[32] Language "itself is the insubstantial tie" where the meaning of the spoken words is only a secondary and consequent effect of the tie itself, insofar as it is the original meaning.[33] In other words, it is the knot of speech, the fact that we are our dialogue, the between-us of lan-guage, which makes meaning. Every other meaning, every other process of signification, presupposes this meaning. Like Levinas and Arendt, Nancy therefore privileges the relationality of Saying instead of the universal hori-zon of the Said. He thus claims that the event of politics "could be called the seizure of speech [*prise de parole*]," which should not be understood as either a democratic principle of free speech, or as a plurality of "multiple wills competing to define a Sense."[34] It is, in fact, the singular entry—al-ways singular precisely because it is spoken by someone—into the con-catenation of speech, into the *legein* or bond. This concatenation is indis-soluble, reticular, infinitely interrupted, and tied again. It tends toward the

most naked function of language, toward what one calls its phatic function—the maintenance of a relation that communicates no other meaning
than the relation itself.[35]

Nancy's *prise de parole* thus seems to lead toward the vocal. Although
it does not thematize the voice directly, the phatic function of language alludes to an acoustic sphere where the relationality of the voice cannot help
being heard. Moreover, Nancy's interest in the voice is explicit elsewhere,
particularly in his essay "Sharing Voices" [*La partage des voix*] cited earlier.
In that text we read that meaning is a sharing of logos and that "we are the
meaning of the sharing of our voices."[36] Although he emphasizes that these
voices are singular and valuable precisely because of this singularity, Nancy
still does not problematize the uniqueness of their sound or the material
relationality of the acoustic sphere. Rather, he is interested in rejecting logos as an abstract system of signification. He understands logos instead as
a sharing "which brings us together only by splitting us."[37] In a certain
sense, therefore, the voice stands as a metaphor for the uniqueness of the
speaker, for the singularity of his announcement that "we are a dialogue."
Obviously, this does not contradict the fact that each speaker has a unique
voice, but it still ends up considering this vocal uniqueness as a given that
does not merit further speculation. For what Nancy really cares about is a
community that "remains to be thought according to the sharing of *logos*."[38] As yet another figure for the "knot," logos is political because it
binds us and splits us, it shares us, it is shared.

For Nancy, there is not so much a relation between logos and politics—rather, there is a coincidence between them, as with all figures for the
knot. Nancy is convinced that—as Giorgio Agamben puts it—"every ontology implies a politics."[39] And so Nancy works against the individualistic ontology of modernity by contrasting it with the ontology of the knot
that finds in logos one of its many figures. The immediate political nature
of this knot, however, ends up denying a proper sphere to politics. The result is a community that, because of its coincidence with ontology, extends
as far as the human condition of plural singularity—namely, everywhere
and anytime. Although the modern state, which is founded on the ontology of the unbound individual, must mobilize its resources in order to recuperate this bond, the ontology of bound (tied, knotted) singularities that
Nancy seems to evoke need spend no resource in order to cut out a specific
space for politics. Even the classical relation between logos and politics
loses its tension here. For politics is the tying up of plural singularities—

the very knot that is represented in the phatic function of language that ties the speakers to one another.

In spite of her common interest in a relational ontology of uniqueness, Arendt's position is rather different. For her, the political sphere of action is clearly distinct from the ontological state of plural uniqueness of which action itself, as interaction, is both consequence and response. Ontology and politics are in a necessary relation, but they are not the same thing; they do not coincide. By the same token, in Arendt's horizon, only in the public sphere of plural action does the relation configure itself in terms of power. This power—in Greek *dynamis*, and in Latin *potentia*— has a "potential" character: "Wherever people gather together, it is potentially there, but only potentially, not necessarily and not forever."[40] Power is generated by interaction, and exists only when actualized. It lasts as long as the time and space of the active relation. It cannot be accumulated; when plural action ceases, power dissolves. Thus, the realm of politics, unlike that of ontology, has constitutive characters of intermittence. In other words, all human beings are unique, but only when and while they interact with words and deeds can they communicate to one another this uniqueness. Without such communication, without action in a shared space of reciprocal exhibition, uniqueness remains a mere ontological given—the given of an ontology that is not able to make itself political.

3.4

The Reciprocal Communication
of Voices

> The question of knowing what is understood by the word "political," and if
> the borders of this concept still today resist analysis, remains an open question.
> —Jacques Derrida, *Adieu to Emmanuel Levinas*

It is language that makes man a political being. For Arendt, this sense allows for a radical rethinking of the classical relation between politics and speech. Having lost its general substance as a species, man is in fact now presented as the embodied singularity of a unique being. The ontology that regards him requires plurality and relation. By communicating this plural relationality on an interactive scene, speech shifts the plane of ontology to that of politics. The specificity of the political sphere is constituted through speech. And speech in turn, is an act that falls together with nonverbal actions under the category of action. It is the act of speaking to one another, rather than language. It is the act with which some unique beings do not simply signify something, but rather communicate to one another who they are. Arendt's homage to Aristotle's *Politics*, however explicit it may be, is therefore not as faithful as it might appear. Indeed, her innovation with regard to Aristotle leads to an unusual question—although it is not as bizarre as it might at first seem: this question asks if, in the political horizon that entrusts uniqueness to speech, the voice can finally cut a role out for itself.

As for the reciprocal communication of speech, nothing in fact communicates uniqueness more than the voice. This happens not only in speech, and even earlier in the infantile vocalizations that precede and inaugurate speech, but above all in the relational resonance that the musicality of every (living) language preserves. From a vocal perspective, the reciprocal communication of the speakers lies in the symphony of a double relationality. One regards the uniqueness of a voice that is for the ear; the other resounds in the musicality of language itself. Both have a physical, corporeal substance. The logos that is shared in the voices—if we want to use Nancy's lexicon—is a logos that vibrates in throats of flesh. In this sense, the distinction between the semantic and the vocalic alludes to the ineludible bond between the universality of a linguistic register, which organizes the disembodied substance of signifieds, and the particularity of an embodied existence, who makes herself heard in voice. Speech—voice and signified, rather than signifying voice—bridges these two shores. Even when it begins to communicate something, obeying the universal codes of language, it still communicates singular voices and, at the same time, the rhythmic cadence of a resonance that links these voices.

Because they are sensitive to the semantic side of speech, and thus to the phonological side rather than the phonic, philosophers and linguists agree that the first organizing cell of language lies in the sentence [*frase*]. Logos, in its minimal form, joins a noun and a verb. It joins them according to a certain disposition, apparently indifferent to the driving cadences of the vocalic. In the sentence, very different rules from the horizontal reciprocity of resonance hold sway. The sentence, as Roland Barthes notes, "is hierarchical: it implies subjections, subordinations, and internal regencies."[1] It is a disciplined and disciplining structure that, not by chance, finds precise correspondences in the way in which the tradition thinks politics. Politics and language also have this connection, lucidly investigated by Michel Foucault in all its multiple aspects and nicely synthesized by Deleuze when he notes that "a grammatical rule is a countersign of power, before being a countersign of syntax."[2] It is enough to think how Plato edifies the *polis* according to the principle of "right joinings" founded on the ideas, and operative in the sentence as the minimal form of *legein*, in order to be convinced of the constitutive nexus between language and politics. By joining nouns and verbs, the sentence places them according to an impersonal, objective hierarchical order that coincides with the principle of discipline to which politics, traditionally, aspires. It is precisely in this context that the sphere of vocality can again gain a politically subversive role. As voice, notes Barthes, speech reveals language to be "the grain of the throat, the patina of the consonants, the guttural vowel, a stereophony of the flesh: the articulation of the body or the tongue, not of meaning or language."[3] For Barthes, this means that the drives of the body, of which the voice is an expression, makes the voice ideal for subverting the order of language and thus of politics.

Like Kristeva and Cixous, when he deals with the vocalic, Barthes insists on pleasure as a prelogical and antilogical site where, together with language, even the linguistically produced and politically functional reality of the individual and the subject gets dissolved. By way of its subversion of the normative system of language, vocalic pleasure is above all understood as the register of a desubjectivized, deindividualized body that disorganizes the system of the "I." As methodologically obvious as this may be, the result is phenomenologically surprising: the most proper character of the corporeality of the voice is overlooked—namely, that of being the voice of a singular body. Understanding pleasure as the site of the individual's or the subject's dissolution—if not of the political order on which they are founded—thus ends up paying yet another homage to the binary economy of metaphysics. For this economy not only seeks to subordinate the voice to the signified and the body to the mind, but above all, it prohibits the voice from making itself heard as the corporeal communication of uniqueness. In other words, in the devocalization of logos that accompanies the history of metaphysics, the repression of vocal pleasure is above all a repression of the pleasure that characterizes resonance as the primary, spontaneous rhythm and drive of the reciprocal communication of unique voices. It is, simply put, the repression of the echo. The system that is constructed on the disembodied rationality of the semantic not only fears the voice because it is bodily, obscurely carnal, sensuous, passionate. It fears the voice above all, because the voice requires speech in order to make itself the carrier of an embodied and musically relational uniqueness that speech itself, as an element of a universal code of signification, would rather ignore, if not expel. In the struggle of semantic rationality against vocalic pleasure—of which certain contemporary strategies risk being merely the reversal—what is really at stake is the uniqueness-in-resonance.

A radical rethinking of the classical relation between speech and politics must therefore begin from an awareness of these stakes. There are many symptoms, so to speak, that encourage such an undertaking. Because it is inherent to speech in a tradition that understands politics as logocentric, the voice has a political—or, better, antipolitical—power that certain philosophers could not help but point out. Plato's hostility toward

Homer because of his song, because of the power of the acoustic sphere, is a good example—indeed, hardly by chance. The order of the *polis*, described in the *Republic*, rejects the vocal as politically dangerous, destabilizing, and subversive. The position of those who, in recent times, valorize the destabilizing function of vocalic pleasure with respect to the disciplining effects of language is analogous, even if it is the "reverse" of Plato. And yet it is worth repeating: what really matters now is not how to think a politics of pleasure that breaks down the relation between politics and speech, but rather how to think a politics that does not continue to expunge the vocal from the realm of speech. One could call it a politics of Saying where the uniqueness of each speaker makes itself heard as a plurality of voices that are already linked to one another in resonance. Rather than simply mobilizing the destabilizing power of pleasure, resonance in fact alludes to the musicality of a reciprocal communication that, from the very first cry, tastes the pleasure that lies in the vocal sphere of relation. This does not mean that this pleasure does not stand in contrast to the rigidity of the codes that organize the system of language. Nor does it mean that speech, because of its association with this system, must be sacrificed on the "liberating" altar of pure pleasure.

The revaluation of the vocalic that I am here proposing, although it has good reasons for opposing itself to the history of political logocentrism, does not aspire to a definitive liberation from politics, but rather posits a different way of thinking the relation between politics and speech. In a certain sense, it is simply a matter of focusing on speech from its vocal site. Listening to its vocalic matrix, Saying shows that it consists in a reciprocal communication of unique voices, whose relational nature is utterly unconcerned with the Said's tendency to dominate. As Arendt invites us to consider, the question lies precisely in thinking the elementary criterion of a politics that valorizes the relationality of the unique beings that manifest themselves actively through speech, leaving aside the imperialism of the Said. The voice not only announces this relation, but it announces it as corporeal, material, and rooted in the always embodied singularity of an existent that convokes the other with the rhythmic and sonorous breath of his or her mouth. Actively and reciprocally communicating their uniqueness, the speakers above all make heard a mutual dependence on a voice that is invocation, no longer autonomous or self-sufficient individuals in search of something that binds them, but already "tied" (to use Nancy's term) by an acoustic dialogue that takes its cadences from the very rhythm of breath. Their logos is oriented toward resonance, rather than toward understanding. Like a kind of song "for more than one voice" [*come una specie di canto a più voci*] whose melodic principle is the reciprocal distinction of the unmistakable timbre of each—or, better, as if a song of this kind were the ideal dimension, the transcendental principle, of politics.

The modern state has a song all its own: the national anthem. In this song, the individuals are not called to distinguish themselves; nor, even less, are they called to distinguish themselves as voices. Rather, they are called on to lose themselves in it. The national anthem, as its name says, regards the "nation" more than the state. The nation, indeed, constitutes the other face of the state; they are conflated in the problematic, if not contradictory, figure of the nation-state. This contradiction is already clear from the foundational moment of the first modern state, when the French revolution combines the declaration of the rights of man (or the individual, understood to be universal), with the proclamation of national sovereignty that makes the (male) citizens of France entitled to these rights. Beyond the sexual discrimination, the contradiction of the nation-state is thus first inscribed in a logic that claims to reconcile universality with territoriality. The decisive side of the problem lies precisely in the question of territory. The modern state is a territorial state. This contradiction not only stands in contrast with the principle according to which the individual, any human being regardless of nationality, is entitled to the "rights of man"— but, moreover, it makes territoriality decisive, leading modern political doctrine to produce a double meaning. Understood in the juridical and administrative terms whereby, according to Arendt, the legal order produced by the state is "open to all who happen to live on its territory"—territory in fact superimposes itself on the idea of a homeland that unites all those who belong to the same land in a common national identity.[4] The etymology of the term *nation*—which derives from the Latin verb *nascor*—evokes the identificatory bond of the "natives" on their own land; that is, "it is attached to the soil which is the product of past labor and where history has left its traces."[5] As the ideological matrix of all nationalisms and their excesses, the nation is thus presented as the "main factor of a precarious equilibrium between a centralized State and an atomized society, the only efficient link between the individuals and the national State."[6] The state, which sees individuals as unbound to each other, leaves the task of binding them to the nation. According to a contradictory logic, which is however quite intrinsic to modernity, the warm bond of the mystique of the nation corrects the cold juridical, procedural, rational bond of the state.

The national anthem carries the fusing heat of this bond. The words of the anthem, which often deal with the struggle from which the nation originates, are moreover dedicated to exalting the historical roots of the homeland and to emphasizing continuity, homogeneity, and shared values. What counts the most is not the words, which are usually ridiculous or rhetorical, but rather the fusion of individuals in the song that symbolizes their union. The song of the nation is lifted by a people who sing in unison.

Nothing in the age of globalization has a more nostalgic or reactionary feel than this song. The contemporary scenarios of politics that now go by the name of globalization in fact propose a postnational constellation. This means, among other things, that rethinking politics is today an unavoidable and yet difficult undertaking. Not only the national anthem, but its entire emotional and conceptual apparatus, which belongs to the historical unfolding of modernity, take on the aura of a past from which the present time constitutes a definitive break. In the light of this break, nation and people, state and individual, appear as concepts of an obsolete political lexicon. Moreover, it is symptomatic that the various indices of this crisis have to do with the question of territory. Clearly, the phenomenon of globalization is in fact presented as a deterritorialization of the cartographic state, and the map of nations. "Territoriality is fast becoming an anachronistic delimitation of material functions and cultural identities," notes Seyla Benhabib.[7] Obviously, this does not mean that states and nations have disappeared, but it suggests that the contradictory model of the nation-state no longer provides the conceptual horizon that defines the political problem of the bond.

Global is, not by chance, a neologism from the perspective of the traditional language of politics. This new term pertains to an era of transition whose formulas already judge the categories of modernity from a postnational perspective. In contemporary debates, "global" is not contrasted to "territory," but rather to "local." This concerns the well-known, apparently paradoxical, phenomenon of the so-called glocal: the globalization of the market and technologies sees a resurrection of identity localism that appeals to ethnic and religious communities. Nationalism, fragmenting and rearticulating itself in more "original" spheres of belonging, takes on another face and gives itself over to instances of fundamentalism. The identity that is denied by the deterritorializing process of the global is thus rediscovered in a mythologization of the territorial history of local communities that are antistate or antimodern: pockets of identity that assert their identity in an exclusive way, through ethnic cleansing and so forth. Globalization and localization, through a double movement of inclusion and exclusion, therefore seem to work together for the definitive liquidation of the state, the first by frustrating the territorial cartography of sovereignty and the second by exalting the territorial roots of a community identity that breaks with the nation-state.

Disturbed by the resurgence of strict tribal nationalisms in the pincers of the glocal, the present crisis thus imposes the difficult task of thinking political categories that pass over the threshold of modernity. In contemporary debates, this task is often configured as an effort to take democracy beyond the historical destiny of the nation-state. At bottom, the hypothesis is that the universal and rational "individual," as the basic element of the democratic model, not only constitutes an unquestionable value, but is moreover methodologically separable from the state and its unforeseen decline. Precisely because it is pervasive, decentered, and deterritorialized, globalization offers an opportunity to think a planetary democracy whose universality is no longer bound by the territorial borders of the nation. This not only allows the ontology of modernity to preserve its individualistic grammar in a postnational world—and, indeed, to realize the universal rights of man without having to entrust these rights to the nation—but it also acts as a stimulus for a definitive valorization of the discursive aspect of democracy. In this theoretical horizon, the Habermasian perspective, which insists on the communicative rationality of the democratic paradigm, looks like the most coherent thesis. Having already been called on to resolve the problem of the political bond in the state framework of modernity, logos again presents itself as the political bond of a planetary democracy, claiming to be an essential medium, capable of orienting the conflicting identities that characterize the era of globalization toward understanding. As the guarantor of essential democratic principles and its discursive practices, the ideal linguistic community separates its fate from that of the state.

There are a number of understandable reasons for this appeal to the values of democracy and to the politics of speech, which react to the crisis of modernity by trying to join globalism and universalism. And yet precisely this insistence on the unquestionability of universal (sharable) values shows that within this theoretical horizon, the categories of modernity still anchor the nucleus of the project. And this constitutes a serious limit, if not a contradiction. The present challenge of globalization in fact calls for a more radical theoretical effort. In order to respond to this challenge, it not only appears necessary to extend the crisis of modernity, without exceptions, to all of its categories, but also to strive to rethink politics, starting with a radical rethinking of ontology and thus of the paradigmatic relation between speech and politics.

In the era of globalization, there is, in effect, an antimodern possibility of revaluing—in a democratic sense—the political role of speech, a possibility that contemporary debates should today try to fully exploit in all of its radical potential. The task is to bring about a revolutionary perspective—or, rather, to challenge the identificatory pretenses of the local, rather than counting on the universalizing promises of the global. The phenomenon of deterritorialization, beyond liquidating the nation-state, in fact allows for an elaboration of the concept of a local without territory. Although it is apparently unusual, a concept of this sort can be traced back to Arendt's reflections on the territorial inconsistency of the political space. Indeed, at stake is the basic principle of politics that Arendt understands as interaction and the sharing of a common space that is generated by interaction itself. The in-between regards a space, not a territory. Politics takes place, but it is not a place.

"Wherever you go, you will be a *polis*," says Arendt, citing a famous sentence that bears witness, according to her, to the way in which for the Greeks the political consists in a space created by acting and speaking together "which can find its proper location almost any time and anywhere."[8] The *polis*, according to Arendt, is not physically situated in a territory. It is the space of interaction that is opened by the reciprocal communication of those present through words and deeds. In the era of globalization—which seems to require neologisms in order to withstand the collapse of the modern political lexicon—this interactive space could therefore be called an absolute local [*locale assoluto*], "absolute" because freed of the territoriality of place and from every dimension that roots it in a continuity. The absolute local is thus the name of a taking-place of politics that has no predefined borders, nor any fixed or sacred confines. It is not a nation, nor a fatherland, nor a land. It extends as far as the interactive space that is generated by reciprocal communication. It is a relational space that happens with the event of this communication and, together with it, disappears. The place and the duration are contingent and unforeseeable.

The horizon of the absolute local is not the direct consequence of the global, but rather an opening that globalization, as an extraterritorial and deterritorializing force, allows. In other words, once the cartography of states that makes of the world a coherent system has been taken away, and once the topographic parameters that make of the world a geography of borders has imploded, the world finally presents itself as a space available for the contextual and contingent insurgence of the absolute local. Because it is without communal substance, and because it is not bound to territory, the local can now take place in any place. This means that the local—like Nancy's "knot"—is immediately anywhere—almost as if it were a global condition of human plurality that, of itself, is a political community. The absolute local is there, and only there, where in any part of the globe, some human beings actively and reciprocally communicate their uniqueness and show this uniqueness as the material given that constitutes the contextuality of their relation. As Arendt would say, the local is a relational space that does not concern what those who share it are, but rather who they are.

The politics of the local, having finally been liberated from the cartography of nations and the individualist ontology, in fact avoids imposing cultural identities on the unrepeatable uniqueness of every human being. Because it is faithful to the ontology of plurality, the local puts in play uniqueness without belongings and entrusts the sense of the relation to this alone. And this, in addition to evoking a passivity, implies first of all the preliminary activity of stripping ourselves of our western, eastern, Christian, Muslim, Jew, gay, straight, poor, rich, ignorant, learned, cynical, sad, happy—or even guilty or innocent—being. Indeed, the politics of the absolute local includes as a preliminary act the deconstruction of belongings, the marginalization of qualities, and the depoliticization of the what. What remains, because it was always there, is the question "who are you?" addressed to the "you who are here." This local, contextual space—which can be actively inaugurated anyway—is opened by this question in which the regulative principle of politics already resounds—namely, the priority of the who with respect to the what.

In spite of appearances, this is not a utopian politics, nor is it an ethics of good will. Rather, it is a position that, taking inspiration from Arendt's thought, finds the generative and symbolic nucleus of politics in the ontology of plural uniqueness and relation. This position of mine is also supported by the thought of sexual difference, which is elaborated—and practiced—by the predominant stream of Italian feminism. As their work shows, Italian feminists focus most of all on the relational matrix of politics and on the desire for symbolic existence that, in the "relation among women," every woman puts in play "starting with herself" [*partire da sé*]. Beyond such formulas—which belong to a feminist idiom that derives from the lexical formalization of a theory that is never disconnected from political practices—the affinities with the Arendtian horizon are notable and, moreover, hardly casual. According to Ida Dominijanni, one of the more lucid minds of the thought of sexual difference, it is precisely Arendt who occupies the primary position in "a feminine genealogy that traverses the century, keeping the thread of the relation between politics and language in hand."[9] Symptomatically, the essay from which this citation is taken is called "Speech is Our Politics" ["*La parola è nostra politica*"]. Speech here is not understood as the Said, or a codified system of language, but rather as that which alludes to the contextual and material sphere of Saying. In other words, the speech that is politics explicitly stands in opposition to the universal abstractions of the semantic and its disciplining valence; this speech emphasizes the corporeal roots of the very practice of speaking, along with the embodied existence as she is communicated in speech. Italian feminism responds to the binary economy of the patriarchal order—which catalogs man in the sphere of thought and women in the sphere of the body—by making speech the reciprocal communication of women in flesh and bone who communicate themselves contextually "starting with themselves." It is thus not a communal belonging—in the sense of identity politics—to the feminine sex that determines the political quality of this communication. It is not Woman, which is just as fictitious as Man, which is here expressed and represented. Rather, this politics consists in the relational context or, better, the absolute local where reciprocal speech signifies the sexed uniqueness of each speaker in spite of patriarchal prohibitions—even before signifying something.

This speech is not only voice, but precisely in the voice it is already given as that embodied uniqueness that the metaphysical ear does not want to hear. Arendt's view, along with that of Italian feminism, significantly allows for the opening of a theoretical horizon in which the relational valence of speech finally makes itself heard as voice. The advantages of this opening of the vocalic sphere are evident. By rooting speech immediately in the body, which is the voice's source and chamber of resonance, the vocal first of all situates the act of reciprocal communication over and against a universal conception of language that turns the speakers into fictitious entities. As Rosenzweig knew well, this goes for whoever speaks, no matter their sex. But it goes all the more for women, because their sex is traditionally represented under the sign of a body that only comes to speech through idle chatter. On closer inspection, there is a subtle plot between the stereotype of the idle chatterer who gets silenced, and the woman who is pure voice without speech. There is a sort of affinity between the nymph Echo's fate and the wife whose husband forces her to keep silent.[10] It would seem that these female figures have in common the fact that they are denied access to the rational universality of a language reserved only for the male subject. The binary economy of the patriarchal symbolic order would be, in this sense, rather simple: on the one hand, the body and the voice, and on the other, the mind and speech. However, the framework is anything but simple, for speech, *phone semantike*, cannot help but reduplicate within itself the dichotomy that splits it into vocalic and semantic. Through the corporeality of the voice, the feminine is thus reinsinuated in the register of masculine speech. In other words, speech— whether understood as signifying voice or as vocalized signified—is sexually ambiguous, from the perspective of the patriarchal ideology. Although the semantic guarantees to speech a rationality that is privileged by man, the vocal keeps speech rooted in the body, which is assigned to woman. The devocalization of logos aims to eliminate this very ambiguity by leaving the feminine figures to embody what remains—namely, the voice.

For a radical rethinking of the classical connection between speech and politics, especially from a feminist perspective, recuperating the theme of the voice is therefore an obligatory strategic gesture. It is not a matter of feminizing politics; nor is it a question of making politics coincide with the pure voice by insisting on the subversive power of vocal pleasure. Rather, it is a matter of tracing speech back to its vocalic roots, extricating speech at the same time from the perverse binary economy that splits the vocalic from the semantic and divides them into the two genders of the human species. In the voice—which is always the voice of someone, essentially destined to speech, and which resonates according to the musical and relational laws of the echo—it is not Woman who makes herself heard; rather, it is the embodied uniqueness of the speaker and his or her convocation of another voice. The antipatriarchal valence of the vocalic already lies in this simple recognition, which demands that the political essence of speech is rooted in the corporeal uniqueness of the speakers and in their reciprocal invocation. Indeed, it is only possible to imagine a politics of speech that continues to attach itself to general subjects like "Man" or the "Individual" if the sonorous plurality of voices is neglected. The vocalic attacks the traditional connection between politics and speech, first, from the site of ontology. Moreover, it is not by chance that the tradition of thought that runs from Aristotle to Habermas, while it insists on the political valence of language, obstinately leaves the vocalic out of consideration. Nor is it any less significant that in this framework, the communicativity of speech is entrusted to the rational order of the semantic rather than the relationality of Saying.

It is interesting to note the way in which the tradition removes the corporeal realm of the voice assigned to woman from the political sphere of universal subjects (which are modeled on "man") assigned to man. In its vocalic matrix, the relationality of speech—as the western macrotext from Homer to today testifies—alludes to the maternal scene. In this sense, the devocalization of logos appears as yet another figure of the symbolic matricide of which patriarchal culture leaves many transparent traces.[11] On the political level, however, the consequences of this are particularly significant. The erasure of the first acoustic space of resonance, in which the voices of the mother and the infant communicate with each other, in fact eradicates speech from the vocalic relationality that, at the origin, allows speech to come into being. Thus, there results the strange problem of entrusting the political bond to a speech that, having been preventatively separated from the voice, can no longer count on the vocalic bond that both nurtures speech and continues to make itself heard in the musicality of language. Saying is "relational" not only well before the order of the Said imposes the disciplining rules of communication, but even before there is a Saying intentioned to say something, or meant to express a signified. What in speech convokes the relation among speakers is, first of all, the voice. This relation belongs to a context that has its material dimension in sonority. As the Homeric Sirens knew, speakers do not speak at a distance if the space that separates them renders the exchange of voices ineffectual for the ear. The intercom and the telephone—where communication "invites the other to make his whole body converge in the voice and which lets me gather everything in my ear"—annul this distance, but they do not negate the material relationality of the vocalic.[12] Although this may seem obvious, it evokes that model of active relation—in a space shared by those present (technically in a hall that is big enough to contain them all)—that Arendt calls politics, and that could take the name of an absolute local.[13]

In fact, the vocalic helps not only to think in ever more radical and corporeal terms the ontology of uniqueness, but it helps above all to conceive of politics in terms of a contextual relation, entrusted to speech, which does not appeal to territory or identity myths of community. The protagonist of this politics is a speaker who, leaving aside his or her belonging to this or that identity group, this or that language, communicates him- or herself first of all as voice. Thus, this speaker does not correspond to the universal, disembodied individual of the modern political fiction that relies on the communicative rationality of language. The reciprocal communication of voices implies the figure of a speaker who exposes first of all herself as a singular body. This is also true—as Levinas would say, and in a certain sense, Arendt too—for the face to face of those who, by looking at each other, expose their embodied uniqueness to the other's gaze. But as I have emphasized repeatedly, the acoustic sphere, unlike the visible sphere, is characterized by an essential adherence to Saying. And it is thus the most proper manifestation of that uniqueness and relationality that are announced as already inscribed criteria for the political essence of speech.

It is therefore worth insisting on this decisive point. The voice is sound, not speech; but speech is its essential destination. Significantly, this can also be reversed. Speech carries in itself that which the voice has destined to it. The embodied uniqueness and the musical rhythm of the relation are part of this destiny. And this requires a more radical rethinking of the *zoon logon echon* that inaugurates, in the west, the history of ontology and thus of politics. Because it unhinges the ontological and political status of modernity, the age of globalization makes this undertaking easier—or, at least, globalization allows us to finally lend an ear to that which the voice destines to speech. For outside of this destination, the speech that sacrifices the voice to the universal laws of the semantic remains imprisoned by metaphysics—and, at the same time, the voice that sacrifices speech to the subversive effects of an absolute pleasure risks crossing the threshold of the animal realm. Not by chance does Aristotle, in the very passage from the *Politics* where he makes a *zoon logon echon* of the *zoon politikon*, feel the need to distinguish men from animals when it comes to the *phone*. Animals and men have a voice—but the destination of the human voice to speech is what distinguishes them. The humanity of human beings plays out precisely along the division (which is rooted in the vocalic) of this destination. Which means that the interweaving of voice and speech, which is not necessary synchronous, cannot be severed without sacrificing humanity itself; this goes for both the animal voice and the devocalized logos.

The politics of the absolute local—in contrast to those contemporary tendencies that celebrate the advent of the posthuman—implies an ontology that is rooted in this vocalic meaning of the human. The voice is invoked here because of its destination to speech, but in such a way that speech is never authorized to erase the reciprocal communication of uniqueness that the voice announces and destines to it. It could thus be called a politics of voices [*una politica delle voci*], or a politics where the speakers, no matter what they say, communicate first of all their vocalic uniqueness and the echo of a resonance as the essential prerequisites of verbal communication. Again, it is not a matter of overcoming or erasing speech, but rather of keeping the primary sense of speech in proximity to the relational plurality of voices that originate speech, or that materialize it, as it were, by making it sing. In every word that is pronounced or exchanged, no matter the language, there is the irremediably singular—yet already modulated through an echo that calls the other's voice—sonorous vibration of this song. Truth sings in key, as Cixous says. Unique and relational, the voice gives its truth to speech in the form of music.

In the Nazi experiment of total domination, in which the *lager* constitutes the laboratory for transforming human nature itself, the last decisive step—according to Arendt—concerns "the methods for dealing with this uniqueness of the human person."[14] "After murder of the moral person and annihilation of the juridical person," the triumph of the system requires that uniqueness be destroyed—until the human beings, by losing that which renders them human, are transformed into "ghastly marionettes" in which every specific character of humanity is absent.[15] This is what Primo Levi calls the drowned, the so-called Muslims, the "anonymous mass, continually renewed and always identical, of nonmen who march and labour in silence, the divine spark dead within them, already too empty to really suffer."[16] The problem—inasmuch as the *lager* can be assumed to be the paradigm of the "extreme situation" that allows us to rethink the essential principles of ontology—regards precisely this transformation of man into nonman, or their being defined "by what they are not," so to speak. Significantly, the last straw lies in the uniqueness that, once eliminated, turns the human into the no longer human. Or, as Giorgio Agamben puts it, it forces all thought that comes after Auschwitz to investigate an "'underman' [who] must matter to us more than the 'overman.'"[17]

Primo Levi recounts that, in the days that followed the liberation and the first transfers of the survivors, there appeared in the "big camp" of Auschwitz a child of about three years of age who "could not speak and had no name."[18] They called him Hurbinek, trying perhaps to interpret "with those syllables one of the inarticulate sounds that the baby let out now and again."[19] In fact, the child—destined to die shortly after, "free but not redeemed"—continually repeated a series of sounds, a word, "or better, several slightly different articulated words, experimental variations of a theme, on a root, perhaps even on a name" that no one in the camp was able to understand, although many languages were represented among them.[20] The sound articulated by Hurbinek, adds Levi, was something like *mass-klo* or *matisklo*. Those present hypothesized that it was an attempt to say his name, or else that it meant "to eat," or "bread," or perhaps "meat." The other deportees therefore attribute to the articulated sounds of the child the intention to signify. Hurbinek's voice, precisely because it modulates variations on a theme, already makes its destination to speech perceptible. Now, as for the communication of a content, or the comprehension that comes from sharing a language, Hurbinek's is a nonlanguage that sinks into the abyss of the nonman, or "underman."[21] However, as far as the reciprocal communication of uniqueness goes, it is an act that—in Hurbinek's sonorous articulations—already intones the truth of a voice that is destined to speech and that is thus peremptorily human.

The *lager* is an "extreme situation" because it is precisely the destruction of uniqueness, of that which is human in the human species, that constitutes the extremity toward which totalitarian domination tends. The "ghastly marionettes," the Muslims, the drowned—all reveal that the extreme limit, the discretion between the human and nonhuman, has been challenged. In this sense, Hurbinek is saved. Rather than being the tragic little exemplar of the nonman, he is the announcement, under infernal conditions, of the quintessence of the human that the voice destines to speech. "The speech he lacked," notes Levi, "which no one had bothered to teach him, the need of speech charged his stare with explosive urgency" in the will "to break his muteness."[22] *Mass-klo, matisklo*—although it is an incomprehensible word—is also the acoustic correspondent of this explosive, living gaze that is neither apathetic nor inexpressive nor defeated. Hurbinek is not "bare life" [*nuda vita*] and his voice is not an inarticulate cry. Rather, his is a voice in which the acoustically perceptible phenomenon of uniqueness, here emphasized by the lack of access to the semantic, modulates itself with experimental variations on a theme; it mimes the musicality of speech, the relational fabric of resonance, the echo that comes from the mouth for the ear of the other. We do not know the circumstances of Hurbinek's early infancy. Perhaps he was born in Auschwitz. We know only that he died early, but not without tasting the human intonation of speech. And yet precisely the capacity for this intonation tells us that his tragedy is not like that of the "children of the wild" who are raised without human contact. Rather, in the horror of the camps, his is the different tragedy of a missing mother who was replaced in a precarious and discontinuous way—until the final encounter with Hanek, the Hungarian who "as a mother more than a father," looks after him and speaks to him.[23] *Mass-klo, matisklo* is the incomprehensible speech (that is, however, intoned to the truth of the vocalic) that—by testifying to the existence of an infancy among humans—keeps Hurbinek on this side of the threshold that the "drowned" have crossed. He is the warning—albeit extreme—to every rethinking of ontology that aspires to radically reestablish the bond between speech and politics.

Appendix: Dedicated to Derrida

> Such is at least the experience—or consciousness—of the voice: of hearing (understanding)-oneself-speak [*s'entendre-parler*]. That experience lives and proclaims itself as the exclusion of writing, that is to say of the invoking of an "exterior," "sensible," "spatial," signifier interrupting self-presence.
> —Jacques Derrida, *Of Grammatology*

Appendix, coda. *In cauda venenum* or, perhaps more ambiguously, *pharmakon*. This is, rather, first of all a dedication—a recognition and a critique expressly dedicated to Derrida. It is important that the accent fall, in the first place, on the recognition. What we recognize in Derrida is the original theoretical gesture with which he—detaching himself from the interpretative canons of the tradition, in the 1960s—identifies in the voice the fundamental question, one would be tempted to say the "matrix," of metaphysics. His theoretical originality, which is well known and which inaugurates a new style for contemporary hermeneutics, should be understood. On the surface, at least, some of the categories that the young Derrida refers to were, at the time, already known and current. Albeit by intersecting them in complex ways, he uses on the one hand the Heideggerian notion of philosophy as a metaphysics of presence, and on the other hand, the distinction—which had been broadly thematized by the studies on orality—between speech and writing. If the debt to Heidegger, while full of reservations, is explicit, then the debt to the studies on orality—and more generally to the modern rediscovery of the voice, if not of writing—is, however, rather deceptive.[1] Derrida maintains the opposition between voice and writing, but he is not interested in the voice in order to safeguard the specificity of oral cultures as distinct from alphabetical ones. Rather, for him the voice becomes precisely the metaphysical feature par excellence, the very thing that metaphysics privileges, over and against writing, in order to construct itself as a system of presence. It is in fact in writing that Derrida finds an antimetaphysical valence, insofar as writing works around and against the system of presence, in a way that destabilizes its construction. At issue is a writing [*écriture*] that, according to Derrida, passes over the usual meaning of that term, and is instead proposed as the site of the proliferation of signs, the infinite deferral of one sign to another, the unstoppable movement of deferral and differentiation—namely, of *différance*, a neologism coined and made famous by Derrida that is almost impossible to translate.[2]

In fact there is also a terminological problem. Derrida's lexicon and syntax, if not the entire working of his theoretical machine, are characterized by a complexity that does not lend itself to simplifications and that often puts translations into crisis. It is well known that "whoever engages with Derrida's work, whoever tries to speak about it, cannot avoid bracketing the risks that such an attempt must confront."[3] Still, by proceeding with caution, it is possible to indicate with a certain precision the speculative thread that links together Derrida's writings in the 1960s—namely, a strategy of counterposing *différance* to presence, rooting the former in writing and the latter in the voice. His framework is something like the reverse of that used in studies on orality. The voice is not investigated because of its pertinence to a culture or an age that is opposed to metaphysics, which gets understood as the historical product of a civilization of writing. Rather, the voice is identified by Derrida as the constitutive feature of metaphysics itself, while the task of destabilizing the phonocentric order of metaphysics is reserved for writing. The crucial—and original, to say the very least—point is this: for Derrida, metaphysical logocentrism is a phonocentrism. Rather than devocalize logos, philosophy in Derrida's view focuses on the voice in order to make it so that in logos itself, truth is configured as a realm of presence.

His thesis, therefore, has some truly surprising features—features that are, for an effort that wants to theoretically redeem the *phone*, somewhat ambivalent. One could in fact argue that Derrida's decision to rethink the role of the voice in the realm of traditional metaphysics is, in and of itself, worthy of merit. However, this rethinking produces some conclusions that risk nullifying the merit. In any event, what is worth recognizing here is the fact that Derrida forces philosophy to take account of the theme of the voice, a crucial theme that philosophy itself has tried to ignore for millennia through a strategy of neutralization. And yet the theoretical results to which Derrida's rediscovery of the voice gets reduced risk canceling out the merit of the undertaking. Derrida's thesis on the phonocentrism of metaphysics in fact ends up discouraging any type of research that aims to valorize the antimetaphysical potential of the voice that, starting with Plato and in spite of strategic reticences, the philosophical tradition itself continually evokes. Put simply, Derrida opens the philosophically disturbing theme of the voice and, at the same time, imprisons it in the very metaphysical box that it was meant to disturb. Given the importance of the question, not to mention its truly ancient roots, a supplemental investigation is necessary. Indeed, when dealing with Derrida, a supplemental inquiry, even a brief and simplifying one, is technically necessary. As already indicated, to synthesize his thought into a few lines and to reduce his complicated speculative procedure into a series of formulas is an impossible task that only increases the risk of misunderstanding his texts. It is therefore necessary to confront the difficult task of at least reconstructuing the general theoretical horizon in which the master of deconstruction moves. The problem, in this dedication, is essentially to understand what this voice—which the metaphysical ear, according to Derrida, privileges—is, or rather, to ascertain whether this voice—to which philosophy listens and to which it entrusts the category of presence (rather than rely on the celebrated power of the eye)—is really a sonorous voice.

Obviously, the problem, thus stated, is neither casual nor neutral. To state it like this, in a critique dedicated to Derrida—placed as the appendix of a book that reads the history of metaphysics as a devocalization of logos, instead of as a triumph of phonocentrism—explicitly mobilizes, so to speak, an anti-Derridean perspective. However, this does not mean that this critique, by offering itself in the place of a conclusion, takes advantage of an oversimplification. Rather, I must confess that this critical confrontation with Derrida, although it comes at the end of the book, has accompanied the work that has been developed until now from the very beginning. The Derridean speculation on the *phone*, not to mention on *écriture*, has oriented, unsettled, and challenged the entire course of my research.

One must go back several decades in order to find the work in which Derrida inserts the famous affirmation that metaphysic logocentrism is a phonocentrism. In a single year, 1967, he provides his contribution to the general twentieth-century war against traditional metaphysics in three formidable books: *Speech and Phenomena*, *Writing and Difference*, and *Of Grammatology*.[4] With these three books, an original style of thought and a new lexicon, whose influence has grown progressively, quickly began to inundate a broad section of international philosophical debate. Although these three texts are complex, and are hardly reducible to a simple, univocal position, Derrida's basic thesis is that western metaphysics is essentially a metaphysics of presence—or rather that the concept of a pure and immediate presence functions in metaphysics as the guarantee of an evident and necessary truth, and thus this concept of presence is "foundational." The Derridean critique of the notion of presence, which is essential to his formulation of metaphysical phonocentrism, has a very broad spectrum. It includes, at a minimum, "the presence of the object, the presence of meaning to consciousness, the presence to oneself in so-called living speech and in self-consiousness."[5] As a consequence, this critique comprehends both platonic-inspired systems centered on the object (Being, the idea, the original form) and modern philosophies centered instead on the subject (consciousness, self-consciousness). Because of his initial interest in Edmund Husserl, however, Derrida privileges the wholly modern ambit of the subject, in which the evidence of the foundation corresponds to a form of immediate self-presence that sees the protagonist as pure consciousness. In short, this is the evidence of the Cartesian cogito—recuperated by a phenomenological project that takes as true only that which can be verified in the realm of pure consciousness—which acts as foundation and principle of philosophy as a rigorous science. Derrida's attention thus goes, first of all, to the "modern" metaphysics of presence understood as self-consciousness" that "defines the very element of philosophical thought, it is evidence itself, conscious thought itself, it governs every possible concept of truth and sense," including the truth of the idea in classical ontology.[6]

Typical of the metaphysics of presence is, as Derrida emphasizes, the famous binary system that opposes intelligible entities to sensible entities. This opposition is also hierarchical, in that the former—conceived as necessary and evident, because present—functions as the origin of the latter and therefore subordinates it. The value of presence is thus to be found in a series of opposed pairs that serve to underscore the foundational valence of the first term: origin/derivation, model/copy, signified/signifier, and so forth. This last pair is, for Derrida, particularly important for his thesis on metaphysical phonocentrism's opposition to the work of writing. He in fact emphasizes that even Saussure's modern linguistics ends up belonging to the metaphysics of presence because, according to the typical system that subordinates the sensible to the intelligible, he works on the signified/signifier pair, making the latter (the phonic sign) depend on the first (the concept), whereas the written sign appears as the sign of a sign—or, rather, according to a conception that goes back to Greek philosophy, as the graphic sign of a phonic sign.[7] Derrida's interest in linguistics is, in effect, due to the centrality of the sign in that discipline. For this is the modern recuperation of the traditional doctrine of the sign, which is totally in keeping with the binary economy of the metaphysical system. Starting from its origins in ancient Greece and its foundations in the realm of truth, this system understands the sign "as re-presentation, derived and modified from simple presentation" or from the signified as presence."[8] In this system, symptomatically, the sign thus implies the absent presence of the signified—in the sense that the full presence of the signified is not here, because there is only a sign that supplements it and shows it to be absent. Therefore in the last analysis, suggests Derrida, the presence of the signified—or, rather, the signified-as-presence—only gets presupposed or constructed vis-à-vis the deferral of the sign to this presence, a deferral that attests to its absence. If the binary pair presence/absence is one of the most genuine and coherent fruits of the metaphysics of presence, then the metaphysical conception of the sign allows for a movement that puts into crisis the claimed originarity of presence, namely, the pretense that is presence—the present signified—lies at the origin of the sign. This makes the sign one of the most interesting "critical concepts" on which Derrida concentrates his work of deconstruction, not before having designating "rigorously their intimate relationship to the machine whose deconstruction they permit."[9]

As it now gets reread according to the method that Derrida calls "deconstruction," the text of western metaphysics in fact turns out to be unsettled by a rather different notion of the sign—namely, the sign, or trace, as Derrida understands it. Significantly, for Derrida, the very distinction between signifier and signified, in whose horizon metaphysics thinks the sign, is fictitious. Deconstruction shows this distinction to be fictitious because the whole area in which meaning proliferates—whether as an articulation of difference or as relation among these differences—is nothing but a continual movement of signs that defer to one another, in an interminable play of referential traces that have no origin. The metaphysical text bears, precisely, the traces of this movement of *différance* and, in large part, is constructed on an attempt to block this very movement and to hide its traces.

This construction of the full presence of the signified as origin and foundation in fact follows, according to Derrida, from metaphysics' incapacity to fully tolerate the play of signs that defer to one another—a play of signs that never ends because the deferral is incessant. *End, beginning, telos, archè* are terms that moreover belong to the metaphysical system of presence. According to the celebrated Derridean *différance*, there is nothing but signs, deferrals, deviations; there is no origin, or fixed point, or stable presence that lasts or that originates and concludes the movement. There is no signified but only signifiers—or, rather, signs. Metaphysics, in a certain sense, knows all of this, and in any case takes account of this. If it is well deconstructed, then metaphysics reveals itself to be clearly obsessed with the infinite play of signs, and to react to this obsession through an "exigent, potent, systematic and irrepressible desire" for presence as origin and end.[10] Precisely because it is characterized by the instability of this continual deferment, the movement of signs generates the need for fixedness; or, rather, it generates the desire for that which is immediately present and no longer defers elsewhere. The signified, and the traditional theory of the sign, respond to this desire.

In Derrida's deconstructive horizon, the metaphysics of presence is therefore a reactive product of the movement of the trace. This does not mean that the trace directly produces presence, or that it necessarily postulates it, as metaphysics and the traditional notion of the sign maintain. Rather, it means that the desire for a present entity, which is capable of arresting the movement of *différance*, produces the necessity of constructing the category of presence. And (finally, this is the point), this "presence" is an effect of the metaphysical privileging of the voice.

This thesis regarding phonocentrism—which is bound up with his critique of the metaphysics of presence—constitutes the most original aspect of Derrida's early work. For many reasons, which perhaps have to do with the critical reception of Derrida's work in the United States, this originality has not received the attention it deserves.[11] The growing success of Derrida's work in speculative (especially Anglo-American) circles, in both analytical and continental philosophy, has in fact ended up making the importance of his initial reflections on the theme of the *phone* take a back seat to other issues. In *Speech and Phenomena*, he takes up this theme through a deconstructive reading of Husserl's phenomenology. As already indicated, the general problematic is that of consciousness. In other words, the Derridean reflections on the voice move in a sector of modern philosophy that is heavily influenced by a Cartesian inheritance. Here, the object of deconstruction is "the idea of knowledge as the transparency of consciousness to itself, of a controllable and masterable knowledge on the part of a knowing, self-conscious subject which speaks and acts always knowing what it does and says, master of its speech, of its discourse."[12]

The category of presence, says Derrida in the text in question, is an effect of the specifically human practice of speech. At least for the moment, it is a question of speech in its most obvious sense—the speech proffered in voice by a speaking subject. The effect of presence depends on the fact that "it is implied in the very structure of speech that the speaker *hears himself* [*s'entende*]: both that he perceives the sensible form of the phonemes and that he understands his own expressive intention."[13] The effect of presence is therefore double. On the one hand, the one who hears himself speak is present to himself in a circuit of "pure auto-affection" between voice and ear.[14] On the other hand, what he wants to say (the signified) is immediately present in the words that he says (the acoustic signifier). In general, it could be said that the former instance tends to found consciousness as the self-presence of the speaker, whereas the latter tends to affirm the extreme proximity of the verbal signifier to the signified that are present, at the same time, to the one who speaks. Both instances end up coinciding, however—and the site of this coincidence is precisely consciousness, or the phenomenological subject who has in mind what he wants to say.

It is worth recalling, again, that the material under investigation here—namely, Husserl's phenomenology—imposes certain prejudicial limits on Derrida's argument. Put simply, he is basically working on a solipsistic concept of subjectivity and consciousness. As happens in Descartes, this is a subjectivity that completely folds back on itself, closed and self-referential, and that does not need any exterior world in order to found the realm of truth. Its interiority is presupposed as absolute. It thus becomes obvious that the exercise of speech is understood as a hearing oneself speak [*s'entendre-parler*]; or, rather, it gets conceived as a soliloquy, almost as if human beings opened their mouths to speak to themselves, or, as if when they speak to others, they concentrate their attention on what they themselves say and not on what others say. For phenomenology, focused on the presence of sense to the intentionality of the transcendental consciousness, it does not matter that speech is communication. Rather, dialogue becomes a duplication of monologue: "to speak to someone is doubtless to hear oneself speak, to be heard by oneself; but, at the same time, if one is heard by another, to speak is to make him repeat immediately in himself the hearing-oneself-speak in the very form in which I effectuated it."[15] Phenomenologically, because of the suspension [*epoche*] of the existence of the external world, every speaker is a circuit of autoaffection—supposing, in any event, that this speaker truly speaks.

There is in fact the rather serious risk that the voice of phenomenological consciousness, here deconstructed by Derrida, is a voice of thought,
totally insonorous. Or there is the justifiable suspicion that "the voice privileged by Husserl is not the physical voice, a sonorous substance, but rather
the phenomenological, transcendental voice that continues to be present to
itself, in the absence of the world."[16] As Mikhail Bakhtin would say, philosophy is structurally monological, not dialogical or polyphonic.[17] In-
clined to be interested in the Said, philosophy ignores the relationality of
Saying, and thus the plurality of voices. The ancient metaphor of the voice
of the soul, recuperated here by the Husserlian consciousness, alludes
moreover to an interior monologue where there is no sound. Indeed, the
genuine circuit of noetic autoaffection in the insonorous Cartesian cogito
would be more than sufficient for investigating the effects of presence in
the "modern" metaphysical system focused on consciousness. In other
words, although it does not use the physical voice and therefore does not
hear itself speak, the Cartesian subject is capable of producing both the
self-presence of the thinker and the immediate presence of that which it
intends with its own thought. Even without the work of the mouth and
the ear, the self-transparency and the immediacy of the effect of presence
produced by the cogito are already perfect. So why does Derrida—who
obviously knows all this quite well—insist on the voice?

For anyone who knows Derrida's writings from this period, the answer to this question is not difficult. What matters to him, what orients his
deconstructive labor, is the philosophy of *différance*—or a theory on the interminable deferral of a trace, understood as the movement of signs, whose
concept basically coincides with writing. Writing, generally understood, is
in fact the privileged realm of the movement of a trace that, not by chance,
acquires the name of *arche-écriture* in Derrida's lexicon. Derrida's interest
in the *phone*, his discovery of the theme of the voice, emerges precisely
from this prejudicial interest in a writing conceived "as a texture of differ-
ential traces, as an open system of deferrals and deviations, which do not
allow access to any presence."[18] In other words, it is the speculation on
writing as *différance* that orients the theoretical axis in which Derrida
places the theme of the voice, making it play a metaphysical role in opposition to the antimetaphysical valence of writing. He can thus read the ancient platonic condemnation of written discourse as a demonstration of
this thesis, or as a symptom of the system of presence. And the proof for
this is a tenacious tradition that, down to Saussure, subordinates writing to

speech: "the history of truth, of the truth of truth, has always been . . . the debasement of writing, and its repression outside 'full' speech."[19] According to Derrida, in fact, this is precisely the most symptomatic aspect of the metaphysical construction—namely, that it reserves for writing the status of "a sign of a sign" and thus an already dead, second-grade sign, while "full" speech, speech in voice, gets the status of a sign that is so close to the present entity that it makes transparent in its sonorous substance the living presence of that entity. In other words, given that, as far as construct of metaphysics is concerned, the original and fundamental sphere is that of the signified (fully present, fixed, universal, ideal, intelligible, immaterial), it follows that in the same construction, the acoustic signifier is given the privilege of an immediate proximity to the signified.

Yet the heart of the problem lies precisely in the measure of this proximity, a problem that, for Derrida, has at least two sides. The first concerns the extreme diminution of this measure, which ends up putting the classical distinction between signifier and signified into crisis. The second concerns the resulting effect of contamination, which makes it so that living speech brings the meaning to life [*che la parola viva passi a vivificare il senso*].

According to Derrida, in the emblematic case of the speaker who hears himself speak, the proximity between speech and meaning tends to be "absolute" and, basically, to disappear. The acoustic signifier becomes "diaphanous," transparent.[20] The one who speaks and listens to himself at the same time perceives "the sensible form of the phonemes" and understands "his own expressive intention."[21] The acoustic signifier and the intelligible signified seem to coincide, and the realm of this coincidence is precisely time in form of the present: "What constitutes the originality of speech, what distinguishes it from every other element of signification, is that this substance seems to be purely temporal."[22] Put in the terms of Husserlian phenomenology, the phenomenon of autoaffection, which is due to the circuit between the voice and ear of a subject who hears himself speak, does not seem to imply any space—or, at least, any space outside of consciousness, the externality that characterizes the world. Captured in the present of its interior time, consciousness claims to be detached from external space and, thus, from the world.

Emblematically, Derrida insists on this question, not so much because he wants to liberate the speaker from his solipsistic prison in order to open him to the world and the plurality of voices, to the relational horizon of Saying, but rather because writing, unfairly downgraded by metaphysics, belongs to the order of space. The written sign is, by definition, external, and it implies a system of spacing [*espacement*]. The absolute proximity of the signifier to the signified "is broken when, instead of hearing myself speak, I see myself write or signify through gestures."[23] In the Derridean economy, this means that unlike the voice, writing, trace par excellence—spacing, movement, genuine play of signs—cannot generate an effect of presence. Writing thus reveals a subversive potential with regard to the system of presence built on the voice. And for this very reason, the metaphysics of presence—centered on a logos in which "the originary and essential bond with the *phone* has never been broken"—casts writing in a subordinate role.[24]

This point is crucial. By emphasizing the link between writing and space, in opposition to the link between the voice and time, Derrida is in fact not only arguing here that the metaphysics of presence depends on the privileging of the faculty of speech, but also that this metaphysics does not at all depend on the privileging of the faculty of sight. Despite the platonic idea and a whole philosophical tradition that insists on the evidence of truth, for Derrida, metaphysics would not be videocentric. In other words, his thesis on metaphysical phonocentrism supplants the far more plausible, and philologically documentable, centrality of videocentrism. This is even more curious because we hardly need to be convinced that, in the macrotext of western philosophy, the category of presence is explicitly traced by many philosophers back to the faculty of sight. Obviously, Derrida knows all this. But for many reasons, he tends to undervalue, if not deny, this simple fact.

The first of these reasons is doubtless the already indicated antihistorical perspective with which Derrida investigates the question of the metaphysics of presence. The notion that a modern conception of "consciousness" or the "subject" can be simply applied backward, so to speak, to a Greek ontology that is centered on the object is, to say the least, questionable. This is all the more so if, as Derrida himself notes in *Margins of Philosophy*, presence as "evidence entrusted to the faculty of sight"—typical of platonic metaphysics—is rephrased in Cartesian language. The way out of the famous hyperbolic doubt is guaranteed by "the axioms that the natural light shows me to be true"—or, as Descartes writes in the *Meditations*, "the light of nature lets us see clearly."[25] According to Derrida, this is one of the innumerable philosophical texts in which the metaphors of light, secondary variations on the heliotropic metaphor centered on the sun, are revealed to be constitutive tropes for the metaphysics of presence.

The *parousia*, as the self-presence of the idea in its light, characterizes a metaphorical trajectory of philosophy that extends "from the platonic *eidos* to the Hegelian Idea."[26] Philosophy as *theoria* in fact owes its own construction to this metaphorical trajectory that is articulated through the analogy between the intelligible sun and the sensible sun, between the eye of the soul and the eye of the body. Thus, states Derrida, "philosophy, as a theory of metaphor, is first of all a metaphor for theory"; and he quickly adds that "this circulation does not exclude, on the contrary it permits and provokes the transformation of presence into self-presence, in proximity or propriety of subjectivity to itself."[27]

It thus seems that Derrida, in a text that was written only a few years after the texts of 1967, ends up recognizing the fundamental role of the eye in the construction of the metaphysics of presence. The effect of presence that is produced by the metaphors relating to the faculty of sight—he says—are announced in Greece with the very emergence of metaphysics and continue down to the modern metaphysics of the subject. The point is that, according to Derrida, this does not at all prove the basic videocentrism of the metaphysics of presence, nor does it require a revision of the famous thesis on metaphysical phonocentrism.

As usual, the explanation for this is very complex and refined; but it stems from a basic assumption. For Derrida, the most significant feature of the heliotropic metaphors is not that they privilege the faculty of sight, but rather that they are metaphors. As Aristotle says, "metaphor is the transference to some thing of a name that designates something else."[28] Metaphor "lets the semantic go astray."[29] In other words, metaphor belongs to the interminable movement of *différance*, and thus it prevents the system from stabilizing itself, from enclosing itself within the margins of a form. This is why, according to Derrida, philosophers—while they erect their system on the heliotropic metaphor—distrust metaphor as a figure of speech. And this is why the heliotropic metaphor "troubles" philosophy from the very start. In fact, "the very opposition of appearing and disappearing, the entire lexicon of the *phainesthai*, of *aletheia*, and so on, and of day and night, of the visible and the invisible, of the present and the absent—all this is possible only under the sun."[30] And yet in the heliotropic metaphor, the sun itself, in a symptomatic play between luminosity and blindness, is already held in the typical movement of substitution and supplementation that turns on itself endlessly *mise-en-abîme*. In the final analysis, the Derridean account of the clear metaphysical videocentrism is thus based on an argumentative strategy that displaces the problem of the heliotropic metaphor onto the problem of metaphor as such. This allows him to understand videocentrism as symptomatic—and yet also as secondary, or nonconstitutive, for a metaphysics of presence that insists on founding itself on the voice.

Actually, Derrida's position on this problem—especially if one compares the texts from 1967 with *Margins*—appears rather ambiguous. On the one hand, he cannot fail to recognize that the evidence of the present object is an effect of the experience of seeing. (The very term *idea* makes this clear, but for Derrida, these are superficial etymologies that do not get at the heart of the problem.) On the other hand, he emphasizes that the effect of presence still owes to the experience of speaking. An interpreter who approaches Derrida's texts without malice, benignly worried about the incoherence of his position, could thus hypothesize the following: for Derrida, in the history of metaphysics, the effect of presence due to the videocentrism of classical ontology, founded on the object, meets up with, and then reinforces, the effect of presence produced by the phonocentrism of modern philosophy, founded on the self-presence of consciousness. Still, this is not Derrida's position. His position, among other things, contests the very category of "history" as a metaphysical category. Every critique of Derrida's work from a historical point of view therefore risks being invalidated, precisely by Derrida's own invalidation of this point of view.

And yet for the critique of metaphysics, and the focus on the theme of the voice, that Derrida himself encourages, the question remains crucial and unavoidable. It is not so much a matter of revindicating the primacy of the gaze over the voice in order to respect—in the name of a certain interpretive "coherence"—the explicit representation that metaphysics gives of itself. Rather, it is a matter of responding to Derrida's solicitations through the unforeseen, and much more interesting, possibility of recuperating a theme that metaphysics sacrificed to the videocentric and mute realm of thought—namely, the theme of the voice, provided that we understand what is meant by the term *voice*.

Derrida, inspired by Husserl, understands the voice as relating to the speech of a self-referential subject who basically speaks to himself. It is worth stressing, yet again, that the field of consciousness, to which the choice of deconstructing Husserl's phenomenology confines Derrida, forces him to continually oscillate between two rather different scenarios. One is the genuinely Cartesian scenario in which there is no speaker, let alone a vocal emission, but rather a silent thinker. The other is a scenario that is more in keeping with the notion of acoustic autoaffection, in which there is a speaker who truly speaks. Here it is helpful to stress again that, in the first scenario, the effect of presence—if this is the point—is produced without any difficulty. Of course, this is not at all an effect of the voice. It is, rather emblematically, the effect of a highly particular voice that is well known to the metaphysical imaginary—namely, the voice of consciousness, or, rather, a metaphorical voice. Therefore, the discourse on phonocentrism is complicated, and even drags the *phone* into the energy field of metaphor. Although Derrida does not seem to make much of this, the play of *différance*—which is inscribed in metaphor as such, not just in a vocal, as opposed to a visual, metaphor—once again shows its subversive power with regard to the metaphysics of presence.

Indeed, Derrida's deconstruction of a metaphysics, which he characterizes as phonocentric, arrives at an analogous conclusion. However, he does not go on the attack against phonocentrism as a system constructed on the metaphor of the voice, but rather as a system constructed on the physically sonorous voice, of a speaker who hears himself speak. In fact, Derrida does not illustrate the phonocentrism of metaphysics in order to defend it, but rather to show how it futilely attempts to hide the work of *différance*, of writing, that it bears in its heart. As we read in *Speech and Phenomena*, Derrida's aim is to reveal that "hearing oneself speak is not the inwardness of an inside that is closed in upon itself; it is the irreducible openness in the inside; it is the eye and the world within speech."[31] The self-presence of consciousness, produced by the phenomenon of hearing oneself speak, shows itself—in a somewhat Hegelian way—not as an identity, but rather as a difference: "auto-affection as the exercise of the voice, auto-affection supposed that a pure difference comes to divide self-presence."[32] Or to put it even more drastically, "the self of the living present is primordially a trace."[33] Even the scenario of the voice thus belongs to the field of *différance*. The phonocentric matrix of the metaphysics of presence consists precisely in the effort of hiding this work of *différance*.

In the horizon of Derrida's speculations—whether metaphysical videocentrism is deconstructed by being traced back to the heliotropic metaphor, or metaphysical phonocentrism is deconstructed by being traced back to the experience of a speaker who hears himself speak—the result is thus the same. Still, Derrida seems to regard the second deconstruction as being more significant. The theme of the voice allows him to focus more easily on what really interests him, and it functions as an explicit proof of his thesis on the privilege that the metaphysical tradition accords to speech over writing. Again, as is evident from the theoretical architecture of *Of Grammatology*, it is his interest in writing as the sphere of the *trace, arche-trace, différance* that orients Derrida's analysis toward the voice. Unlike the mute Cartesian scenario, Derrida wants the scenario to be sonorous—and not just metaphorical—because his critique has in its sights above all the effect of life [*vivezza*] that speech claims to transmit to the category of presence. It is worth noting that in this sense, the self-present object of Greek ontology would be of absolutely no use. Apparently at least, nothing is less live than the platonic idea, frozen in the immobility of its eternal present.

Derrida writes, "*The voice is heard.* Phonic signs ('acoustical images' in Saussure's sense, or the phenomenological voice) are heard [*entendus*] by the subject who proffers them in the absolute proximity of their present. The subject does not have to pass forth beyond himself to be immediately affected by his expressive activity."[34] Thus described, the framework of phonocentric metaphysics consists in a compacting that leaves no interval, and thus no difference; no space of differentiation and of deferment. The absolute proximity of the speaker to the proffered phonic signs is in fact combined with the absolute proximity of such phonic signs to the signifieds. All this happens in the speaking subject, and it takes on the character of a live presence. Having eliminated all exteriority and all spacing, the live present reigns supreme in the metaphysical system. If the voice were the metaphorical voice of consciousness, obviously, there would be much less life in circulation. Only the voice that is perceptible sound and breath is capable of transferring an effect of living presence to the phonic sign, rendering it an animated signifier.

To the eyes of metaphysics, however, the written signifier, as Derrida notes, appears as dead. It lies immobile, lifeless and breathless. In the very same operation with which it vivifies presence through the voice, metaphysics mortifies writing, the trace, *différance*—or rather, it mortifies precisely that movement of infinite deferral, inscribed in the play of signs, that was the origin of the "exigent, potent, systematic and irrepressible desire" to construct presence.[35] Thus, in the end, the reversal is complete. In the economy of Derrida's deconstruction, phonocentric metaphysics shows itself for what it is: a system that hides the trace, and that not only seems to ignore that metaphysics always already bears the trace itself in its heart, but also devalues the trace by freezing writing in the posture of a dead body. With his explicit condemnation of writing, Plato is, in this sense, an exemplary metaphysician.

The problem of the subordination of writing to speech, which is central for the whole history of metaphysics, begins with Plato, above all in the *Seventh Letter* and in the *Phaedrus*. Not unlike Aristotle in *De Interpretatione*, Plato maintains that written letters are the sign of a sign—or, rather, they are the graphic signifier of an acoustic signifier. This is almost obvious in the sphere of a phonetic writing that derives the letters of the alphabet from the sounds of the voice. If the problem is to stay as close as possible to the ideas, speech will thus be better than writing. Very platonically, it is worth recalling, the pure presence of the signified occupies the first place; in the second place lies speech that constitutes its acoustic signifier; third comes writing, which translates the acoustic signifier into graphic signs.

Just as the origin of names was interrogated in the *Cratylus*, so too in the *Phaedrus* the origin of writing is interrogated. This investigation, strangely, leads to Egypt, the homeland of hieroglyphic writing, the ancient culture to which Plato often refers when he deals with the articulation of sounds and their correspondence to the letters of the alphabet. In the *Phaedrus*, Socrates recounts how the letters were invented by the Egyptian god Theuth.[36] Already the mythical discoverer of the number, of geometry, of astronomy, and of the game of dice, Theuth gives to King Thamus the written characters [*grammata*] and announces their power to found a new type of knowledge. He in fact declares that they are a remedy [*pharmakon*] for forgetfulness and for the lack of learning.[37] The king, however, does not agree; on the contrary, he declares that if men trust written characters, then they will become more forgetful, because they will cease to exercise their memory. Their knowledge will thus consist in a counterfeit learning, turned toward appearances rather than truth. According to the Egyptian legend narrated by Plato, writing is thus presented as a good and as an evil. For Theuth it is a remedy; for Thamus it is a poison. As Derrida points out, this ambiguity is rendered possible by the term *pharmakon* that, in Greek, means both remedy and poison.

Published for the first time in 1968, the long essay "Plato's Pharmacy" is dedicated by Derrida to an analysis of writing as *pharmakon*.[38] Deconstructing the *Phaedrus* and broadening his analysis to other texts by Plato, Derrida stresses the importance of the *pharmakon*'s structural ambiguity.

What is significant is that in the platonic tale of the Egyptian legend, the term is mise-en-scène as an undecidable opposition of meaning. This opposition does not simply privilege the positive meaning over its contrary, but rather plays on the simultaneity of their difference. The *pharmakon*, at once both remedy and poison, is the site of a difference that never stabilizes into an opposition; it is the movement of differing itself as the precondition of metaphysics as a binary system of opposites. By telling the Egyptian legend and qualifying writing as *pharmakon*, Plato—according to Derrida's reading—thus puts his own system at risk. On the one hand, he tries to construct a hierarchical relationship between speech and writing on a series of binary oppositions (good/evil, true/false, essence/appearance, inside/outside, and so on) that are typical of the metaphysical system. On the other hand, by tracing this series of binary oppositions back to the ambivalence of the *pharmakon*, Plato still remains unable to hide that which threatens, and also stimulates, the edification of the system itself. In other words, the platonic text lets both the figure of its construction and of its deconstruction, come to light. By thinking of writing as *pharmakon*, Plato finds himself in the paradoxical position of understanding it "correctly"— in Derrida's sense—as trace, and for this very reason, of raising a barrier against the work of the trace itself by constructing a metaphysical system in which writing appears as the negative pole of an opposition that subordinates it to speech.

Inaugurated by Plato and Platonism—which, according to Derrida, "sets up the whole of Western metaphysics in its conceptuality"—the condemnation of writing ends up being in keeping with a system that, if well deconstructed, shows itself to be always already built on the removal of the trace.[39] This means, in Derridean terms, that the metaphysical condemnation of writing is only the explicit figure of the metaphysical condemnation of the trace. The trace, also called *arche-écriture*, has the very characteristics that Plato imputes to writing when he accuses it of being the sign of a sign, the supplement of a supplement, the deferral of a deferral. The problem is that—precisely on this crucial point of the platonic mechanism of deferral—Derrida seems to indulge a symptomatic reticence. He fails to emphasize that this deferral, after having passed through speech, finds its fixed point, its origin in the pure presence that the videocentric horizon guarantees to the idea. Derrida's interest here, in other words, turns out to be prejudicially indifferent to the platonic foundation of the idea in the visual sphere. Given the attention that goes to the effect of presence that speech, as living voice, would assure to the "speaking subject," in the Derridean reading of Plato, the fundamental difference between speech and the idea, or between the acoustic signifier and the intelligible signified—and, thus, their crucial hierarchical relation—ends up being ignored in favor of a proximity that tends toward identification. This allows Derrida to apply to Plato as well the thesis that claims that the condemnation of writing follows from the essential solidarity between logocentrism and phonocentrism—and thus to count Plato among the philosophers of the *phone*.

In order to corroborate this rather surprising (to say the least) thesis, Derrida goes on to read in detail the final part of the *Phaedrus*. In this text, after having recounted the Egyptian legend, Socrates claims that the signs of writing, not unlike those of painted figures, have the defect of seeming alive when they are in fact dead, immobile, and always the same. If they are interrogated, "they maintain a dignified silence."[40] This rigidity and muteness of written discourse is aggravated by the fact that writing is in everyone's hands, experts and laymen, to whose attacks it must submit: "when it is faulted and attacked unfairly, it always needs its father's support; for, alone it can neither defend itself nor come to its own support."[41] "The specificity of writing," notes Derrida at this point, "would thus be intimately bound to the absence of the father."[42] Written discourse is an orphan; indeed, as Socrates declares soon after, it is an illegitimate offspring. The passage deserves to be cited in full:

> SOCRATES: So, we want to consider another logos, which is the legitimate brother of this one, in order to see how it is generated [*gignetai*] and how it is by nature/birth [*phyetai*] better and more powerful than this one?
>
> PHAEDRUS: Which one is that? And how do you think it is generated?
>
> SOCRATES: That which is written [*graphetai*], with science [*episteme*], in the soul of the listener; it can defend itself by itself, and it knows for whom it should speak and for whom it should remain silent.
>
> PHAEDRUS: You are speaking of the living, breathing [*zonta kai empsychon*] logos of the one who knows [*eidotos*], of which the written one [*gegrammenos*] can rightly be called a simulacrum [*eidolon*]?
>
> SOCRATES: Precisely.[43]

Taking for granted that this legitimate offspring is spoken discourse, Derrida underscores that it is living because there is "a father that is *present, standing* near it"; in fact, "one could say anachronously that the 'speaking subject' is the *father* of his speech," a father who is absent when speech is consigned to written signs.[44] In Derridean terms, this means that Plato's

text inaugurates metaphysical phonocentrism, and the consequent condemnation of writing because it founds the superiority of speech on presence, on living presence. Derrida's spontaneous indication of the anachronistic use of the concept "speaking subject," however, reveals that—as far
as his thesis on metaphysical phonocentrism goes—his reading of Plato's
text is a cause of some embarrassment. In fact, in this case, the living presence is not the effect of "a speaker who hears himself speak"; still less is it
an effect of a circuit of autoaffection owing to the *phone*. Supposing, but
not admitting, that Socrates is illustrating spoken discourse, here the voice
and the acoustic sphere are irrelevant. After all, the father's defense and as-
sistance of his own speech implies at least a dialogic situation where, unlike
what happens in the written text, the father responds when interrogated.
In this passage from the *Phaedrus*, the problematic of speech—illustrated,
not by chance, in terms of attack and defense—shows that the "speaking
subject" always speaks to another and with another. What matters is precisely what the interlocutors say to one another and how their discourse
proceeds—not their voices and the phenomenon of the acoustic sphere.
Nor could it be said that self-presence as consciousness comes into play
here. If anything, it is the signifieds—or the ideas—that are proposed as
pure presence. Far from being an effect of the phonic substance of speech,
this presence is of a visible, mute character—just like writing.

   In contrast to what Derrida seems to believe, the legitimate offspring—rather than corresponding to speech proffered in voice—is in fact
a descendent of the ideas. The logos that is written in the soul of the one
who apprehends, with science [*episteme*], is precisely the devocalized logos
that coincides with the visible and mute order of ideas. Its status as legitimate offspring, instead of being surprising, recalls the notorious figure of
Socrates as midwife, who fertilizes the souls of the young, inducing them
to procreate beautiful and immortal offspring.[45] In fact, it is worth remembering that in Plato's texts, the metaphorical field that describes logos
as an offspring is often characterized by an imposition of the paternal function on the maternal function. Symptomatically, this is borne out in the
Phaedrus. Precisely in order to clarify his discourse on the legitimate offspring, Socrates claims that through the art of dialectic, the logoi that are
accompanied by science get inseminated in souls that are fit to receive
them until, by propagating themselves from one soul to another, their seed
becomes immortal.[46] Like the uterus, the soul is therefore a site of insemi-
nation. Although it is often practiced according to rules that preside over

homosexual-pederast relations, the risk that the young—or at least the souls of the young—recoup a feminine role is always latent in Plato's speculation. Moreover, here the position of the young is ambiguous. First he gets inseminated and lets the seeds germinate; then he transmits them to others, inseminating them in turn. The organ of the entire operation is the art of dialectic [*dialektike techne*], or an art that is specific to speech and that entertains an exclusive relation with the ideas.

In effect, it is precisely the art of dialectic that functions as a means of transmission between the world of words and the world of ideas. This art belongs to the verbal sphere, but it belongs to it as a method for showing the insufficiency of words and at the same time, their constitutive dependence on the order of ideas. Modeled on Socratic confutation, in a large section of Plato's writings dialectic consists essentially in a dialogue that proceeds through questions and answers. In its simplest form—the one most faithful to the figure of Socrates—it unfolds as a dialogue that puts a series of definitions provided by the interlocutors under examination in order to respond to the initial question that asks for the meaning of one of the words they pronounce. Entrusted to the typical formula of the 'what it is' (the good, the just, courage, and so on), this question takes as its object the idea and, notoriously, never leads to an answer that the interlocutors find satisfying, even as they agree in the end on the necessity of the question itself. Precisely this aporetic outcome of the dialogue—rather than signaling a subjective inability of the interlocutors to find the right answer—gets indicated by Plato as an objective incapacity of spoken discourse to say, or to define through the joining of words, the idea. The ideas, in fact, are not sayable—rather, as is platonically obvious, they are only thinkable, or contemplatable, through the eyes of the mind. The great merit of dialectic consists precisely in actively showing the unsayability of the idea. As we read in the *Seventh Letter*, through the questioning and answering, the task of the interlocutors is to rub the words against one another, until the words themselves reveal their inadequacy and at the same time bring the interlocutors to grasp the luminosity of the idea that suddenly flashes up, present to the eye of the soul.[47] Pure presence does not belong to the realm of speech, and yet it allows the dialectic exercise of speech to prove the necessity that the idea be a pure, visible, and mute presence. In other words, in Plato, the bond between the idea and speech does not only allude to the metaphysical theory of the sign that locates the origin and cause of the phonic signifier in the mental signified, but it is also configured above all as an incommensurable distance between the realm of sight and the realm of sounds. When the silent *dia-logos* of the soul with itself is vocalized, it is transmitted into an extraneous, corporeal, unstable, untrustworthy element. In the dream of what we called major metaphysics—which Plato never gets tired of dreaming—the steady heart of truth can do without the voice, without words or dialogues, and thus without dialectic.

Nicely exemplified in the myth of the cave, the great platonic dream is in fact to find oneself face to face with the idea—in the luminous and mute mirage of the pure vision of a pure presence. An analogous dream can be found, moreover, in the famous myth of the charioteer in the *Phaedrus* where we are told how, during the heavenly sojourn that precedes the incarnation in a mortal body, the soul has the opportunity to directly contemplate the ideas.[48] This is the great dream that inspires the pure and immobile contemplation of major metaphysics—as distinct from the minor metaphysics that is still busy with the movement and verbality of the *dilegesthai*—and that, symptomatically, always makes of philosophy an otherworldly expression that is similar to the desire for death. The limit of this dream lies, significantly, in the fact that major metaphysics must take into account the everyday experience of an ordinary world where human beings live a corporeal existence and share speech. Ideally superfluous, speech is, in other words, necessary in the world—indeed, it is the specific characteristic of the human condition. Plato comes to terms with this "given" through a sort of reversal—in a certain sense, very coherent—of the trajectory that brings the silent *dia-logos* of the soul with itself to make itself sonorous logos through the voice. In other words, in platonic philosophy—which is famously full of two-way streets—there are two trajectories that regard the relationship between the idea and speech. One descends from the idea to speech, from the signified to the signifier, from the heavenly to the world. The other goes (back) from speech to the idea, from the signifier to the signified, from the ordinary world to the eternal world of the forms. This return is possible only through the art of dialectic that rubs the words together until, with a leap out of the acoustic sphere, the eye of the soul can (again) see the luminosity of the ideas.

Along with the rubbing of the words that is modeled on Socratic confutation, the mature Plato goes on to indicate an ulterior and, so to speak, more rigorous and refined form of *dialektike techne*. The text that introduces this formula is, precisely, the *Phaedrus*. Here again there are two progressions, to the letter, of two types of "vision": *eidos*. The first consists in "gathering together multiple and dispersed things into a single idea"; the second consists in "knowing how to divide according to the ideas in conformity with the natural articulation of its members, without splintering any part, as a bad butcher might do."[49] The first progression thus recalls the question with which the confutational model of dialectic begins: a dispersed multiplicity of things that, for example, are designated "beautiful" get traced back to the idea of the beautiful, which such a designation implies. The second progression, however, is totally new: it prevents the interlocutors from freely proposing the sought definition and requires this definition to follow the natural articulation of the body of ideas. Like a natural body, which has members and organs, the logos of the pure forms is characterized by an order that articulates its parts in "right joinings." In the platonic metaphorology—it should be pointed out—this logos is a living, breathing offspring and, at the same time, a cadaver that is ready for the butcher's knife.

In "Plato's Pharmacy," Derrida is naturally very interested in the vitality of this body, but he fails to note that this living body is well articulated and made first of all of ideas, not words. Although it operates with words, dialectic in fact presupposes that its organizing principle depends on criteria that articulate the body of the ideas. And for this very reason, it is possible to retrace, in the system of language, the originary system of ideas—namely, the order of their "right joining." The dialectical art of unification and division, described in the *Phaedrus* and put into practice in the *Sophist* and in the *Republic*, allows the philosopher to let go of a "minor" dream. Although there is no presumption of a direct face to face with the ideas, there is the expectation that a discourse can be constructed that joins words to one another according to an objective order that follows, retraces, and reproduces exactly the jointure of the body of the ideas. The real thesis, already announced in the *Cratylus*, is that language is a perfect verbal map of the heavenly realm of the signifieds. The art of dialectic presupposes, in fact, that it is possible to identify the jointures and to progress accordingly.

Peremptorily videocentric, the platonic metaphysics of presence is therefore preoccupied with organizing speech according to the progression of the *dialektike techne*; it is not worried about the *phone*, except as the inevitable material of vocalized speech. The father of discourse, in the *Phaedrus*, is present in order to assist his own discourse and to make it proceed in the right direction by responding to the objections of the interlocutors.

But he does not at all produce the category of presence—which Plato reserves for the ideas; nor, even less, is he protagonist of a vocal scene where the effects of an acoustic autoaffection come to the fore. Indeed, it is regrettable that, as he reflects on the *Phaedrus*, Derrida does not take the opportunity to note that, at least within the literary fiction of the dialogue, the speakers address one another. Thus, a relational horizon, rather than an autoaffection, would open a polyphony rather than a monologue for the voice—if this is indeed the theme. There would also be an opening where the voice could make itself heard as a vibration in a throat of flesh, which announces the uniqueness of the one who emits it, invoking the other in resonance. For as much as the metaphysicians, and Derrida with them, pretend to ignore it, this is precisely the life—always fragile and singular—which is communicated in the voice. It is enough to listen attentively—something that, evidently, philosophers refuse to do, perhaps because they are concentrated on the silent and solitary work of writing.

Nearly twenty years later, in 1986, Derrida has the opportunity once again to encounter the theme of the voice when he rereads one of the most beautiful texts of the western tradition: William Shakespeare's *Romeo and Juliet*.[50] In the meantime, Derrida's interests have been taken far from the question of metaphysical phonocentrism. After the early Derrida, well represented by the three texts from 1967, there in fact follows a second Derrida, often occupied with the American debate on the performative effect of language—a Derrida who no longer focuses his attention on the relationship between voice and writing. The occasion for reflecting anew on the theme of the voice comes in a brief essay, "Aphorism, Countertime," which he dedicates to the famous balcony scene in the second act of Shakespeare's tragedy. This is, rather tellingly, a missed opportunity. For reasons that are worth considering, Shakespeare's wisdom in constructing a scene centered on vocalic uniqueness escapes Derrida.

In the essay in question, the theoretical perspective with which Derrida reads Shakespeare's text turns on the problem of the proper name and the aphorism. He underscores, first of all, the valence of the "countertime" [*contretemps*] in the aphorism—both in the sense of an inopportune accident, and in the sense of something that goes contrary to the ordinary unfolding of time and is thus identified with a disjointed time. In Shakespeare's tragedy, the aphorism or countertime would be in the mechanism of equivocations and delays—messages that arrive too late at their destination, and at the wrong time—which not only lead to the death of the two lovers, but also allow each one to see and to survive, albeit briefly, the other's death. It is the law of love, emphasizes Derrida, that the one who loves does not want to see the other die; and yet it nevertheless happens that one of them, the one who survives, has this experience. Even double suicide, where the lovers die in the same instant, cannot overcome the temporal rule according to which it is impossible that both survive the other's death. Because of a series of countertimes, however, precisely this happens to Romeo and Juliet: each sees the other dead. This means, according to Derrida, that "what Romeo and Juliet experience is the exemplary anachrony, the essential impossibility of any absolute synchronization" that is typical of desire insofar as desire itself is structurally an aphorism.[51] More precisely, this means that the lovers' desire, like the aphorism, lies in the contradiction between anachrony and synchrony, separation and union.

It is precisely in this context that Derrida analyzes the question of the proper name. Captured in the movement of the aphorism, the proper name is inextricably united with the one who bears it, it coincides with him; but at the same time, it is something distinct from the one who bears it and is separable from him. In effect, in the balcony scene, Juliet evokes precisely this union, as she also invokes this separation. Calling Romeo by name—"O Romeo, Romeo, wherefore art thou Romeo?" (2.2.33)—and thus insisting on the coincidence between Romeo and his name, she invites him to separate himself from the name "Romeo," which is her "enemy" (2.2.38), just as the Montagues are the enemies of the Capulets in a way that makes their union impossible.[52] The problem to which Juliet alludes here is no small matter. Besides the union and separation of the two lovers, and of Romeo in relation to his name, this problem clearly brings into play the ontological status of a unique being whose existence is not reducible to the name, or to language. The crucial point—although Derrida overlooks it—is that this ontological status or, better, the singularity of the human being loved by Juliet, is manifested as voice in the balcony scene. Recognizing Romeo's voice, the young girl recognizes the uniqueness of the loved one, separable from the proper name ("thou art thyself, though not a Montague" [2.2.39]), which is communicated to her vocally. Thus the essential bond between voice and uniqueness—theatrically underscored by a nocturnal darkness that empowers the exclusive role of the acoustic sphere—comes to the fore. And yet it is here that the strange reticence of Derrida appears. Although he dedicates his commentary to this scene, he in fact does not focus on its fundamental theoretical nucleus; he symptomatically misses the opportunity to deepen the theme of vocalic uniqueness along with Shakespeare.

To be sure, there are many interesting and convincing aspects of the reading that Derrida devotes to the Shakespearean masterpiece. What stands out, first of all, is the way in which his interpretation is able to link the logic of desire to its mortal outcome, through the thread of a contretemps that unites and dissociates, passing on the question of the name. In particular, he insists on the relation between the proper name, as aphorism, and death. Asking him to separate himself from his name, Juliet, who would like him to live, is in fact asking Romeo "to die, since his life *is* his name."[53] According to Derrida, this alludes to the "non-coincidence and contretemps between my name and me, between the experience according to which I am named or hear myself called by name and my 'living present.'"[54] This sentence, if for no other reason than the choice of certain terms, deserves attention. For anyone familiar with the lexicon of the early Derrida and with his thesis on phonocentrism, an expression like "living present" cannot but evoke the theme of the voice. Add to this a "hear myself called" that alludes, albeit obliquely, to his earlier formula "hear oneself speak." As already indicated, the context of the essay on Shakespeare is however quite different from that of the writings of 1967. Concentrating on the movement of the aphorism, Derrida wants here to emphasize that there is a union and a separation between the name and the one who bears it. And thanks to this separation, he notes, the name is "destined to survive me"; "in this way it announces my death."[55]

At stake is an aphoristic separation that implies dissociation as much as uniting. It adheres structurally in the coincidence between each one and his name. In other words, caught in a movement that is not unlike that of *différance*, Romeo is and is not his name; he coincides with it and is separated from it. And it is precisely in this horizon that, according to the sentence cited above, Derrida points out the noncoincidence, the contretemps, between Romeo and his name, between the "living presence" of the young man and the experience in which he has a name and "hears himself called by name." Although it presupposes and is rooted in the coincidence between Romeo and his name, the separation thus works between the register of the name and the register of the living presence of the one who bears it. The interesting point is not so much the distinction between the two registers, but rather the fact that this distinction distinguishes, precisely, the "hearing oneself called" from the "living presence." In other words, the living presence seems here not to be an essential effect of the voice and, in turn, the voice itself seems to refer to a phenomenological horizon where the subject, tellingly, "hears himself called" rather than "hears himself speak." The autoaffection of the acoustic circuit is therefore open to the external, to the voice of the other, and the living present comes to allude to the one who at once coincides with his name, and is a singular living being who dissociates himself from his name (pronounced, audible). In sum, rather curiously, the proper name separates or, at least, distinguishes the category of presence from the sphere of the voice.

This curiosity is further piqued, not so much by the brief citation taken from Derrida's essay—which has the tone of an interpolated clause and is not developed further—but rather from the Shakespeare text to which the sentence itself refers. As already indicated, in the balcony scene, the voice is in fact a central element, even aside from the significance of the words that are pronounced. The scene, as Derrida himself stresses, unfolds precisely at night. Although she invokes him, Juliet does not know that Romeo is listening to her in the penumbra, nor can she see him. Although it deals with the theater, and thus with the centrality of the eye, the indisputable protagonists here are the voices. The dialogue unfolds between two people who do not see one another.

For Juliet, who at the outset believes she speaks alone and then hears the words of an invisible interlocutor, this dialogue becomes such when she recognizes, by its sound, Romeo's voice: "My ears have not yet drunk a hundred words/Of thy tongue's uttering, yet I know the sound" (2.2.58–59). Derrida comments at this point that "she *identifies* him . . . by the timbre of his voice, that is to say by the words she hears without being able to see."[56] The uniqueness of the voice as a factor of identification thus comes to the fore. However, without stopping to consider the phenomenon of vocalic uniqueness, Derrida's commentary goes on to underscore the cold light of the moon—the penumbra, the night—which would characterize Juliet's discourse on the separation of the name as the announcement of death. Derrida wants to emphasize that the darkness, the absence of visibility that is so unusual for the theater, functions on the one hand as a metaphor for death, and on the other hand unequivocally places in relief the dissection of the name and thus also of speech and language in general. His thesis is of course rather interesting, and plausible. And yet it ends up overlooking the more relevant aspect of Shakespeare's scene. For the theme

of the proper name here announces, significantly, the question of uniqueness and, more specifically, lets the attention of the spectator concentrate
itself on a uniqueness that makes itself heard as voice, beyond the name itself, beyond speech and even beyond language. In other words, Shakespeare's scene is quite complex and subtle. The spectator, like Juliet, does
not see Romeo's face. The recognition is vocalic. There where the proper
name and the singular existent who bears it are discussed, Shakespeare
makes reference to the voice and the ear.

It is obvious that the proper name evokes uniqueness; this is, so to
speak, the prerequisite of the problem and its theatrical solution. Juliet addresses herself precisely to Romeo, to the one who bears this name, in spite
of this name. She wants Romeo's singularity, the embodied uniqueness of
her lover, to be separated from the name "Romeo" and to take another
name. Or, rather, she postulates the separation of the proper name from
the one who bears it. In this sense, in loving the irreducible uniqueness of
who she loves, the young girl accomplishes a more radical move than the
one suggested by Rosenzweig, who insists instead on the "I, name and surname." In the case of Romeo, in fact, "Romeo" means "Montague"; it
means the irruption of what Romeo, historically and socially, is. But Juliet,
as is natural for lovers, does not love what Romeo is, but rather who he is.
She loves Romeo's uniqueness, and she asks him to separate himself from
that proper name that, while it announces the uniqueness of the one who
bears it, renders the reality of their love improper, in the context of the
feud between Montague and Capulet. "What is Montague? It is nor hand
nor foot/Nor arm nor face nor any other part/Belonging to a man"
(2.2.40–42). It is obvious that, for Juliet, the loved one is an embodied
uniqueness. Thus, the reciprocal communication of this uniqueness functions all the more in the physical, corporeal element of the voice—in contrast to a proper name, which belongs instead to the verbal register. The
name is not flesh; still less is it singular flesh. The voice, however, is.

Shakespeare could have set the scene in the light of day. By day, the
sense of the dialogue, the request to separate Romeo from his name, would
not have changed. But he set the scene at night—not, or not only, because
the penumbra foreshadows their death, but above all because the voice of
Romeo, unseen and therefore unidentifiable through the gaze, is the immediate, sonorous revelation that is proper to that embodied uniqueness
that Juliet wants to separate from the name. Significantly, she recognizes
Romeo by his voice. And she recognizes him by a voice that pronounces

words that are totally irrelevant to the act of this recognition. Shakespeare's lesson is, therefore, quite subtle: if the problem is how to separate the embodied uniqueness from the name—from that word, the proper name, that already alludes to the uniqueness—then the voice is what allows for this separation. This reveals a uniqueness that is such beyond the register of speech and above all, in this context, beyond the name. The problem, introduced by Juliet, of the separation between the proper name and the one who bears it thus finds a solution that reverses its terms. In the first place—or, rather, in the second place according to the narrative development of the dialogue—it in fact seems that the solution lies in parting from the proper name and in separating it from the embodied uniqueness of the one who bears it. So that this very uniqueness, finally freed from the name Romeo, can take another name. In the second place, more significantly, after the recognition of the voice, there follows a second solution: its point of departure is what is always already given and perceptible— namely, that uniqueness that the voice announces. This uniqueness can leave the name aside, can unite or separate itself from any name. In other words, the crucial twist in the balcony scene shows us that who Juliet loves communicates himself to her in a unique voice, with respect to which the proper name is nothing but an inessential, and thus modifiable, addition. Indeed, Juliet does not love one of the Montagues, but rather the one who is now communicating himself in his own, singular voice. In this context, it becomes obvious that Romeo's singularity—which is absolute because it is absolutely loved—can take any name; it can separate itself from the name that it bears and take on another.

In a certain sense, the tragedy in Verona is simple. It tells how a name—"Romeo," and thus "Montague"—prevails and determines the plot. It is basically a tragedy of the name. Still, Shakespeare is not satisfied with this simplicity. He finds a way to show us that underneath a plot centered on the name, there is a broken thread that alludes to another possible plot and a happier outcome, even if it is not carried to conclusion. This is a plot, barely begun and then interrupted, in which the uniqueness that makes itself heard in the voice overcomes the name; or, in which love, as a community of lovers in their bare singularity, would prevail over a social order that has determined their name as the mark of belonging to two feuding families. In the final analysis, the true tragic side of *Romeo and Juliet* lies in the impotence of the community of lovers in the face of the political community of the name. The historically determined sociality of the name wins, in the tragedy, over the socially undisciplinable uniqueness of the voice. The community of lovers, we know, is fragile. "Call me but love, and I'll be new baptis'd," exclaims Romeo in the balcony scene (2.2.50). But this is precisely the point: love is not a proper name. It is the name of a passion that exposes the lovers to one another in the embodied uniqueness of their being who they are. Insofar as in the voice there resounds a singularity that can leave speech aside, the voice itself is the active, reciprocal communication—we could say the bare, reciprocal communication that has not yet been vested in the semantic—of this reciprocal passion.

"What is in a name?" asks Juliet at a certain point; and she quickly observes that "that which we call a rose / By any other word would smell as sweet" (2.2.43–44). At this point, Derrida notes that "rose," like "love," is a common name, not a proper name. In addition to the aporia inscribed in the aphorism of the proper name, there would therefore be the aporia of the exchange of a proper name for a common name. However, what escapes Derrida—who, again, misses the appointment with the voice to which Shakespeare invites the reader, or the spectator—is that the rose is named here in order to pull Romeo's voice into a curious analogy. The play between the olfactory and the auditory, or between smell and phonic emission, unfolds between the nose and the ear without any intervention from sight. If what is proper to the rose, its odor, is revealed as such regardless of the name by which we call it and regardless of the fact that we see it, then the uniqueness that is proper to the lover, too, is revealed as such regardless of his name and regardless of whether or not we see his face. The voice corresponds to the smell. More than a perfect rhetorical figure, the analogy is curious because it is constructed as a series of suggestions. The common name rests on the rose that smells just as the proper name rests on Romeo who, by speaking, makes his voice heard. The verbal register, which covers both names, is not bound by any necessity to the two sources of emission—odorous and sonorous—which constitute the "dear perfection," or the proper of that to which the two names refer (2.2.46). This proper, unlike the amorous impropriety of his name, is for Romeo an embodied uniqueness that is manifested vocally. The name "Romeo" says nothing of this proper, just as the name "rose" says nothing of the smell of a rose. In the first case, listening is enough; in the second, smelling. The voice is the way in which the exquisitely human uniqueness emits its essence.

It is superfluous to point out that, in the balcony scene, there is also the acoustic work of a resonance. This resonance lies not only in the *aria della canzone* by Shakespeare, but moreover in the theatrical construction that solicits the audience's ear, hindering the power of the eye. The dialogue between the two lovers develops on two intersecting registers. In one sense it is a dialogue of words, fully semantic, which connects the phrases of Romeo and Juliet, often in the form of question and answer, to the thread of a meaning. In another sense, however, it is a dialogue of voices, an exchange of sonorous emissions that reciprocally communicate two embodied uniquenesses whose reality, in their "dear perfection," can do without the name, and even without speech. After all, does not the discourse on the rose allude to this too? Its smell remains sweet, not only if we give it another name, but if we give it no name at all. Juliet lets the *nomina* alone, and looks at the *res*. Yet this *res* is not a thing that can be subsumed under the wing of the universal; rather, it is a living, unrepeatable, unsubstitutable, and therefore lovable singularity. This lovability of the singular being—in fact loved because "thou art thyself, though not a Montague"—gets configured in the balcony scene as an exchange of voices. Beyond the words, two voices invoke and convoke one another; they resound according to the musical rhythm of the relation. Rather than a regression to the vocalic pleasure of infancy, this is an allusion to a lost, ahistorical time of an infancy in which—as far as the bare uniqueness that makes everyone a dear perfection is concerned—the world of speech and names, of linguistic and social rules, is as yet nothing. This nothing sustains the love dream of Romeo and Juliet. It allows them—it allows us—to imagine another story for the community of lovers who want neither to be separated nor to die.

It is precisely Shakespeare who suggests for the story a second, improbable plot. For our ears that are opened in the dark, he has left a duet of two voices and the amorous echo of their resonance.

Notes

TRANSLATOR'S INTRODUCTION

1. Cavarero provides an original and insightful rereading of this passage from Aristotle's *Politics* in the pages that follow. She shows that Aristotle does not simply claim that man is political "because he speaks and thus mobilizes the intrinsic communicativity of language." Instead, she shows how for Aristotle, speech is, so to speak, that which distinguishes man from other political animals (like bees) because man is able to perceive and hence to speak of things that belong to the *koninonia politike*.

2. Hannah Arendt, *The Human Condition* (Chicago: University of Chicago Press, 1958), 179.

3. See, respectively, Rosi Braidotti's introduction to my *In Spite of Plato*, trans. Serena Anderlini-D'Onofrio and Aine O'Healy (New York: Routledge Press, 1995); my own introduction to *Relating Narratives: Storytelling and Selfhood*, trans. and with an introduction by Paul Kottman (New York: Routledge Press, 2000); and Deanna Shemek's introduction to my *Stately Bodies: Literature, Philosophy, Gender*, trans. Robert de Lucca and Deanna Shemek (Ann Arbor: University of Michigan Press, 2002).

4. For more on this tragedy of the name, see my introduction to Cavarero, *Relating Narratives*, xxiii–xxv.

5. All references to William Shakespeare's *Romeo and Juliet* are taken from the Arden edition of the play, ed. Brian Gibbons (London: Metheuen, 1980).

6. The story itself—retold in poems, novels, films, and musicals—clearly has a life that extends well beyond Shakespeare's text. Indeed, films like *Shakespeare in Love* (1999) go so far as to suggest that the force of the story or myth fully determine the actual composition of Shakespeare's dramatic script. The extraordinary popularity of the Romeo and Juliet mythos might also account for the not insignificant fact that *Romeo and Juliet* has replaced *Julius Caesar* as the play most often taught in high schools in the United States. See Jonathan Goldberg's chapter on *Romeo and Juliet* in his collection of essays, *Shakespeare's Hand* (Minneapolis: University of Minnesota Press, 2002).

7. Arendt, *Human Condition*, 188.

8. One of the themes to which Cavarero repeatedly returns in *For More than One Voice* is the extent to which, in her view, the reciprocal exchange of voices implies a material, contextual relation between embodied, singular existents more fully than does the gaze. Through reference to Emmanuel Levinas' notion of the "face to face," she underscores that a more radical response to the metaphysical tradition of thinking about ethics and politics requires an entirely different lexicon, one not indebted to the primacy of vision, seeing (*theoria, idea,* etc.).

9. See Kenneth Muir, *Shakespeare's Sources* (London: Metheuen, 1977); and Joel Fineman, *Shakespeare's Perjured Eye* (Berkeley: University of California Press, 1986), 161 and passim.

10. This is, of course, how the scene has traditionally been read by critics from Northrop Frye to Jacques Derrida; indeed, in my experience of teaching the play, this is what many students of the play come to realize right away. See, respectively, *Northrop Frye on Shakespeare* (New Haven: Yale University Press, 1988); and Jacques Derrida's essay "Aphorism, Countertime," in *Acts of Literature*, ed. Derek Attridge (New York: Routledge Press, 1994).

11. I develop more fully this notion of the "scene" in relation to, and in contradistinction to, the dramatic work or tragic myth in my essay "Memory, Mimesis, Tragedy: The Scene Before Philosophy," *Theatre Journal* 55, no. 1 (2003).

12. Cavarero makes a similar claim, revising Arendt's notion of the "space of interaction" under the name of "local"—"the *local* is a relational space which does not concern *what* those who share it are, but rather *who* they are."

13. Cavarero writes: "In the uniqueness that makes itself heard as voice, there is an embodied existent, or rather, a 'being-there' in its radical finitude, here and now."

14. This may in fact be a more precise way of accounting for the popularity of the story itself, over and beyond any particular version.

15. Responding to an orally delivered version of this preface, Kaja Silverman objected to this claim, suggesting instead that the role of the voice in the scene I am describing is an effect of Shakespeare's text. Her objection, as I understood it, was that my interpretation is antitextual, or too essentialist in the way that it attributes to the singularity of Romeo's voice an ontological status that precedes and exceeds Shakespeare's text. I recall her objection here because I can imagine other readers (particularly those for whom the theme of *écriture* in poststructuralist thought has been of particular influence) responding in a similar fashion to some claims made by Cavarero in *For More than One Voice*. My position, which I share with Cavarero, is that the embodied singularity of each speaker as it is manifested in the voice is an ontological given that, significantly, resists figuration and inscription in general. Instead, this "vocal ontology of uniqueness" (to use Cavarero's phrase) belongs irrevocably to the here and now of its acoustic resonance between speaker and listener. Indeed, it is this irrevocability that is—I believe—at stake in Shakespeare's balcony scene. For it is precisely what no sign, mark, inscription, or trace can reveal—namely, Romeo's embodied singularity—on which Shake-

speare's script depends for the plot of the story and for this particular scene's efficacy in relation to that plot.

16. It is telling in this regard that Cavarero's reading of Levinas' theme of the face to face is quite literal. Rather than focusing on those passages where Levinas appears to be referring figuratively to a mode of transcendence that is not visible to the eye of the body, she takes his descriptions of a reciprocal gaze as a literal reference to a visual horizon.

17. The full passage reads: "Speechless action would no longer be action because there would no longer be an actor, and the actor, the doer of deeds, is possible only if he is at the same time the speaker of words. The action he humanly discloses by the word, and through his deed can be perceived in its brute physical appearance without verbal accompaniment, it becomes relevant only through the spoken word in which he identifies himself as the actor, announcing what he does, has done, and intends to do." Arendt, *Human Condition*, 178–79.

18. This very distinction is articulated by Arendt, tellingly, through reference to the voice. She writes: "In acting and speaking, men show who they are, reveal actively their unique personal identities and thus make their appearance in the human world, while their physical identities appear without any activity of their own in the unique shape of the body and sound of the voice." Ibid., 179.

19. It is worth pointing out, although I do not have the space to elaborate, the extent to which Cavarero's methodology differs from "deconstruction" of a Derridean sort. (Her reading of Derrida in the Appendix of this book explains her dissent with Derrida's account of the voice. However, she does not address the question of methodology explicitly.) Like Derrida, Cavarero is interested in "overturning" (Derrida's phrase) classical, hierarchical philosophical oppositions—like speech and writing, or the voice and the semantic. But unlike Derrida, she does not proceed through an analysis of the aporias or "undecidables" (Derrida's term again) that mark the history of such oppositions, or through textual attention to whatever figures resist these oppositions. Rather, her work simply presumes the absolute failure of metaphysical philosophical discourse and instead seeks to recuperate its figures not by analyzing their figurality but by *literalizing* them. For her, the "voice" or the "body" are not simply tropes or themes, but rather the literal, phenomenological horizon of an ontology in which there is no distinction between body and soul, or being and appearing. (I have quoted here from Derrida's own account of the methodology of deconstruction. See Jacques Derrida, *Positions*, trans. Alan Bass [Chicago: University of Chicago Press, 1981], 41–43 and passim.)

20. Cavarero employs a similar dis-figuring methodology in her earlier works, *In Spite of Plato* and *Stately Bodies*.

21. As Giorgio Agamben claims, "every ontology implies a politics." Giorgio Agamben, introduction to Emmanuel Levinas, *Alcune riflessioni sulla filosofia dell'hitlerismo* (Macerata: Quodlibet, 1996), 14.

22. Symptomatically, not only is the voice not understood primarily through the Arendtian category of action in Cavarero's text, but it even comes close to

identifying itself with those features of biological life (reproduction, breathing, etc.) that Arendt classifies as "labor." See, for example, Cavarero's discussion of breath/voice in ancient Hebrew, or her discussion of the maternal *chora* in the work of Julia Kristeva and Hélène Cixous below.

23. To be precise, for Arendt, the embodied singularity of each actor (the fact that each is born unique) is the ontological precondition for the "the startling un-expectedness [that] is inherent in all beginnings and origins." In other words, the "newness" of each action "is possible only because each man is unique, so that with each birth something uniquely new comes into the world." Implicit here, again, is a disjunction between the ontological horizon of a plurality of embodied, singular actors and the political sphere of action that this horizon makes possible. Arendt, *Human Condition*, 178.

24. The term *condition* plays a crucial role in Arendt's discourse, where she at-tempts to articulate the extent—and the limit—of how humans are "condi-tioned." She remarks that "the conditions of human existence—natality and mor-tality, worldliness, plurality . . . never condition us absolutely." Ibid., 11.

25. Ibid., 177. To avoid confusion, it should be quickly emphasized that this "initiative" is not the same thing as the self-conscious "will" or "intention" of the actor. For Arendt, the actor never "knows" what he or she is doing; action does not spring from the willing subject or from the intentions of an autonomous "self." In-deed, for Arendt, action represents a crucial "limit" of the actors' will and self-knowledge.

INTRODUCTION

1. All citations from "A King Listens" are taken from Italo Calvino, *Under the Jaguar Sun*, trans. William Weaver (New York: Harcourt Brace, 1988), 33–64. The privileging of the acoustic sphere and the importance in the story of a woman who sings are not coincidences. In its original form, Calvino's story is in fact the reelab-oration of a text explicitly adapted by Calvino for a work of musical theater by Lu-ciano Berio, which bears the same title. The project, which was developed between 1979 and 1983, was taken forward by Berio and Calvino independently; the libretto in three acts sketched out by the writer was only used in part. *A King Listens*—mu-sical action in the texts of Calvino, Auden, Gotter, and Berio—debuted in 1984 at the Salzburger Festspiele under the direction of Lorin Maazel.

2. Paul Zumthor, *Oral Poetry: An Introduction*, trans. Kathryn Murphy-Judy (Minneapolis: University of Minnesota Press, 1990), 44.

3. Paul Zumthor, preface to Corrado Bologna, *Flatus vocis: Metafisica e antropologia della voce* (Bologna: Il Mulino, 2000), vii.

4. See Bologna, *Flatus vocis*, xiii and passim. The book, edited for the first time in 1992, is, according to Zumthor himself, who wrote the preface, an exemplary and pioneering text for the study of vocality. Although insisting on the physical and bodily nature of the voice, Bologna nevertheless means by voice something like the potentiality of signification, "a confused push towards *meaning*, towards

expression, that is towards *existing*" (23). (This expression is taken, to the letter, from Zumthor, who writes that "the voice is in fact *vouloir-dire* and the will to exist"; *Oral Poetry*, 7.) Precisely this push to signification, or to the end of which the voice would be a potentiality, thus ends up keeping the vocal bound to the decisive category of speech. This is the criticism that Vicenzo Cuomo makes of Corrado Bologna. See Cuomo, *Le parole della voce: Lineamenti di una filosofia della phonè* (Salerno: Edisud, 1998), 52. Other works in Italian on this topic include an anthology of texts that analyze the voice from different disciplinary perspectives, generating a number of suggestions but also a certain confusion. It can be found in a collection called *Fonè: La voce e la traccia*, ed. Stefano Mecatti (Florence: La casa Husher, 1985). Finally, it is symptomatic that in order to find a text in recent Italian writings that is dedicated to the uniqueness of the voice, one must turn to a literary text: *Voci* by Dacia Mariani (Milan: Rizzoli, 1994).

5. Roland Barthes (in collaboration with Roland Havas), "Ascolto," in *Enciclopedia Einaudi* (Turin: Einaudi, 1977), 1:247.

6. Ibid.

7. Ibid., 1:272.

CHAPTER I.I

1. Bologna, *Flatus vocis*, 31.

2. [TN: For more on the Pythia, see Walter Burkert, *Greek Religion*, trans. John Raffan (Cambridge: Harvard University Press, 1985), 116–17.]

3. See Vicenzo Cuomo, *La parola della voce*, 27–31.

4. Franz Rosenzweig, *Philosophical and Theological Writings*, trans. and ed. with notes and commentary by Paul W. Franks and Michael L. Morgan (Indianapolis, IN: Hackett, 2000), 83.

5. I take this definition from J. Botterweck and H. Ringgren, eds., *Theological Dictionary of the Old Testament*, trans. John T. Wills (Grand Rapids, MI: Eardmans, 1977).

6. Franz Rosenzweig, *The Star of Redemption*, trans. William Hallo (New York: Holt, Rinehart and Winston, 1971), 190.

7. Gershom Scholem, *On the Kabbalah and Its Symbolism*, trans. Ralph Manheim (New York: Schocken Books, 1996), 11.

8. Ibid., 12–13.

9. Walter Benjamin, "On Language as Such and on the Language of Man," in *Selected Writings*, ed. Marcus Bullock and Michael W. Jennings (Cambridge: Harvard University Press, 1996), 1:67.

10. Ibid., 1:65.

11. See Jean Bottero, Clarisse Herrenschmidt, and Jean-Pierre Vernant, *Ancestor of the West: Writing, Reasoning and Religion in Mesopotamia, Elam and Greece*, trans. Teresa Lavender Fagan (Chicago: University of Chicago Press, 2003).

12. Rosenzweig, *Star of Redemption*, 178.

13. Gianfranco Ravesi, *Bereshit . . . En archè*, in AA.VV., *Il Libro sacro: Letture e interpretazioni ebraiche, cristiane e mussulmane* (Milan: Mondadori, 2002), 1.

14. As is well known, at least until the time of Augustine, even for the Christians the reading of the sacred text was done aloud. Augustine himself was in fact stunned that Ambrose, transgressing the norm, read in silence, "saving his voice" (*Confessions*, VI, 3.3). For more on the contradistinction of the visual and acoustic sphere in this regard, see Maria Tasinato, *L'occhio del silenzio* (Padua: Esedra, 1997).

15. Rusmir Mahmutcehajic, *Rijeci kao boje zdjela* (Sarajevo: DID, 2000), 15.

16. Scholem, *On the Kabbalah*, 22.

17. Rosenzweig, *Philosophical and Theological Writings*, 109.

18. Ibid.

CHAPTER I.2

1. Emmanuel Levinas, *The Levinas Reader*, ed. Sean Hand (Oxford: Blackwell, 1989), 217.

2. Emmanuel Levinas, *Basic Philosophical Writings*, ed. Adriaan Peperzak, Simon Critchley, and Robert Bernasconi (Indianapolis: Indiana University Press, 1996), 41.

3. Levinas, *Levinas Reader*, 84.

4. Ibid.

5. Ibid., 265.

6. Ibid.

7. Emmanuel Levinas, *Otherwise than Being or Beyond Essence*, trans. Alphonso Lingis (Pittsburgh: Duquesne University Press, 1998), 17.

8. Levinas, *Basic Philosophical Writings*, 34.

9. Ibid., 56.

10. Ibid., 20.

11. Ibid.

12. Ibid., 55.

13. Ibid.

14. Ibid., 61.

15. Ibid.

16. Ibid., 96.

17. Ibid., 201. The link between Saying and Giving appears, for example, in the Latin equivalence of *dic* and *da*, in certain contexts; and it is the reason for the substitutability with the same form *cedo*. See Johann B. Hoffmann, *La lingua d'uso latina* (Bologna: Patron, 1985), 143.

18. Ibid., 223.

19. Ibid., 225.

20. Ibid.

21. Ibid.

22. Ibid., 221.

CHAPTER I.3

1. Ibid., 45.

2. Aristotle, *Poetics*, 1457a5–30.

3. Aristotle, *Politics*, 1253a9–19.

4. See Hannah Arendt, *The Life of Mind* (New York: Harcourt Brace, 1973).

5. Ibid.

6. Parmenides, B 1.29; see Jonathan Barnes, ed., *Early Greek Philosophy* (New York: Penguin Books, 1987), 131.

7. See Giovanni Semerano, *L'infinito: Un equivoco millenario*, 3, n. 1.

8. See Bruno Snell, *The Discovery of the Mind: The Greek Origins of European Thought* (Cambridge: Harvard University Press, 1953), 1–17.

9. For more, see Linda Napolitano Valditara, *Lo sguardo nel buio* (Rome: Laterza, 1994), 3–12.

10. I discuss Derrida's work at more length in the Appendix to this book.

11. Hans Jonas, *The Phenomenon of Life* (Evanston: Northwestern University Press, 2001), 137.

12. Ibid., 138.

13. Ibid., 146.

14. Ibid., 144.

15. Arendt, *Life of Mind*, 144.

16. Ibid., 129–51.

17. See Plato, *Seventh Letter*, 342a–344b.

18. Plotinus, *Enneads*, DK B 8.

19. Parmenides, DK B 8.

20. Maria Zambrano, *I beati* (Milan: Feltrinelli, 1992), 83.

21. Levinas, *Basic Philosophical Writings*, 111.

CHAPTER 1.4

1. Plato, *Sophist*, 263e. [TN: The translations of Plato's and Aristotle's texts cited by Cavarero are her own. For this reason, I have throughout relied loosely on the English translation of Plato's *Complete Works* published by Hackett (1996) and the English translation of Aristotle's *Basic Works* published by Random House (1941), but I have often amended these translations in order to preserve the sense of Cavarero's translation.]

2. Plato, *Theaetetus*, 190a.

3. Ibid.

4. Giovanni Gentile, *Genesi e struttura della società* (Florence: Sansoni, 1975), 37. On the complexity of the problems relative to the figure of consciousness, see Fabrizio Desideri, *L'ascolto della conscienza* (Milan: Feltrinelli, 1998).

5. Jacques Derrida, *Speech and Phenomenon*, trans. David Allison (Evanston: Northwestern University Press, 1973), 80 and passim. Again, I discuss Derrida's work at more length in the Appendix to this book.

CHAPTER 1.5

1. Citations taken from Jorge Luis Borges, *Labyrinths* (New York: New Directions, 1964), 59–66.

2. Hannah Arendt, *Life of Mind*, 170.

3. Desideri, *L'ascolto della conscienza*, 36. Desideri refers here to Wittgenstein's critique of Platonism.

CHAPTER 1.6

1. I am referring here to the classic distinction according to which "phonology" is the science that studies the sounds of language from the point of view of their function in the system of linguistic communication, whereas the "phonetic" is the science that studies the sounds of language in their concrete realization, inde-

pendent of their linguistic function. See David Crystal, *A Dictionary of Linguistics and Phonetics* (Cambridge: Blackwell, 1997).

2. Aristotle, *Poetics*, 1456b 30–34.

3. Ibid., 1457a 10–27.

4. Plato, *Philebus*, 17b.

5. Ibid., 17e–18c.

6. Plato, *Cratylus*, 388e–389a.

7. Ibid., 424b–c.

8. Ibid., 432e, 433b.

9. Ibid., 408b–c.

10. See Giovanni Manetti, *La teoria del segno nell'antichità classica* (Milan: Bompiani, 1987), 105.

11. Lia Formigari, *Il linguaggio* (Rome-Bari: Laterza, 2001), 36.

12. Aristotle, *De Interpretatione*, 1.

13. Emile Benveniste, *Problems in General Linguistics*, trans. Mary Elizabeth Meek (Gables, FL: University of Miami Press, 1971), 34.

14. Ibid.

15. Plato, *Sophist*, 253a.

16. Ibid., 262c.

17. Ibid., 262d.

18. Ibid., 262a.

CHAPTER 1.7

1. R. B. Onians, *The Origins of European Thought About the Body, the Mind, the Soul, the World, Time, and Fate: New Interpretations of Greek, Roman and Kindred Evidence Also of Some Basic Jewish and Christian Beliefs* (Cambridge: Cambridge University Press, 1988), 44.

2. Empedocles, DK B 105; Barnes, *Early Greek Philosophy*, 191.

3. Onians, *Origins of European Thought*, 46.

4. Ibid.

5. Ibid., 156.

6. Ibid., 158.

7. Alfred A. Tomatis, *L'oreille et le langage* (Paris: Editions du Seuil, 1991), 56.

8. Ibid.

9. Plato, *Timaeus*, 73c–d, 44d.

10. Onians, *Origins of European Thought*, 65.

11. Plato, *Timaeus*, 91b.

12. Ibid., 46d.

13. Onians, *Origins of European Thought*, 78.

14. Plato, *Symposium*, 209b–e.

15. Plato, *Phaedrus*, 278b.

CHAPTER 1.8

1. Plato, *Symposium*, 221c.

2. Martha Nussbaum, *The Fragility of Goodness* (Cambridge: Harvard University Press, 1986), 232.

3. Plato, *Symposium*, 221c–e.

4. Ibid.

5. Ibid., 215b.

6. Ibid., 215b–c.

7. Ibid., 216c.

8. Ibid., 216a.

9. On the explicit and implicit inferences to Alcibiades' biography, see Martha Nussbaum, *Fragility of Goodness*, esp. chap. 6.

10. Plato, *Symposium*, 218a.

11. Ibid., 221c.

12. Ibid., 222a.

13. Plato, *Cratylus*, 508b–c.

14. Plato, *Apology*, 31d.

15. See Arendt, *Human Condition*, 193; see also my *Relating Narratives*, 11–12, 27.

16. Robert Browning, "The Pied-Piper of Hamelin," in *The Poems* (London: Penguin, 1981), 1:383–91.

17. Friedrich Nietzsche, *The Birth of Tragedy*, trans. Francis Golffing (New York: Doubleday, 1956), 82. In the excellent commentary to the Italian translation, edited by Vicenzo Vitiello and Ettore Fagioli, it is noted that the parallel drawn by Nietzsche between Socrates and Orpheus concerns above all the "'demonic' aspect, that is, the persuasive and enchanting power that is linked to rationality." *La nascita della tragedia*, ed. Vitiello and Fagioli (Milan: Mondadori, 1996), 156, 152.

18. Ibid., 146.

19. Giorgio Colli, *La nascita della filosofia* (Milan: Adelphi, 1981).

20. Ibid., 34.

21. Ibid., 46.

22. Ibid., 81.

CHAPTER 1.9

1. Milman Parry, *The Making of Homeric Verse: The Collected Papers of Milman Parry* (Oxford: Clarendon Press, 1971). See also Walter Ong, *Orality and Literacy: The Technologizing of the Word* (New York: Routledge, 1982).

2. Ong, *Orality and Literacy*, 13.

3. Ibid., 21.

4. For more on the functional specialization of the two hemispheres of the brain see, among others, Roman Jakobson and Linda R. Waugh, *The Sound Shape of Language* (New York: Mouton de Gruyter, 1987). A suggestive hypothesis on the prevalence of the left hemisphere over the right, owing to the historical advent of writing that "breaks" the original bicamerality of the mind, can be found in Julian Janes, *The Origin of Consciousness in the Breakdown of the Bicameral Mind* (Boston: Houghton Mifflin, 1977).

5. See Janes, *The Origin of Consciousness*.

6. Eric Havelock, *Preface to Plato* (Cambridge: Harvard University Press, 1963), 5.

7. Snell, *Discovery of the Mind*, 229.

8. Ong, *Orality and Literacy*, 12.

9. See Plato, *Phaedrus*, 275c–277a; Plato, *Seventh Letter*, 344c–d.

10. Bruno Gentili, *Poesia e pubblico nella Grecia antica* (Rome: Laterza, 1995), 15.

11. Plato, *Sophist*, 263e.

12. Havelock, *Preface to Plato*, 150.

13. Ibid., 151–52.

14. Plato, *Republic*, 606d.

15. Ibid., 475d–e.

16. Gentili, *Poesia e pubblico nella Grecia antica*, 216 and passim.

17. The following represents a slight revision of an essay that has already been published in English under the title "The Envied Muse: Plato Versus Homer," in *Cultivating the Muse*, ed. Efrossini Spentzou and Don Fowler (Oxford: Oxford University Press, 2002), 47–67.

18. Nancy, "Sharing Voices," in *Transforming the Hermeneutic Context: From Nietzsche to Nancy*, ed. Gayle L. Ormiston and Alan D. Schrift (Albany: State University of New York Press, 1990), 201.

19. See Maria Tasinato, "Dalla parte di Ione: Frustoli per un dialogetto platonico," *Esercizi Filosofici* 5 (2000): 15–34.

20. Plato, *Ion*, 533d.

21. Ibid., 534c.

22. Ibid., 534b.

23. Plato, *Republic*, 601a.

24. Plato, *Ion*, 534d.

25. Ibid., 534e.

26. Jean-Luc Nancy, "Sharing Voices," 220; Martin Heidegger, "On the Way to Language," in *Basic Writings*, ed. David Krell (New York: Harper Collins, 1993), 393–426. The etymology obviously alludes to the god Hermes who, as Plato says in the *Cratylus* (408a), is "a messenger and deeply knows the power of speech."

27. Plato, *Ion*, 535a.

28. See Andrew Ford, *Homer: The Poetry of the Past* (Ithaca: Cornell University Press, 1992), chap. 5.

29. Alessandro Portelli, *Il testo e la voce* (Rome: Manifestolibri, 1992), 29.

30. Nancy, "Sharing Voices," 221.

31. The term *voice*, whose singularity Nancy continues to emphasize, has a multivocal and ambiguous application in his text. One reads, for example, that "Plato himself is nothing but the difference of the voices of his characters, and the general difference—general and always singular—of each voice with respect to *logos*." The singularity of voices thus does not regard, in this case, the materiality of the acoustic sphere. Significantly, Nancy goes on to declare that logos "articulates itself on the margins of silence and the voice. It articulates 'before' each voice the sharing of voices." See Nancy, "Sharing Voices," 223.

CHAPTER 2.1

1. Homer, *Iliad*, book 2, vv. 484–86. [TN: Here and throughout I use the English translation of the *Iliad* by Robert Fagles (New York: Penguin, 1990). At times I modify this translation in order to adhere more closely to the Italian translation cited by Cavarero.]

2. Ford, *Homer*, 49–50.

3. Homer, *Iliad*, book 2, 488–90.

4. Arendt, *Human Condition*, 184.

5. Gilles Deleuze, *A Thousand Plateaus: Capitalism and Schizophrenia*, trans. and foreword by Brian Massumi (London: Athlone Press, 1988), 35.

6. Jean-Pierre Vernant, "Aspects mythique de la mémoire en Grèce," *Journal de psychologie* 56 (1959): 1–29.

7. Thomas Bernhard, *The Voice Imitator*, trans. Kenneth J. Northcott (Chicago: University of Chicago Press, 1997), 13.

8. Plato, *Republic*, 607a.

9. For more on this, see my *Relating Narratives*.

10. Hannah Arendt, *Life of Mind*, 85.

11. Borges, *Labyrinths*, 64.

12. Ibid., 63.

13. Ibid.

14. Plato, *Phaedrus*, 245a.

15. See Giovanni Ferrari, *Listening to the Cicadas* (Cambridge: Cambridge University Press, 1987).

16. Plato, *Phaedrus*, 259b–c.

17. Ibid.

18. Ibid., 259d.

19. Ida Travi, *L'aspetto orale della poesia* (Verona: Anterem, 2000), 30.

CHAPTER 2.2

1. Homer, *Odyssey*, book 12, line 44. [TN: Here and throughout I use the English translation of the *Odyssey* by Richard Lattimore (New York: Harper Collins, 1965). At times I modify this translation in order to adhere more closely to the Italian translation cited by Cavarero.]

2. Ibid., line 158.

3. Ibid., line 181.

4. Pietro Pucci, *The Song of the Sirens* (Boston: Rowman and Littlefield, 1998), 2 and passim.

5. Homer, *Odyssey*, book 12, line 189.

6. I have written on this elsewhere, in regard to the Sirens, in *Stately Bodies*, 152–60.

7. René Magritte, *The Collective Invention*, 1934 (private collection, Belgium).

8. Franz Kafka, "The Silence of the Sirens," in *The Complete Stories* (New York: Schocken Books, 1971), 431.

9. Ibid.

10. Ibid.

11. Ibid.

12. Max Horkheimer and Theodor Adorno, *Dialectic of Enlightenment*, trans. John Cumming (New York: Verso, 1997), 46.

13. Ibid., 47, nn. 5, 46.

14. Ibid., 54.

15. Ibid., 59.

16. Ibid.

17. Ibid., 63–64.

18. Ibid., 46.

19. Edward Said, *Musical Elaborations* (New York: Columbia University Press, 1991), xviii.

20. Ibid., 68.

21. Ibid., 78–80.

22. Ibid., 79.

23. Ibid.

CHAPTER 2.3

1. [TN: In Italian, the adage is "alle donne si addice il silenzio," literally, "silence suits women."]

2. Isak Dinesen [Karen Blixen], "The Dreamers," in *Seven Gothic Tales* (New York: Smith and Haas, 1934).

3. Ibid., 332.

4. Ibid., 331.

5. Augusto Illuminati, *Il filosofo all'Opera* (Rome: Manifestolibri, 1999), 8.

6. Carlo Emilio Gadda, "Teatro," in *La Madonna dei filosofi* (Turin: Einaudi, 1973), 14.

7. Wayne Koestenbaum, *The Queen's Throat: Opera, Homosexuality and the Mystery of Desire* (New York: Poseidon Press, 1993).

8. Hélène Cixous, *Entre l'écriture des femmes* (Paris: Gallimard, 1986), 146.

9. Wolfgang Amadeus Mozart, *Lettere* (Milan: Guanda, 1981), 181.

10. Koestenbaum, *Queen's Throat*, 79.

11. Illuminati, *Il filosofo all'Opera*, 55.

12. Catherine Clément, *L'opéra ou la défaite des femmes* (Paris: Grasset, 1979).

13. See Kaja Silverman, *The Acoustic Mirror* (Bloomington and Indianapolis: Indiana University Press, 1988).

14. See Umberto Curi, *Filosofia del Don Giovanni: Alle origini di un mito moderno* (Milan: Bruno Mondadori, 2002). Concerning Mozart's masterpiece, the third chapter of this book is particularly interesting. There Curi emphasizes the different elaborations of the myth by Da Ponte and Mozart, showing how "Mozart's choice of conferring to music not the function of *accompanying* the libretto, or of *illustrating* it, nor of *translating* it or *commenting* on it, but rather of *systematically contradicting its importance*, deliberately introduces conflicts and dissonances, irregularities and anomalies into the elementary geometry of the delineated universe of Da Ponte" (230).

15. Said, *Musical Elaborations*, 40.

16. Augustine, *Confessions*, trans. R. S. Pine-Coffin (New York: Penguin, 1961), 238.

17. Henrich Besseler, *L'ascolto musicale nell'età moderna* (Bologna: Il Mulino, 1993), 39.

18. Antonio Savezzi, introduction to the Italian edition of Henrich Besseler, *L'ascolto musicale nell'età moderna*, 10.

19. See Roland Barthes, *S/Z*, trans. Richard Miller (New York: Hill and Wang, 1974), 107–13.

20. See Meri Franco-Lao, *Musica strega: Per la ricerca di una dimensione femminile della musica* (Rome: Edizioni della donna, 1976), 41–50.

21. [TN: "Drag" is in English in the original.]

22. See Judith Butler, *Gender Trouble* (New York: Routledge Press, 1990).

23. See Marco Beghelli, "Erotismo canoro," *Il saggiatore musicale* 7 (2000): 131 and passim.

CHAPTER 2.4

1. Friedrich Nietzsche, *Birth of Tragedy*, paragraph 21.
2. Julia Kristeva, *Revolutions in Poetic Language*, trans. Margaret Waller (New York: Columbia University Press, 1984), 201.
3. Gilles Deleuze and Felix Guattari, *Milles Plateaux* (Paris: Editions de Minuit, 1980), chap. 11.
4. Plato, *Republic*, 620a.
5. [TN: In French: "le Mot présent, dans ses voyelles et ses dipthtongues, comme un chair; et, dans ses consonnes, comme une ossature délicate à disséquer." Stéphene Mallarmé, "Les mots anglais," in *Oeuvres Complètes* (Paris: Gallimard, 1996), 901.]
6. Plato, *Timaeus*, 50d.
7. Ibid., 52b; I have developed the question of the platonic *chora* in greater detail in my *Stately Bodies*, 70–89. See also Judith Butler, *Bodies that Matter* (New York: Routledge Press, 1993).
8. Kristeva, *Revolutions*, 34.
9. Ibid., 247.
10. [TN: In French, the entire passage reads: "en le Vers, dispensateur, ordonnateur du jeu des pages, maître du livre. Visiblement soit qu'apparaisse son intégralité, parmi les marges et du blanc; ou qu'il se dissimule, nommez-le Prose, néanmoins c'est lui si demeure quelque secrète poursuite de musique, dans la réserve du Discours." Stéphane Mallarmé, "Quant au livre," in *Oeuvres Complètes*, 375.]
11. Kristeva, *Revolutions*, 200.

CHAPTER 2.5

1. Hélène Cixous, "Sorties," in Catherine Clément and Hélène Cixous, *La jeune née* (Paris: UGE, 1975), 118–19. Translated into English as *The Newly Born Woman* by Betsy Wing (Minneapolis: University of Minnesota Press, 1986), 65.
2. Ibid., 93.
3. Ibid.
4. See Cixous, *Entre l'écriture*, 32.
5. Hélène Cixous, *Coming to Writing and Other Essays*, ed. Deborah Jenson (Cambridge: Harvard University Press, 1991), 20.
6. Ibid., 21–22.
7. Ibid., 21.
8. See Maria Zambrano, *All'ombra del Dio sconosciuto* (Milan: Pratiche, 1997), 132.
9. Clément and Cixous, *Newly Born Woman*, 94.
10. Hélène Cixous and Mirelle Calle-Gruber, *Rootprints*, trans. Eric Prenowitz (New York: Routledge Press, 1997), 46.

11. Citation taken from an interview with Hélène Cixous that appears in the appendix to a thesis (*tesi di laurea*) written by Monica Fiorini, "Scrittura e dicibilità dell'esperienza: Sulla poetica di Hélène Cixous" (University of Bologna, 1995–96), 175.

12. Cixous and Calle-Gruber, *Rootprints*, 46.

13. [TN: The phrase that "truth sings in key" is rendered in English by the translator Eric Prenowitz as "I have the impression that the truth sings true." I have here modified Prenowitz's translation in order to correspond more closely to Cavarero's Italian translation, which is itself closer to the French sense.] The phrase is taken from Hélène Cixous, *L'heure de Clarice Lispector* (Paris: Des Femmes, 1989), 134.

14. Fiorini, interview with Cixous, "Scrittura e dicibilità dell'esperienza," 175.

15. Hélène Cixous, "Quand je n'écris pas, c'est comme si j'étais morte," in Jean Luis de Ramboures, *Comment travaillent les écrivains* (Paris: Flammarion, 1978), 58.

16. See especially Cixous, "Clarice Lispector: The Approach," in *Coming to Writing*.

17. For more on this process, see Clarice Lispector, *La passione secondo G.H.* (Milan: Feltrinelli, 1991). In part because of Cixous, Lispector's work has now become an essential point of reference for feminist reflections. I dealt with Lispector's work myself in my *In Spite of Plato*, 114–19; and in my essay "La passione della differenza," in *Storie delle passioni*, ed. Silvia Vegetti Finzi (Rome: Laterza, 1995), 297 and passim.

18. Cixous and Calle-Gruber, *Rootprints*, 63 and passim.

19. Hélène Cixous, "Contes de la Différence Sexuelle," in *Lectures de la Différence Sexuelle*, ed. Mara Negron (Paris: Des Femmes, 1994), 59.

20. Actually, in a text called *L'ange au secret* (Paris: Des Femmes, 1994), which is structured like a polyphonic song, Cixous describes each of the various voices, and recognizes in each an unmistakable timbre. There are the voices of writers with whom she feels an affinity, such as Ingeborg, Bachman, Maria Cvetaeva, and Kafka.

21. Cixous and Calle-Gruber, *Rootprints*, 89.

22. Cixous, *Coming to Writing*, 42.

CHAPTER 2.6

1. Cixous, *Coming to Writing*, 13.

2. Jacques Derrida, *Monolingualism of the Other; or, The Prosthesis of Origin*, trans. Patrick Mensah (Stanford: Stanford University Press, 1998), 36.

3. Cited by Derrida; ibid., 79.

4. Cixous, *Coming to Writing*, 11.

5. Derrida, *Monolingualism of the Other*, 93, n. 9.

6. Edward Kamau Brathwaite, *History of the Voice: The Development of Nation Language in Anglophone Carribean Poetry* (London: New Beacon Books, 1984), 8. For more on Brathwaite's work, and the cultural, literary, and political problems to

which it attends, see Timothy J. Reiss, *Against Autonomy: Global Dialectic of Cultural Exchange* (Stanford: Stanford University Press, 2002), 296 and passim.

7. Brathwaite, *History of the Voice*, 10.

8. My thanks to Timothy Reiss for introducing me the work, and the person, of Kamau Braithwaite. After having read the draft of this book, Reiss rightly pointed out that my argument here might have been developed as well in reference to the negritude movement that was at the center of a well-known debate between Jean-Paul Sartre and Franz Fanon regarding precisely this question of "voice" versus "language." For more on this, I refer the reader to Reiss, *Against Autonomy*, 69 and passim.

9. Ibid., 46.

10. Travi, *L'aspetto orale della poesia*, 24.

11. Brathwaite, *History of the Voice*, 17.

12. Ibid., 18–19.

13. See, for example, Edward Kamau Brathwaite, *Barabajan Poems* (Kingston: Savacou North, 1994).

CHAPTER 2.7

1. Plato, *Charmides*, 166a. See also Paolo Zellini, *Gnomon: Un'indagine sul numero* (Milan: Adelphi, 1999), 131. In this excellent and detailed study, Zellini analyzes the problems of ancient mathematics and their development in modernity.

2. See Plato, *Republic*, 525c.

3. Ibid., 516b.

4. Jean-Pierre Vernant, "Geometry and Astronomy in Early Greek Cosmology," in *The Origins of Greek Thought* (Ithaca: Cornell University Press, 1984).

5. Vladimir Jankélévitch, *La musica e l'ineffabile* (Milan: Bompiani, 1998), 78.

6. Hippasus, DK B 12; see Barnes, *Early Greek Philosophy*, 214.

7. Archytas of Tanantam, DK 47 B 1.

8. Julius Stenzel, *Platone educatore* (Laterza: Bari 1966), 42.

9. See Pierre Sauvanet, *Le rythme grec d'Héraclite à Aristote* (Paris: PUF, 1999), 70.

10. Martin Heidegger, *On the Way to Language*, trans. Peter D. Hertz (San Francisco: Harper and Row, 1971), 174.

11. Plato, *Laws*, 665a. See also Benveniste, *Problems in General Linguistics*, 397–98.

12. See Leo Spitzer, *L'armonia del mondo* (Bologna: Il Mulino, 1967), 188.

13. Plato, *Gorgias*, 507e–508a.

14. Hannah Arendt, *Between Past and Future* (New York: Penguin, 1993), 159.

15. Plato, *Republic*, 500c–501c.

16. Damon, DK B 4.

17. See Said, *Musical Elaborations*, 12–13.

18. Plato, *Republic*, 411a.

19. See Henrich Besseler, *L'ascolto musicale nell'età moderna*, 57–61.

20. Vladimir Jankélévitch, *La musica e l'ineffabile*, 7.

21. Sauvanet, *Le rythme grec d'Héraclite à Aristote*, 67.

22. Plato, *Republic*, 398d.

23. Arendt, *Between Past and Future*, 157–58, and passim. See also Simona Forti, *Vita della mente e tempo della polis* (Milan: Francoangeli, 1994), 121–34.

24. Beghelli, "Erotismo canoro," 124.

25. Plato, *Republic*, 617b.

CHAPTER 3.1

1. The myth of Echo and Narcissus is narrated in Ovid's *Metamorphoses*, book 3, verses 339–510. [TN: Citations of Ovid's text are taken from *The Metamorphoses of Ovid*, trans. Mary M. Innes (New York: Penguin, 1955).]

2. See especially Samuel Beckett, "The Unnamable," in *Three Novels by Samuel Beckett* (New York: Grove Press, 1995). As Didier Anzieu puts it, Beckett "defended the obstinance of breathing, as that which sustains the constancy of saying." See Didier Anzier, "Beckett, Self-Analysis and Creativity," trans. Pierre Johannet, in *Self-Analysis*, ed. James Barron. Hillsdale (New Jersey: The Analytic Press, 1993), 44.

3. Luisa Muraro, *L'ordine simbolico della madre* (Rome: Editori Riuniti, 1991), 43.

CHAPTER 3.2

1. Rosenzweig, *Philosophical and Theological Writings*, 262.

2. Ibid., 270.

3. Zambrano, *I beati*, 97.

4. Rosenzweig, *Philosophical and Theological Writings*, 271.

5. Ibid.

6. For more on the classic, inexhaustible theme of narcissism in psychoanalysis and contemporary thought, see, as a start, Paolo Gambazzi, *L'occhio e lo sguardo* (Milan: Cortina, 1999).

7. Koestenbaum, *Queen's Throat*, 14.

8. Diane Ackerman, *A Natural History of the Senses* (New York: Vintage Press, 1991), 179.

9. See Bruce Chatwin, *The Songlines* (London: Penguin Books, 1987). For an interesting reading of *The Songlines* as a narrative paradigm of a open and fluid horizontality that is contrasted to the rigid verticality of metaphysics, see Olivia Guaraldo, *Storylines: Politics, History and Narrative from an Arendtian Perspective* (Sophi: Jyvaskyla, 2001), 17–18.

10. Maria Zambrano, *Chiari nel bosco* (Milan: Feltrinelli, 1991), 69.

11. Carmelo Bene, '*L mal de' fiori: Autointervista dell'autore*. Available at http://www.alice.it/cafeletterario/152/cafelib.htm, p. 3.

12. Arendt, *Human Condition*, 176.

13. See Licinia Ricottilli, *Gesto e parola nell'Eineide* (Bologna: Patron, 2000), 81–83.

CHAPTER 3.3

1. See, respectively, Aristotle, *Poetics*, 1457a5–30; and *Politics*, 1253a9–19.

2. Aristotle, *Politics*, 1252a27.

3. Ibid., 1253a9.

4. Ibid., 1253a17–18.

5. Ibid., 1253a37–38.

6. Roberto Esposito, *Communitas* (Turin: Einaudi, 1998), xxiv. Esposito has extrapolated and developed this argument in another text entitled, emblematically, *Immunitas* (Turin: Einaudi, 2002).

7. See Adam B. Seligman, *Modernity's Wagner* (Princeton: Princeton University Press, 2000), 120.

8. Hannah Arendt, "The Nation," in *Essays in Understanding: 1930–1954* (New York: Harcourt Brace, 1994), 209.

9. For those interested in the varied aspects of "Communitarian" thought, which I cannot analyze here, there is an excellent volume of essays that represents the most significant figures. See *Comunitarismo e liberalismo*, ed. Alessandro Ferrara (Rome: Editori Riuniti, 2000), li.

10. Angelo Bolaffi and Giacomo Marramao, *Frammento e sistema* (Rome: Donzelli, 2001), 57, 121, and passim.

11. Arendt, *Human Condition*, 3.

12. See Jürgen Habermas, "Hannah Arendt's Communications Concept of Power," *Social Research* 44 (1977).

13. See Jürgen Habermas, *Theory of Communicative Action*, trans. Thomas McCarthy (Boston: Beacon Press, 1984).

14. Arendt, *Human Condition*, 179.

15. Ibid., 176.

16. Ibid.

17. Simona Forti, "Hannah Arendt: Filosofia politica," in *Hannah Arendt*, ed. Simona Forti (Milan: Bruno Mondadori, 1999), xx.

18. Hannah Arendt, *Che cos'è la politica?* (Milano, Edizioni di Comunità 1995).

19. Ibid., 7.

20. Arendt, *Che cos'è la politica?* 7.

21. [TN: "In between" in English; italics in original.]

22. Arendt, *Che cos'è la politica?* 7.

23. Arendt, *Human Condition*, 8.

24. Ibid., 58.

25. Ibid., 52.

26. [TN: The following paragraphs appeared in English as part of an article, "Politicizing Theory," trans. John Ronan, in *Political Theory* 30 (2002): 506–32.]

27. Jean-Luc Nancy, *The Sense of the World*, trans. Jeffrey S. Librett (Minneapolis: University of Minnesota Press, 1997), 111.

28. Ibid., 112.

29. Jean-Luc Nancy, *Being Singular Plural*, trans. Robert Richardson and Anne O'Byrne (Stanford: Stanford University Press, 2000), 32.

30. Ibid., 91.

31. Arendt, *Human Condition*, 52.

32. Jean-Luc Nancy, "Calcolo del poeta," in *Luoghi divini* (Padua: Il poligrafo, 1999), 71.

33. Nancy, *Sense of the World*, 115.

34. Ibid.

35. Ibid., 117. For more on the phatic function of language, see Roman Jacobson's essay "Linguistics and Poetics," in *Style in Language*, ed. Thomas A. Sebeok (New York: Routledge, 1960), 350–77.

36. Nancy, "Sharing Voices," 206.

37. Ibid.

38. Ibid., 211.

39. Giorgio Agamben, introduction to Emmanuel Levinas, *Alcune riflessioni sulla filosofia dell'hitlerismo*, 14.

40. Arendt, *Human Condition*, 199.

CHAPTER 3.4

1. Roland Barthes, *The Pleasure of the Text*, trans. Richard Miller (New York: Hill and Wang, 1975), 20.

2. Gilles Deleuze, *Rizoma* (Rome: Castelvecchi, 1997), 113.

3. Barthes, *Pleasure of the Text*, 127.

4. Arendt, *Essays in Understanding*, 208.

5. Ibid.

6. Arendt, *The Origins of Totalitarianism* (New York: Meridian, 1958), 305.

7. Seyla Benhabib, "Dismantling the Leviathan: Citizen and State in a Global World," *Responsive Community* 11, no. 2 (2001): 15.

8. Arendt, *Human Condition*, 198.

9. Ida Dominijanni, "La parola è nostra politica," in *Duemilaeuna: Donne che cambiano l'Italia*, ed. Annarosa Buttarelli, Luisa Murano, and Liliana Rampello (Milan: Practiche, 2000), 210.

10. I allude here to Plutarch's *Coniugalia Preacepta*, according to which—as Maurizio Bettini and Licinia Riccottilli note—"the woman had to hold her tongue among strangers . . . and had to speak only to her husband, or speak through him, expressing herself through a 'tongue' that was not hers, with a lower and more solemn tone, just as the flute-player does." The authors note how this rule evokes the Ovidian framework in which Echo is denied a command of language. See Bettini and Riccottilli, "Elogio dell'indiscrezione," *Studi Urbinati* 60 (1987): 19.

11. For more on this symbolic matricide, as the essential condition for the functioning of the metaphysical system, see Luce Irigaray, *Sexes and Genealogies*, trans. Gillian Gill (New York: Columbia University Press, 1993), 13 and passim. See also my *In Spite of Plato*, 38 and passim.

12. Barthes, *L'ovvio e l'ottuso* (Turin: Einaudi, 2001), 243.

13. Hannah Arendt, *On Revolution* (New York: Penguin Books, 1963), 271–72.

14. Arendt, *Origins of Totalitarianism*, 453.

15. Ibid., 455.

16. Primo Levi, *Survival in Auschwitz and The Reawakening*, trans. Stuart Woolf (New York: Summit, 1986), 90.

17. Giorgio Agamben, *Remnants of Auschwitz*, trans. Daniel Heller-Roazen (New York: Zone Books, 1999), 21.

18. Levi, *Survival in Auschwitz*, 191.

19. Ibid.

20. Ibid., 192.

21. This is the direction taken by Giorgio Agamben's reading of this scene in his book *Remnants of Auschwitz*. Reflecting on the "lacuna" of language that prevents the survivors from testifying, he traces the roots of the impossibility of testifying to "that which has no language"—and, more in general, the question of the lost articulation between the living being and logos.

22. Levi, *Survival in Auschwitz*, 191.

23. Ibid.

APPENDIX

1. Derrida affirms in an interview, "I sometimes have the feeling that the Heideggerian problematic is the most 'profound' and 'powerful' defense of what I attempt to put into question under the rubric of the *thought of presence*." Jacques Derrida, *Positions*, 55.

2. For more on the meaning of *différance* and the spelling of the term, which substitutes an *a* for an *e* (*différence, différance*), an *a* that is lost in the French pronunciation, see Derrida's remarks in *Positions*, 27–29, 40, 44, and passim. See also his "Différance," in *Margins of Philosophy*, trans. Alan Bass (Chicago: University of Chicago Press, 1982), 1–28.

3. Caterina Resta, *Pensare al limite: Tracciati di Derrida* (Milan: Guerini and Associates, 1990), 17. Resta's book happily places itself far from the work of those commentators on Derrida who "limit themselves to imitating his style of writing, often increasing the illegibility and obscurity of his work." Instead, she provides in this book a clear and convincing interpretation that, taking up Gianni Vattimo's invitation, tries to give a systemization of Derrida's work by interrogating "the internal hierarchy of his concepts." See Gianni Vattimo, "Derrida e l'oltrepassamento della metafisica," introduction to Jacques Derrida, *La scrittura e la differenza* (Turin: Einaudi, 1990), ix.

4. [TN: The original French title (and the Italian translation used by Cavarero) of *Speech and Phenomena* is *La voix et le phénomene: Introduction au problème du signe dans la phénomènologie de Husserl*—literally, "The Voice and the Phenomenon."]

5. Derrida, *Positions*, 25.

6. Jacques Derrida, *Speech and Phenomena*, trans. David Allison (Evanston: Northwestern University Press, 1973), 62–63.

7. For more on Derrida's reading of Saussure, see Jacques Derrida, *Of Gram-*

matology, trans. Gayatri Spivak (Baltimore: Johns Hopkins University Press, 1976), 27–73.

8. Derrida, *Speech and Phenomena*, 103.

9. Derrida, *Of Grammatology*, 14.

10. Ibid., 65.

11. This history of the reception of Derrida's work in the United States is long and complex. Of note is the English publication, in 1977, of Derrida's essay "Signature, Event, Context," which had appeared as a chapter in the French collection, *Marges—de la philosophie* (Paris: Minuit, 1972). The reaction of John Searle, and the debate over "speech acts" that followed as part of a larger encounter with so-called continental philosophy, induced Derrida himself to intervene directly, with increasing success, in Anglo-American philosophical and literary circles. See the editor's foreword to Jacques Derrida, *Limited Inc.* (Evanston: Northwestern University Press, 1977).

12. Vicenzo Costa, "Volerne sapere," postscript to Jacques Derrida, *La voce e il fenomeno* (Milan: Java Books, 1997), 161.

13. Derrida, *Speech and Phenomena*, 78.

14. Ibid., 79.

15. Ibid., 80.

16. Sarah Kofman, *Lectures de Derrida* (Paris: Galilée, 1984), 27.

17. See Mikhail Bakhtin, *Problems of Dostoevsky's Poetics*, trans. Caryl Emerson (Minneapolis: University of Minnesota Press, 1984).

18. Resta, *Pensare al limite*, 151.

19. Derrida, *Of Grammatology*, 3.

20. Derrida, *Speech and Phenomena*, 80.

21. Ibid., 78.

22. Ibid., 83.

23. Ibid., 86.

24. Ibid., 84.

25. The first phrase is Derrida's paraphrase of the Cartesian doctrine; the second phrase, cited by Derrida, is from Descartes himself. See, respectively, Derrida, *Margins of Philosophy*, 267; René Descartes, *Meditations on First Philosophy*, in *The Philosophical Works of Descartes*, trans. Elizabeth Haldane and G. R. T. Ross (Cambridge: Cambridge University Press, 1970), 1:168.

26. Derrida, *Margins of Philosophy*, 228.

27. Ibid.

28. Aristotle, *Poetics*, 1457b7–8.

29. Derrida, *Margins of Philosophy*, 233.

30. Ibid., 251.

31. Derrida, *Speech and Phenomena*, 86.

32. Ibid., 82.

33. Ibid., 85.

34. Ibid., 76.

35. Derrida, *Of Grammatology*, 65.

36. Plato, *Phaedrus*, 274c–275b.

37. Ibid., 275e.

38. Jacques Derrida, *Dissemination*, trans. Barbara Johnson (Chicago: University of Chicago Press, 1981), 61–172.

39. Ibid., 76.

40. Plato, *Phaedrus*, 275d.

41. Ibid., 275e.

42. Derrida, *Dissemination*, 77.

43. Plato, *Phaedrus*, 276a.

44. Derrida, *Dissemination*, 77.

45. Plato, *Symposium*, 209c.
46. Plato, *Phaedrus*, 276e–277a.
47. Plato, *Seventh Letter*, 341d, 344b–c.
48. Plato, *Phaedrus*, 247d–e.
49. Ibid., 265d–e.
50. I want to thank Paul Kottman for bringing this scene to my attention.
51. Jacques Derrida, "Aphorism, Countertime," 418.
52. [TN: References to Shakespeare's *Romeo and Juliet* are to the Arden text, previously cited.]
53. Derrida, "Aphorism, Countertime," 427.
54. Ibid., 432.
55. Ibid.
56. Ibid., 431.

Index